INTERNATIONAL COPYRIGHT AND ACCESS TO KNOWLEDGE

The principle of access to knowledge (A2K) has become a common reference point for a diverse set of agendas that all hope to realize technological and human potential by making knowledge more accessible. This book is a history of international copyright that focuses not on the principles of copyright protection, but on the principles of access to knowledge embedded in the international copyright system. Most discussions of international copyright focus on major western countries, but *International Copyright and Access to Knowledge* examines the roles of emerging countries, NGOs, and indigenous peoples in the history of international copyright. Written in a clear and accessible style, the book connects copyright history to current problems, issues, and events.

SARA BANNERMAN is an Associate Professor at McMaster University. She is the author of *The Struggle for Canadian Copyright: Imperialism to Internationalism, 1842–1971* (UBC Press, 2013) and has published numerous articles and book chapters on international copyright and international copyright history, as well as on other topics in new media, traditional media, and communications theory.

CAMBRIDGE INTELLECTUAL PROPERTY
AND INFORMATION LAW

As its economic potential has rapidly expanded, intellectual property has become a subject of front-rank legal importance. *Cambridge Intellectual Property and Information Law* is a series of monograph studies of major current issues in intellectual property. Each volume contains a mix of international, European, comparative, and national law, making this a highly significant series for practitioners, judges, and academic researchers in many countries.

A list of books in the series can be found at the end of this volume.

INTERNATIONAL COPYRIGHT AND ACCESS TO KNOWLEDGE

SARA BANNERMAN

CAMBRIDGE
UNIVERSITY PRESS

CAMBRIDGE
UNIVERSITY PRESS

University Printing House, Cambridge CB2 8BS, United Kingdom

Cambridge University Press is part of the University of Cambridge.

It furthers the University's mission by disseminating knowledge in the pursuit of education, learning and research at the highest international levels of excellence.

www.cambridge.org
Information on this title: www.cambridge.org/9781107023062

First published 2016

A catalog record for this publication is available from the British Library

ISBN 978-1-107-02306-2 Hardback

CONTENTS

ACKNOWLEDGMENTS

A huge circle of colleagues, mentors, and friends have provided feedback and support in the writing of this book, and I have enjoyed wonderful discussions for which I am extremely grateful. I must mention, in particular, Ahmed Abdel-Latif, Benedict Atkinson, Blayne Haggart, Bruce Couchman, Darren Smith, Dwayne Winseck, Eli Maclaren, Eva Hemmungs Wirtén, Graeme Greenleaf, Graham Knight, Heidi Tworek, Heiko Baumgartner, Howard Knopf, Jean-Frédéric Morin, Jeremy de Beer, Jeremy Shtern, José Estanislau do Amaral, Katharine Sarikakis, Katie Boothe, Kenneth Nobrega, Khaled Fourati, Marc Raboy, Margaret Chon, Matthew Rimmer, Maureen Smith, Michael Geist, Michèle Martin, Myra Tawfik, Nadine Attewell, Natasha Tusikov, Norman Hillmer, Pedro Roffe, Peter Drahos, Peter Putnis, Peter Yu, Robin Mansell, Rosemary Coombe, Ross Eaman, Sam Ricketson, Sandra Braman, Stefania Milan, Susan Sell, and Sheryl Hamilton. I'd also like to thank colleagues at the International Development Research Centre and at McMaster University, as well as those who provided feedback to versions and parts of this project at conferences of the International Association for Media and Communication Research, the Canadian Communications Association, the International Communications Association, the International Studies Association, and the International Centre for Trade and Sustainable Development, as well as at the George Washington University Copyright History Conference, the International Society for the History and Theory of Intellectual Property, the Copyright Conference held at Old Parliament House in Canberra in 2009, the Australasian IP Academics Conference of 2011, and many others.

I have had a wonderful team of research assistants whom I cannot thank enough for their work on this project. This includes Nicholas Must, Karim El-Ziftawi, Jordan Baker, Sarah James, Corbin Hartwick, Ryan Prance, Nina Chopra, and Julian Gantt. I especially thank Nicholas Must, whose editing, insight, and assistance have been invaluable.

I'd like to thank my colleagues and the support staff at McMaster University, including in particular Lorraine Redford, Dale Askey, Janice Adlington, Sandra Lapointe, and Jason Brodeur for their support of this project, the staff of the Library and Archives Canada, the WIPO library, the South African national archives in Cape Town and Johannesburg, the National Archives of Ireland, the National Archives of Australia, the United States National Archives and Records Administration, and the Swiss Federal Archives.

This project would not have been possible without the support of the Social Sciences and Humanities Research Council of Canada, the Canada-US Fulbright Foundation, McMaster University, and the International Development Research Centre.

I'd like to thank my editor at Cambridge University Press, Kim Hughes, and assistant editor Helen Francis for their work on this project.

I am indebted to wonderful friends, including Andrew Wolgemuth, Ayse Turak, Chantal Lalonde, Christina Baade, and Alana Hudson, Emily Arrowsmith, Nathalie Quach, Heather Anderson, Henry Dyck, Johanne Boucher, Paul Thorne, Pu Chen, Rebekah Johnston, Sarah R. Evans and Season Osborne.

Most importantly I'd like to thank my family, including my partner Mary Caldbick, who is my bedrock; my sister Molly, my mother Deborah Bannerman and stepfather Dennis Souder, as well as all my treasured aunts, uncles, and cousins. I am also thankful to my father Don Bannerman, and my beloved grandparents, Stewart and Norma Devereux.

"We are all developing countries."[1]

[1] Canadian delegate, Records of the Conference for Revision of the Universal Copyright Convention, UNESCO House, Paris, July 5–24, 1971, 105.

TREATIES

Agreement between the United Nations and the World Intellectual Property Organization. Geneva: WIPO, 1974.

Berne Convention for the Protection of Literary and Artistic Works. Berlin Act of 13 November 1908. Berne: Office of the International Union for the Protection of Literary and Artistic Works, 1908.

Berne Convention for the Protection of Literary and Artistic Works. Brussels Act of 26 June 1948. Berne: International Bureau for the Union for the Protection of Literary and Artistic Works, 1948.

Berne Convention for the Protection of Literary and Artistic Works. Paris Act of 4 May 1896. Berne: Office of the International Union for the Protection of Literary and Artistic Works, 1896.

Berne Convention for the Protection of Literary and Artistic Works. Paris Act of 24 July, 1971, as Amended on September 28, 1979. Geneva: World Intellectual Property Organization, 1979.

Berne Convention for the Protection of Literary and Artistic Works. Rome Act of 2 June 1928. Berne: Office of the International Union for the Protection of Literary and Artistic Works, 1928.

Berne Convention for the Protection of Literary and Artistic Works. Stockholm Act of 14 July 1967. Geneva: World Intellectual Property Organization, 1967.

Convention de Buenos Aires pour la protection de la propriété littéraire et artistique, révisé par la sixième conférence international américaine, 1928. Cuba: Organisation of American States, 1928.

Convention Concerning the Creation of an International Union for the Protection of Literary and Artistic Works (Berne Convention). Berne: Office of the International Union for the Protection of Literary and Artistic Works, September 9, 1886.

Convention Establishing the World Intellectual Property Organization, Signed at Stockholm on July 14, 1967, and as Amended on September 28, 1979. Geneva: World Intellectual Property Organization, 1979.

Convention on Biological Diversity. Adopted on June 5, 1992. Montreal, QC: Secretariat of the Convention on Biological Diversity, 1992.

Declaration on the Granting of Independence to Colonial Countries and Peoples Adopted by General Assembly Resolution 1514 (XV) of 14 December 1960. New York: United Nations, 1960.

Declaration Interpreting Certain Provisions of the Berne Convention of September 9, 1886, and the Additional Act Signed at Paris on May 4, 1896. Berne: Office of the International Union for the Protection of Literary and Artistic Works, 1896.

Final Act Embodying the Results of the Uruguay Round of Multilateral Trade Negotiations, Annex IC: Agreement on Trade-Related Aspects of Intellectual Property Rights. Geneva: World Trade Organization, 1994.

Marrakesh Treaty to Facilitate Access to Published Works for Persons Who Are Blind, Visually Impaired, or Otherwise Print Disabled adopted by the Diplomatic Conference to Conclude a Treaty to Facilitate Access to Published Works by Visually Impaired Persons and Persons with Print Disabilities in Marrakesh, on June 27, 2013. Geneva: WIPO, 2013.

Paris Convention for the Protection of Industrial Property (Paris Convention). Paris Act of 20 March 1883. Berne: Office of the International Union for the Protection of Industrial Property, 1883.

Paris Convention for the Protection of Industrial Property. The Hague Act of 6 November 1925. Berne: Office of the International Union for the Protection of Industrial Property, 1925.

Protocole additionnel à la convention de Berne révisée du 13 novembre 1908. Berne: Bureau de l'Union internationale littéraires et artistiques, 1914.

Universal Copyright Convention of 6 September 1952, with Appendix Declaration Relating to Article XVII and Resolution Concerning Article XI. Geneva: UNESCO, 1952.

Universal Copyright Convention as revised at Paris on 24 July 1971, with Appendix Declaration Relating to Article XVII and Resolution Concerning Article XI 1971. Paris Act of 1971. Paris: UNESCO, 1971.

Universal Declaration of Human Rights. New York: United Nations, 1948.

WIPO Copyright Treaty, Adopted in Geneva on December 20, 1996. Geneva: WIPO, 1996.

WIPO Performers and Phonograms Treaty, Adopted in Geneva on December 20, 1996. Geneva: WIPO, 1996.

RECORDS

Berne Convention records[1]

Actes de la conférence réunie à Berlin du 14 octobre au 14 novembre 1908 avec les actes de ratification. Berne: Bureau de l'Union internationale littéraires et artistiques, 1910.
Actes de la conférence réunie à Paris du 15 avril au 4 mai 1896. Berne: Bureau International de l'Union, 1897.
Actes de la conférence réunie à Rome du 7 mai au 2 juin 1928. Berne: Bureau de l'Union internationale pour la protection des oeuvres littéraires et artistiques, 1929.
Actes de la deuxième conférence internationale pour la protection des oeuvres littéraires et artistiques réunie à Berne du 7 au 18 septembre 1885. Berne: Conseil Fédérale Suisse, 1885.
Actes de la première conférence internationale pour la protection des oeuvres littéraires et artistiques du 8 septembre 1884 à Berne. Berne: Conseil Fédérale Suisse, 1884.
Actes de la troisième conférence internationale pour la protection des oeuvres littéraires et artistiques réunie à Berne du 6 au 9 septembre 1886. Berne: Conseil Fédérale Suisse, 1886.
Documents de la conférence réunie à Bruxelles du 5 au 26 juin 1948. Berne: Bureau de l'Union internationale pour la protection des oeuvres littéraires et artistiques, 1951.
Records of the Diplomatic Conference for the Revision of the Berne Convention (Paris, July 5 to 24, 1971). Geneva: World Intellectual Property Organization, 1974.
Records of the Intellectual Property Conference of Stockholm June 11 to July 14, 1967. Geneva: World Intellectual Property Organization, 1971.

WIPO Internet Treaties records

Diplomatic Conference on Certain Copyright and Neighbouring Rights Questions: Summary Minutes, Plenary. CRNR/DC/101. Geneva: WIPO, 1996.
Diplomatic Conference on Certain Copyright and Neighbouring Rights Questions: Summary Minutes, Main Committee I. CRNR/DC/102. Geneva: WIPO, 1996.
Diplomatic Conference on Certain Copyright and Neighbouring Rights Questions: Summary Minutes, Main Committee II. CRNR/DC/103. Geneva: WIPO, 1996.

[1] The abbreviations "Actes" and "Records" have been adopted in the footnotes of this book to refer respectively to the French and English language records of Berne Convention negotiations.

Diplomatic Conference on Certain Copyright and Neighbouring Rights Questions: List of Participants. CRNR/DC/INF.2 Geneva: WIPO, 1996.

Diplomatic Conference on Certain Copyright and Neighbouring Rights Questions: List of States and Organizations. CRNR/DC/INF.4 Geneva: WIPO, 1996.

Universal Copyright Convention records

Records of the Conference for Revision of the Universal Copyright Convention, UNESCO House, Paris, 5 to 24 July 1971. Paris: UNESCO, 1973.

Records of the Inter-Governmental Copyright Conference, Geneva, August 18 – September 6, 1952. Paris: UNESCO, 1955.

LEGISLATION

Australia

An Act Relating to Copyright No. 25 of 1905.
An Act Relating to Copyright No. 20 of 1912.

UK

An Act for the Encouragement of Learning, by Vesting the Copies of Printed Books in the Authors or Purchasers of Such Copies, During the Times Therein mentioned 8 Anne, c.19 (1710).
Copyright Act 1&2 Geo. 5 Ch. 46 (1911).

US

U.S. Constitution, art. 1, sec. 8, cl. 8.

1

Introduction

The term "access to knowledge" or "A2K" was coined in 2004 and has become a common reference for a diverse set of agendas that all hope to realize technological and human potential by making knowledge of various types more accessible.[1] A2K's sister, "Y2K," signified the year 2000, the new millennium, and the whole set of computer problems expected to arise at midnight on the dawn of the year 2000: the Y2K problem. The new millennium, now upon us, could become known as the age of A2K – an age of wider, broader, and more universal access to many types of knowledge than ever before thought possible. On the other hand, the new millennium may be destined – much like the millennium before it – to become the age of the "A2K problem." It may be the age where the possibility of broad access existed as it never had before, but where this potential was never realized.

Copyright is a bundle of rights, some complementary, some in tension with one another. While many of the rights in the copyright package are granted to copyright owners, the copyright bundle also contains, or should contain, principles intended to protect the interests of users of works, and public interests more generally.

This study engages with a number of contested terms – "civilizing," "emerging," "developing,"[2] – normative concepts tied to a particular economic and cultural agenda that privileges Western law, culture, and

1 Ahmed Abdel Latif, "The Emergence of the A2K Movement: Reminiscences and Reflections of a Developing-Country Delegate," in *Access to Knowledge in the Age of Intellectual Property*, eds. Gaëlle Krikorian and Amy Kapczynski (Cambridge, Mass.: Massachusetts Institute of Technology Press, 2010), 99–125.

2 This book adopts the term "developing countries" with hesitation. Rather than adopting the term uncritically, I have attempted to disrupt to some extent this category, taking the position that all countries are, to some degree, developing in one way or another, although certainly not all on the same path, in the same mode, or toward the same end. For that reason, I do use the term "developing country," but I enclose the term "developed," in reference to the so-called "developed" countries, in quotation marks.

economic interests. Tied to the agendas of "civilization," "modernization," "progress," and "development," copyright is part of a long economic movement to commercialize cultural production, part of a cultural agenda that has motivated the international dissemination of primarily Western cultural goods, and part of a legal agenda that has taken as a goal the universalization of Western law.[3] Within this framework, countries that have not conformed precisely to the dominant framework of international copyright have been classed as "pirates," "backwards,"[4] or "outlaws" among the copyright nations of the world,[5] "underdeveloped"[6] and "outsiders" from the general community of nations.[7]

Many states, until the 1990s, remained outside of, or contested, the dominant system of international copyright. Some adopted copyright in general and adhered to many of the principles that were part of the dominant system, while objecting to or ignoring others, sometimes in favor of alternative norms. Others, for one reason or another, denounced the regime. These events speak counter to the traditional narrative of copyright history – that of progressive expansion – showing the history of copyright to be, instead, one of continual conflict and dispute.

Many histories portray the development of international copyright law as the gradual and rational (and as-yet-incomplete) extension and perfection of authors' rights over a period of 300 years. I take the contrary view. The international copyright system in its current form has enshrined a set of individual and divisible principles that could have been otherwise, and that can be adjusted. It is a set of principles that arose out of chance and path dependency, and that was established under colonialism, cultural imperialism, and conditions of economic and political inequality among interest groups and states. Conditions of colonialism and inequality have shaped the processes by which particular systems were held up as models, displayed, symbolically interpreted, and copied by other states.[8]

Instead of adopting the conventional view of the rise and expansion of the rights granted to owners of copyright, I trace the principles of access

3 Ha-Joon Chang, *Kicking Away the Ladder: Development Strategy in Historical Perspective* (London: Anthem Press, 2002).

4 "Urges Revision of Copyright Laws: Official of British Society says Canada Backward in Protection Legislation: Development Retarded," Montreal Gazette, December 6, 1920, 8.

5 *F.C.T. O'Hara to W.M. Dickson*, June 2, 1919, in Library and Archives Canada, RG20, Vol. 91, File 22655, Vol. 1.

6 "Urges Revision," 8.

7 Canada. House of Commons of Canada, *Debates of the House of Commons, Fifth Session – Thirteenth Parliament 11–12 George V., 1921*, Vol. CXLVI (Ottawa: F.A. Acland, 1921), 3833.

8 John Braithwaite and Peter Drahos, *Global Business Regulation* (Cambridge: Cambridge University Press, 2000), 581.

to knowledge that have been embedded, at various points, in the international copyright system. Viewed in this light, the history of international copyright can be seen, in some cases, as an erosion of the principles of access to knowledge. It can be seen not as a win for authors but as a loss for A2K advocates – as well as a loss *of* A2K advocates as more and more countries joined the dominant international copyright system and gave up struggles for alternate models of international copyright. From this perspective one can view "emerging" countries as "disappearing" countries; as countries "emerge" into the dominant system they disappear from other copyright regimes and models.[9]

In introducing his *Social History of Knowledge*, Peter Burke comments:

> One purpose of this book may be described in a single word: "defamiliarization." The hope is to achieve what the Russian critic Viktor Shklovsky described as *ostranenie*, a kind of distanciation which makes what was familiar appear strange and what was natural seem arbitrary.[10]

My purpose in telling this history of copyright differently is similar. The current regime of international copyright makes it hard to imagine a world with different copyright – let alone a world without copyright. In fact, the current model of copyright is so much embedded in thinking, legal regimes, and interlocking international conventions that it is hard to imagine any truly significant change to that model at all. However, the A2K movement is premised on the demand that significant change is necessary. I hope that by imagining differently the history of the current set of rules and norms known as "copyright" it may be possible to imagine differently its future, and that this book is a contribution to that different imagining.

The Berne system

The *Berne Convention for the Protection of Literary and Artistic Works* was established in 1886 between Belgium, France, Germany, Great Britain, Haiti, Italy, Liberia, Spain, Switzerland, and Tunisia.[11] Though they were

[9] Peter Yu refers to a "crossover point" where a country crosses over from being "a pirating nation to a country respectful of intellectual property rights." "The Rise and Decline of the Intellectual Property Powers," *Campbell Law Review* 34, 3 (2012), 525–577.

[10] Peter Burke, *A Social History of Knowledge: from Gutenberg to Diderot* (Cambridge: Polity Press, 2000), 2.

[11] Actes de la troisième conférence internationale pour la protection des oeuvres littéraires et artistiques réunie à Berne du 6 au 9 septembre 1886 (Berne: Conseil Fédérale Suisse, 1886); Francis Adams and J.H.G. Bergne to the Earl of Iddelsleigh, Report on the Third International Copyright Conference at Berne, September 10, 1886, in Library and Archives Canada, RG6 A3, Vol. 214, File: "Copyright Conference at Berne, 1886."

not listed as signatories, the convention also encompassed the colonies and possessions of Great Britain, France, and Spain. It competed, until the 1990s, with various other copyright systems, including the Pan American copyright system and the *Universal Copyright Convention* (UCC). However, the Berne system established a position of preeminence over alternate models and has come to act as the core of the international copyright system, superseding its alternatives.

The *Berne Convention* has undergone six major revisions, in 1896, 1908, 1928, 1948, 1967, and 1971. Since 1971 the *Berne Convention* has remained substantively unchanged while additional treaties dealing with international copyright, including the *Agreement on Trade-Related Aspects of Intellectual Property* (the *TRIPs Agreement*) under the World Trade Organization (WTO), the World Intellectual Property Organization (WIPO) Internet Treaties, and various bilateral and regional trade agreements, have been established. These more recent treaties build on top of the *Berne Convention*, adopting the main provisions of the *Berne Convention* and adding additional provisions. The *Berne Convention* thus acts as the core of the international copyright system today.

The history of the *Berne Convention* and international copyright generally, though involving a seemingly diverse group of states and other actors, has often been recorded with a focus on the most powerful states involved, including especially Great Britain, France, and Germany. Through international travel and communication, the establishment of transnational networks and centers of certain types of knowledge, culture, governance, and diplomacy, a specific geography of knowledge was formed. These networks constructed distinct cores and peripheries. The historical experiences of the relatively peripheral states, NGOs, and indigenous peoples with the *Berne Convention* are often ignored. Here, I recount a history of international copyright with a focus on the principles of access embedded in the international copyright system, on these more peripheral actors, and on the now dominant Berne system of international copyright.

History and international copyright

The history of the international copyright system has been portrayed as a progressive history of justice for authors and other creators, modernization, and civilization. This historical narrative tends to obscure the inequality and exploitation that also marks the history of international copyright.[12] The *Berne Convention* embeds and reinforces the substantive inequalities of the international system, enshrining rich countries and corporations, the primary producers of copyright works, as the main beneficiaries of international copyright, and locking economically poorer countries and groups into a system that requires the exporting of royalties from relatively poor countries and groups to rich ones with few mechanisms to ensure that local public policy goals are met.[13] The Berne system of international copyright has been called, for this reason, an "ideology . . . exported to the South" – a system that, while appearing just, hides the inequalities and injustices that it actually perpetuates.[14] The particular system of property that is thus constructed – specifically international intellectual property – is the key instrument of exploitation. International copyright replaced, in many senses, the imperial copyright system that came before it by designing a system that would protect the works produced at the core, allowing businesses at the core of the international system to own "property" around the world, to expand, to profit, and to influence via the circulation of their works and ideas in the periphery.[15] The international copyright system is thus intricately connected to colonialism and economic imperialism.[16]

'Postcolonialism' signifies not a world where colonialism no longer exists, but rather a world where colonialism continues to shape international, economic, and cultural systems in new ways. Such processes, embedded in institutions – including in international institutions – continue to perpetuate unequal economic and cultural relations, to create elites, and to inspire resistance.

In the context of decolonization, many thinkers have pointed to the role of international law and international institutions in founding and continuing the colonial project of the European imperial powers. As Antony Anghie points out, today's international law and institutions were founded, in the late nineteenth and early twentieth century, on

[12] Peter Drahos, *A Philosophy of Intellectual Property* (London: Ashgate, 1996), 101; Alan Story, "Burn Berne: Why the Leading International Copyright Convention Must Be Repealed," *Houston Law Review* 40, 3 (2003), 763–803.

[13] Story, "Burn Berne." [14] Ibid., 794; Drahos, *A Philosophy of Intellectual Property*, 101.

[15] Sara Bannerman, *The Struggle for Canadian Copyright: Imperialism to Internationalism 1886–1971* (Vancouver: University of British Columbia Press, 2013).

[16] Alexander Peukert, "The Colonial Legacy of the International Copyright System," in *Staging the Immaterial: Rights, Style and Performance in Sub-Saharan Africa*, eds. Mamadou Diawara and Ute Röschenthaler (Oxford: Sean Kingston, Forthcoming).

legal positivism, which recognizes only Western-style law.[17] Under legal positivism:

> Whether a society has a legal system depends on the presence of certain structures of governance, not on the extent to which it satisfies ideals of justice, democracy, or the rule of law. What laws are in force in that system depends on what social standards its officials recognize as authoritative; for example, legislative enactments, judicial decisions, or social customs. The fact that a policy would be just, wise, efficient, or prudent is never sufficient reason for thinking that it is actually the law, and the fact that it is unjust, unwise, inefficient or imprudent is never sufficient reason for doubting it. According to positivism, law is a matter of what has been posited (ordered, decided, practiced, tolerated, etc.).[18]

According to Anghie, this set of ideas about international law worked to perpetuate colonialism. International law, as formulated by European positivist jurists, first "purported to expel the non-European world from the realm of legality by insisting on the distinction between civilized and noncivilized states," the latter not seen as having the requisite structures of governance, under the positivist legal paradigm, to produce law.[19] Second, following decolonization, international law "proceeded to enact the re-admission of non-European states into international society" by defining "the terms and methods by which they were to be assimilated into the legal framework."[20] This reentry took place "on terms that completely subordinated and crippled non-European societies."[21]

International institutions played prominent roles in the decolonization process by setting these terms, and by spreading new legal, economic, and social norms globally. In a sense, they act as, "'missionaries' of our time, [a]rmed with a notion of progress, an idea of how to create the better life, and some understanding of the conversion process."[22]

The discourse and practices of this process divided the world into categories, classifying societies and peoples according to particular systems and ideas of progress – some societies and peoples as "developed," and

17 See also Martti Koskenniemi, *The Gentle Civilizer of Nations: The Rise and Fall of International Law, 1870–1960* (Cambridge: Cambridge University Press, 2002).

18 Leslie Green, "Legal Positivism," in *Stanford Encyclopedia of Philosophy*, Fall 2009 edition, ed. Edward N. Zalta, http://plato.stanford.edu/archives/fall2009/entries/legal-positivism/.

19 Antony Anghie, "Finding the Peripheries: Sovereignty and Colonialism in Nineteenth-Century International Law," *Harvard International Law Journal* 40, 1 (Winter 1999), 31.

20 Ibid. 21 Ibid.

22 Martha Finnemore and Michael N. Barnett, "The Politics, Power and Pathologies of International Organizations," *International Organizations* 53, 4 (1999), 699.

others as "underdeveloped," some as "civilized" and others as "uncivilized," with the latter regarded as powerless and peripheral.[23] Only the former were deemed to have the requisite sovereignty to participate in the decision-making processes of international institutions.[24]

Reflecting this categorization, only representatives of "civilized" countries were invited to the founding of the *Berne Convention*. In the case of copyright, a draft convention was circulated to the "governments of civilized countries," along with an invitation to a conference in 1884 to discuss its contents.[25] The negotiations that founded the *Berne Convention* took place in the same years as the 1885 conference at Berlin that would divide up the African continent among European powers; no Africans were invited to the copyright conference, nor were representatives of colonies in other parts of the world.[26] Neither were representatives of Asian countries initially invited.[27] The institutions and legal norms associated with Western intellectual property were recognized, engaged, and globalized, while the existing systems of norms and jurisprudence of "uncivilized" countries and indigenous peoples with respect to traditional knowledge, cultural expressions, and genetic resources – not having arisen from the requisite legal and legislative institutions – were expelled from the realm of legality, and forms of knowledge and creativity that were not recognized under the Western intellectual property system were not afforded protection.[28]

Even so, most postcolonial scholars are reluctant to see international law and institutions as either *simply* a continuation of empire, or as institutions of *emancipation* from empire. Pahuja emphasizes this:

> [a]rguably there is something distinctive about the relation implied in the 'postcolonial' – both a break from and a continuity with past forms of

[23] Arturo Escobar, *Encountering Development: The Making and Unmaking of the Third World* (Princeton, N.J.: Princeton University Press, 1995).

[24] Anghie "Finding the Peripheries," 31.

[25] Actes de la première conférence internationale pour la protection des oeuvres littéraires et artistiques du 8 septembre 1884 à Berne (Conseil Fédérale Suisse, 1884, 9; Sam Ricketson and Jane Ginsburg, *International Copyright and Neighbouring Rights: The Berne Convention and Beyond*, 2nd edition (London: Oxford University Press, 2006), 52–58; Max M. Kampelman, "The United States and International Copyright," *American Journal of International Law* 41, 2 (1947), 406–411.

[26] Actes 1884, 9. [27] Ibid.

[28] Madhavi Sunder, "The Invention of Traditional Knowledge," *Law and Contemporary Problems* 70 (Spring 2007), 97; Brad Sherman, "From the Non-Original to the Ab-Original: A History," in *Of Authors and Origins: Essays on Copyright Law*, eds. Brad Sherman and Alain Strowel (Oxford: Clarendon Press, 1994); Story, "Burn Berne."

> domination – and something particular about the capacity of law to be both appropriated to imperial ends and used as a force for liberation.[29]

Some international institutions, by embracing the principle of universality, brought a (somewhat) wider array of groups and representatives to the table of international norm-setting. Pahuja writes:

> international law . . . contains within it what we might call the condition of the postcolonial. Succinctly stated, this can be understood . . . as the paradoxical inclusion of the excluded necessitated by the claim to universality of this constitution. This dynamic accounts for both international law's imperializing effect and its anti-imperial tendency.[30]

Postmodern and poststructural thinkers emphasize the interconnectedness of power and knowledge, the role of power in constructing knowledge, and the role of knowledge in constructing power, viewing the two as sides of a coin that can never be separated. The ability, therefore, to participate in the construction of knowledge – to be a "nodal point" on the networks where meaning is constructed – is an essential source of power.[31] Thus, postcolonialism does not view ideas as purely in the hands of dominant groups; imperial law, culture, and ideas, while working to maintain a hegemonic order, are also appropriated in projects of resistance and change. While imitation, mimicry, and the tendency of dominant groups' ideas to infuse the imaginations of the oppressed are powerful forces, oppressed groups are themselves also recognized as possessing agency and interests that may be poorly expressed, or left unexpressed, by elites empowered to speak on their behalf. This is true in particular of indigenous peoples, whose interests were largely unrepresented within the international copyright regime, and the larger nation-state system, through much of its history, as discussed in Chapters 5 and 9 below.

Postcolonial theory is especially interested in the power of literary and artistic works as a vehicle for spreading the power of the dominant core, and copyright – and international law in general – is a key vehicle for doing so.[32] In relation to copyright, we can see similar trends; legal scholar Michael Birnhack notes that, as with other types of law, copyright

[29] Sundhya Pahuja, "The Postcoloniality of International Law," *Harvard Journal of International Law* 46, 2 (2005), 460.

[30] Ibid.

[31] Jean-François Lyotard, *The Postmodern Condition: A Report on Knowledge.* Minnesota: University of Minnesota Press, 1984.

[32] On international law in general as tool of postcolonialism: Antony Anghie, "Finding the Peripheries," 1–71.

has been appropriated, modified, translated, and used in new ways by postcolonial states.[33] Colonial legal transplants take place on a spectrum, with some transplants being voluntarily accepted, and others externally imposed. The interaction of local and imperial is often complex and sometimes involves a back-and-forth process.[34] In that sense, international copyright is a system containing imperial and potentially anti-imperial tendencies.

Progress

This book differs from some approaches to the political economy of communication in that it takes change to be far more complex than what is portrayed in some more teleological accounts. It does not assume that history progresses in any particular direction. Rather, the direction that history does take is determined in part by institutions that mediate ideas and material interests. This approach leaves open the possibility of a more complex and less teleological history, and the possibility of addressing the embeddedness of power in institutions. Such a conceptual framework allows for the analysis of the expansion of a single copyright regime to be divorced from the idea of unidirectional progress.

"The very use of the language of progress," Alexander Peukert notes, "is an ideological strategy."[35] As Michael Carroll also notes, any particular system represents a different configuration of benefits and costs to the various parties involved, and thus comes with advantages and disadvantages: "The displacement of prior arrangements by copyright should not necessarily be viewed as a form of legal progress."[36] Rather, such changes "should be understood as the outcome of a specific political struggle."[37] As Birnhack points out: "[w]e should ask whose progress is advanced, at what cost, and whether there are alternatives."[38] The "first in Europe, then

[33] Michael D. Birnhack, *Colonial Copyright: Intellectual Property in Mandate Palestine* (Oxford: Oxford University Press, 2012).

[34] Ibid., Chapter 1 "Colonial Transplants."

[35] Peukert, "The Colonial Legacy," 28.

[36] Michael Carroll, "The Struggle for Music Copyright," in Villanova University School of Law: School of Law Working Papers, Paper 31 (Villanova, PA: Villanova School of Law, 2005), 956, http://law.bepress.com/villanovalwps/papers/art31.

[37] Ibid.

[38] Birnhack, *Colonial Copyright*, 45. See alsoMichael D. Birnhack, "The Idea of Progress in Copyright Law," *Buffalo Intellectual Property Law Journal* 1 (2001) and Margaret Chon, "Postmodern Progress: Reconsidering the Copyright and Patent Power," *DePaul Law Review* 43, 1 (1993), 97–146.

elsewhere" version of historical time set a path of European domination and consigned alternatives to the sidelines.[39]

Within this larger context and complex set of processes, it is important to consider the degree to which one international institution or another, or one property model or another, serves or responds to both dominant players and more peripheral actors, and the extent to which a particular institution might contribute to change. Thus, this book takes a meso-level approach that takes on board both the relatively pessimistic perspective outlined above, which portrays countries of the South as the objects of manipulation, and the relatively optimistic perspective of postcolonial appropriation. At the meso-level, it enquires into the particular historical and institutional characteristics of the international copyright system that shore up power while also creating possibilities for change.

Access to knowledge: ideas, interests, and institutions

We can point to three forms of access to knowledge that are key to this study's analysis. The first form of access to knowledge relates to ideas; here, "access to knowledge" means access to the sources of knowledge – to memory and databanks, copyright works, and corpora of scientific and technological knowledge. The second relates to interests: the recognition of the interests of particular groups and their legitimate right to have voice. Here, "access to knowledge" means the ability to be recognized as a source of knowledge, to influence the direction and shape of the discourse that defines what knowledge is, what knowledge is valued, and what knowledge is recognized as being knowledge. The third form of access to knowledge is focused on institutions. Here, "access to knowledge" involves access to the processes and institutions of the creation, circulation, and regulation of knowledge, including the educational, scientific, political, and regulatory institutions that are central to the production of knowledge.

It is important that discussions about access to knowledge should focus on all three forms of access to knowledge, especially since copyright law has too often focused on the first form of access to knowledge to the exclusion of the latter two. Ultimately, all three forms of access are linked. As Willinsky notes, institutional failures, resulting in lack of access to the institutions for the production and dissemination of knowledge, can lead to failure to be recognized as a source of knowledge; such institutional

[39] Dipesh Chakrabarty, *Provincializing Europe: Postcolonial Thought and Historical Difference*. (Princeton, NJ: Princeton University Press, 2009), 7–8.

failures can lead to blindness at the core to knowledge on the periphery, and to the assumption that "no knowledge exists on certain peripheral realities."[40] This is a central problem of access to knowledge.

These three forms of access are important because, in expanding our conception of access beyond a vision of access by the South to the knowledge of the North, and by recognizing the importance of access to the discourse that defines and shapes what knowledge is as well as the institutional mechanisms to shape those definitions, we also expand our conceptualization of what "development" is. Recognizing that visions of development are political and contested, and that dominant conceptualizations and theories of development have changed radically over time, we must also recognize that copyright and copyright norm-setting institutions mediate in historically situated ways between differing visions of development,[41] some dominant, some hegemonic, and others contesting dominant and hegemonic views.[42] Market visions compete with those of various state institutions; still others are the visions of those working in and with international institutions, involving the development of particular international institutions and their place in international relations. Others are based in civil society and relate to the objectives of various civil society groups; competing visions of development are held by producers of scientific knowledge, and by those who might benefit from such knowledge; by teachers, students, parents, and elders about the future of education and what constitutes education; by traditional knowledge holders about the future of traditional knowledge; by Internet users, consumers of digital content, and consumers of news; and by those invested in the translation of knowledge across borders of various kinds.[43] Visions of development and access to knowledge differ not just over time and between countries, but are also contested within the polity of each country, and within particular institutions.

[40] John Willinsky, *The Access Principle: The Case for Open Access to Research and Scholarship* (Cambridge: Massachusetts Institute of Technology Press, 2006), 107. Citing A. Suresh Canagarajah, *A Geopolitics of Academic Writing* (Pittsburgh: University of Pittsburgh Press, 2002), 242.

[41] Benjamin Knutsson, "The Intellectual History of Development: Towards a Widening Potential Repertoire," *Perspectives* 13 (April 2009), 2–46.

[42] Ibid., 2.

[43] Knutsson discusses development discourse as a product of competing visions held by state, market, and civil society, with wars of position ongoing between these three sectors as to whose vision of or role in development is dominant or hegemonic. Ibid., 5–7 and throughout.

Such visions are, for the A2K movement, invested in principles of access. I focus on several principles of access in this book: principles of access to scientific knowledge, education, news, and translations. Principles of access are negotiated within the broader context of conflicting ideas and visions of development, as held and promoted by interested actors within markets, states, international organizations, and civil society, and as mediated by the institutions in which they are negotiated. Over time, dominant conceptualizations and theories of development, as well as the recognition of principles of access in international copyright, have been affected by the rise and fall of interested state, market, and civil society actors, as well as by the institutional processes of their negotiation.

Outline

The following three parts of this book are organized around the three "I"s discussed above: ideas, interests, and institutions.[44] In Part I, I focus on key ideas that are central to the history of access to knowledge within the international copyright system. First, Chapter 2 focuses on the concept of "development" and the various "development agendas" that have been tied to the history of international copyright. Chapter 3 focuses on the history of principles of access to scientific and medical knowledge, Chapter 4 on the history of principles of access to education, libraries, and traditional knowledge, Chapter 5 on the history of the principle of access to news, and Chapter 6 on the history of access to works in translation. Throughout this part, we can see competing, changing, and often narrowing visions of development – or of the future of news, science, education, and translation more generally – reflected in the history of international copyright. The A2K movement, whether operating at local and private or international levels, challenges many of the particular visions of development that have been entrenched in the international copyright system, as new or alternative visions of the future of access to knowledge are developed.

Part II focuses on the second "I": interests. It examines the history of nondominant interest groups, whose involvement at the World Intellectual Property Organization (WIPO), in part as a result of the A2K movement, has grown in recent years: In Chapter 7, I examine the role of

[44] Hugh Heclo, "Ideas, Interests, and Institutions," in *The Dynamics of American Politics: Approaches & Interpretations*, eds. Lawrence C. Dodd and Calvin Jillson (Boulder: Westview Press, 1994), 366–392.

developing country representatives in the history of international copyright; Chapter 8 examines the role of nongovernmental organizations (NGOs), and Chapter 9 examines the changing role of indigenous peoples in the history of international copyright. While such groups have always been, and continue to be, underrepresented, they have made significant challenges to the visions of the future and of development that have been inscribed in international copyright at WIPO.

Part III focuses on the third "I": institutions. It examines the institutional features of WIPO and its predecessor, the *Bureaux Internationaux Réunis pour la Protection de la Propriété Intellectuelle* (BIRPI), as well as the institutional features of the *Berne Convention,* in shaping the role that nondominant actors could and can play in the history and future of international copyright. It is here, in the institutionalized rules and procedures of the making of international copyright, in the battleground that lies on the border between the foundation – the material and economic direction that governs international copyright – and the ideals and visions of how international community might be achieved, that the A2K movement fights many of its key battles.

PART I

Ideas: principles of access

Introduction to Part I

In the early days of the *Berne Convention*, from the 1880s to the 1920s, four of what I will call "principles of access to knowledge," also commonly termed "limitations and exceptions to copyright" or "users' rights," were ascendant. First, copyright, it was agreed, should not stand in the way of the reproduction of scientific articles. Second, provisions were put in place that would permit copying for educational uses. Third, there was broad agreement among the countries party to the negotiations that copyright should not stand in the way of the free flow of news, and that provisions allowing the reproduction of newspaper articles by other newspapers or by the press should be in place. Finally, the translation of works from one language to another was, after a short term of ten years, permitted.

By the 1920s these principles had gone into decline. The provisions on access to scientific publications would be eliminated; the provisions for educational use would be narrowed; the provisions on access to news would be narrowed (but not eliminated); and translation would be assimilated fully to authors' rights. By the 1960s, access to knowledge provisions had come to be seen as appropriate more so to *developing* countries than to "developed" countries. Rather than provisions that might apply to all countries, special provisions were put in place for developing countries in particular.

Principles of access have become increasingly important, not only to developing countries, but also to some developing technologies and business models. While the view arose in the 1950s and 1960s that some countries – the US most particularly – were "developed," having reached some end goal of development, the digital revolution of the 1990s and 2000s has opened new internal and external frontiers, thrusting the "developed" world into a somewhat revived awareness that "development" has not yet been achieved, that it is an ongoing process, rather than a goal, that new possible social and technological arrangements, whether better or worse than those presently in place, might await, and that high levels of copyright protection, or current concepts of how copyright works, may stand in the way, at times, of certain technological and social developments. Here, firms invested in developing areas butt up against those invested in established business models, even as the two merge and integrate. Some consumer and public interest groups also see copyright as a hurdle to new public projects and forms of culture. The state-centric approach, that divides developing from "developed" according to state boundaries, and that views developing country states as the primary actors seeking access to knowledge and copyright works, seems ill-fitting in light of such changes.

The digital revolution has also brought awareness that "development" does not necessarily bring improvements to quality of life, human potential, or solutions to the great environmental problems of our age. "Development" can be, but is not necessarily, coincident with social or economic improvements.

This alignment between developing technologies and developing countries has inspired, at the turn of the twenty-first century, a great deal of new reflection on copyright's relationship with technology and history. Choices in the development of both law and history are political and path dependent; neither is predetermined. They are made by political actors invested both politically and ideationally in particular mappings of moral and cultural norms, economic flows, world geographies, knowledge, and expertise that shape legal and technological landscapes. The turn of the twenty-first century, therefore, has inspired a reexamination of the particular mappings in which copyright is rooted.

The turn of the twenty-first century has also inspired a search for new concrete models of both state and private regulation of knowledge upon which broader visions of the development of access to knowledge could be realized. These include new legislative models, models in indigenous peoples' customary law, new business models, and new models of regulation by contract. On the copyright maximalist side, new models of knowledge governance include the legal enforcement of technological protection measures, content paywalls, and protectionist copyright licensing terms. Associated with the A2K movement, new models include legislative provisions allowing greater fair use and fair dealing, business models that involve open-access publishing, and private regulation such as Creative Commons licensing.

In some ways, copyright is a field of competing models of knowledge governance, both public and private.[1] However, international copyright treaties limit the possibilities of access-oriented legislative innovation, preventing the testing and implementation of models that make use of greater limitations and exceptions to copyright than those currently permitted under international treaties. This has created a form of path dependency – the proliferation of proprietary models, alongside stringent restrictions on access-oriented models – that the A2K movement aims to address.

The chapters that follow trace some of the fundamental ideas that have shaped the history of international copyright within the Berne system. This begins, in Chapter 2, with the history of the idea of "development" at WIPO and its predecessor BIRPI. Then, in the chapters that follow, I return to the roots of the principles of access to scientific works, educational and library materials, traditional knowledge, news, and works in translation.

[1] Braithwaite and Drahos, *Global Business Regulation*, Chapter 25.

2

Access and development

In his 1949 inaugural address, US President Harry Truman called for a new era in world affairs involving a "program of development" for world economic recovery.[1] Within a few years this vision was almost universally embraced. A United Nations Department of Social and Economic Affairs (UN-DESA) report in 1951 suggested the total restructuring of "underdeveloped" societies, and such plans to transform two-thirds of the world, while possibly arrogant and certainly naïve, became hegemonic, making their way into the mandates of international institutions such as the UN, the World Bank, the International Monetary Fund (IMF) and, eventually, the World Intellectual Property Organization (WIPO).[2]

When development was introduced into the vocabulary of intellectual property protection, it became a contested term, inextricably linked to debates about political ideology, decolonization, and globalization. Many international institutions, including the international unions established in the nineteenth century in the areas of copyright, patents, the postal services, and telecommunications, had been founded before the project of "development" became hegemonic, and none had been established with development as a core mandate. Even the IMF, when established in 1944, did not distinguish between its members based on level of development.[3] When development was ultimately introduced into the missions of international intellectual property institutions, it therefore existed in tension with preexisting mandates that related primarily to the protection of intellectual property rights.

In some ways, the classification systems that have emerged remain fraught; how does one measure something as amorphous as "development?" The United Nations General Assembly has never established a

[1] Harry S. Truman, Inaugural Address, January 20, 1949.

[2] Escobar, *Encountering Development*, 3–5.

[3] Lynge Nielson, *Classifications of Countries Based on Their Level of Development: How It Is Done and How It Could Be Done* (Washington, DC: IMF, 2011), 14.

taxonomy of development for its full membership; it established a list of least developed countries (LDCs) in 1971, but otherwise has left precise definitions to other international organizations.[4]

While the term "developing country" was informally used prior to the mid-twentieth century, formal country classification systems related to the concept of "development" arose only after the Second World War, along with decolonization and the rise of development economics tied to Truman's vision.[5] Various terms came to be used: "pioneers," "latecomers," "Third World," "low-income," "low-development," "less developed," and "developing," to name a few.[6]

Such categories have become conceptual maps or regimes of representation that guide the work of actors in international affairs, including states, NGOs, and international institutions, with complex implications and consequences. Insofar as they take "development" and related projects as their mission, international institutions, states, and NGOs often work to foster coalitions and communities with common interests and endeavors in various visions of development. They also perpetuate not only the legal and economic dominance of countries considered to be "developed," but also the hegemonic idea of those countries' superiority and the superiority of their specific policies and ideas.[7]

In this chapter, I examine WIPO's historical engagement with "development." First, drawing on a content analysis of the records of international conferences to negotiate international copyright agreements, I trace the long roots of WIPO's recent emphasis on development by examining the ways that the concept of development has been addressed in diplomatic conferences to negotiate and revise international intellectual property treaties between 1884 and the present. The concept of "development," I note, has been used in many contexts during the negotiation of international copyright norms, some of which continue to be emphasized, while others have fallen into relative disuse.

Second, I outline the rise of the A2K movement, the 2004–2007 battle that resulted in a formal Development Agenda for WIPO, and the battles, since 2007, over its implementation. The negotiation of the Development Agenda for WIPO has also brought to the surface a deep ideological divide relating to the relationship between WIPO and development in particular, and intellectual property and development more generally, discussed further in Chapter 7.

[4] Ibid., 7. [5] Ibid. [6] Ibid., 7–16. [7] Escobar, *Encountering Development*, 8.

I argue that, while the Friends of Development and the A2K movement have had some significant successes in influencing WIPO's relationship with development, strong forces inhibit the erasure of the particular concept of "development" that arose in the 1950s and 1960s. As the future chapters of this book demonstrate, ideas, interests, and institutions interact in historical time to "lock in" an agenda of development that built on Truman's vision.

WIPO and development: a history

The general assemblies of WIPO and the UN, on September 27 and December 17, 1974, respectively, approved an agreement that made WIPO a specialized agency of the UN.[8] The groundwork for this move had been laid during the establishment of WIPO's founding convention in 1967, which came into effect in 1970, transforming what had been the international office of the *Berne Convention*, BIRPI, into WIPO, a member-state international organization. In adopting specialized agency status, WIPO followed organizations such as the United Nations Educational, Scientific and Cultural Organization (UNESCO), the Universal Postal Union, and the International Telecommunication Union.[9]

The proposal for WIPO to become a UN specialized agency was put forward by the Brazilian delegation to WIPO, supported by developing and socialist country delegates, who prevailed over country delegations that objected based on concerns that such membership might mean a weakening of intellectual property laws.[10] The proposal was criticized – wrongly, as it turned out – by countries concerned that an increase in developing country membership might mean a weakening of intellectual property laws.[11] The success of this proposal laid important groundwork for, thirty years later, attempts to more fully incorporate "development" into the core of WIPO's mandate.[12]

8 Agreement between the United Nations and the World Intellectual Property Organization (Geneva: WIPO, 1974); Arpad Bogsch, *The First Twenty-Five Years of the World Intellectual Property Organization from 1967 to 1992* (Geneva: International Bureau of Intellectual Property, 1992).

9 Bogsch, *The First Twenty-Five Years*, 29.

10 *Geneva to Ottawa*, teletext, May 7, 1973, in Library and Archives Canada, RG25, Vol. 10902, file 55–19-WIPO 1970, Vol. 5–2; *Geneva to Ottawa*, teletext, October 5, 1971, in Library and Archives Canada, RG25, Vol. 10902, file 55–19-WIPO 1970, Vol. 5–1.

11 *Geneva to Ottawa*, teletext, May 7, 1973, in Library and Archives Canada, ibid., Vol. 5–2.

12 For example, in 1928 the Brazilian and French delegations had together composed a *voeu* calling for the ultimate unification of the Berne and Havana conventions. Actes

In the 1970s, proponents of incorporation into the UN system saw three advantages in the move. First, this status would allow WIPO to inherit the UN's worldwide recognition; second, it was felt that WIPO might also inherit many UN members, particularly developing country members; and, finally, special agency status would allow WIPO to adopt the UN salary and pension system, relieving WIPO member states of the administrative burden of fixing salaries.[13] While the third of these goals was achieved, the first two were not completely realized at the time; only following the negotiation of the WTO's *TRIPs Agreement* in 1994, which required adherence to the substantive elements of WIPO's *Berne Convention* and *Paris Convention*, did WIPO's membership or profile begin to approximate that of the United Nations.[14] Putting intellectual property (IP) in the service of development was not among the primary stated motives for WIPO's becoming a specialized agency of the UN.

Many feared that the move to join the UN, insofar as it encouraged developing countries to join WIPO, would "weaken" the WIPO intellectual property system. However, proponents felt that the possibility of such "weakening" was a worthwhile tradeoff for the possibility of broader and more universal membership in WIPO treaties.[15] Thus, differing state and institutional interests were in tension as parties agreed on WIPO's move to join the UN.

WIPO's move to join the UN system would mean grafting concepts of "development" from the UN system onto WIPO, where various concepts of "development" were already established. "Development" had begun to move from a peripheral to a central position in the WIPO system in the 1960s and 1970s. Prior to that, when the term *was* used, it was in more diverse and often different senses from the "development agenda" associated with Truman's project and the mission of the UN.

Turning to the history of international copyright, we can see several "agendas of development" rooted in the particular visions of economic, state, and civil society actors. These "agendas" have shifted dramatically over time.

The *Berne Convention* itself, until 1967, contained only a single mention of the word "development." It pertained not to "developing" countries or to economic, social, or cultural development, but to the development of the Berne Union – the "Union" established by the member states of the

de la conférence réunie à Rome du 7 mai au 2 juin 1928 (Berne: Bureau de l'Union internationale pour la protection des oeuvres littéraires et artistiques, 1929), 350.

13 Bogsch, *The First Twenty-Five Years*, 28. 14 Ibid., 29–30. 15 Ibid., 29.

Berne Convention "for the protection of the rights of authors over their literary and artistic works" – itself.[16] The convention stated that the improvement, *development*, and perfection of the Union would be addressed in periodic revision conferences.[17] Thus, the first "development agenda" with which international copyright was concerned – the one written into the *Berne Convention* itself – was the development and "perfection" of authors' rights.

At the same time, the first "development agenda" competed, in the first decades of international copyright, with several other "development agendas." The second "development agenda" of the Berne Union was grounded in a concern with the formation of international law and institutions of globalization. When the word "develop" or "developing" arose in the context of the initial negotiations that established the *Berne Convention* in the nineteenth century, it was most often in reference to the development of international norms relating to copyright and, second, in reference to the development of a spirit of international cooperation and international relationships – to the development of international relations. "Development" was undertaken by building international institutions that would "perfect" international law, which itself embodied "civilization" while simultaneously expelling "uncivilized" countries from the "realm of legality."[18] The development of national laws and institutions in the Western image and the development and growth of the membership of the Berne Union were both tied to this project.

Third, the term "development," at the founding negotiations, was also used in reference to the development of literature, the arts, and culture.[19] This "development agenda" would remain present but tertiary during Berne Union negotiations up to the 1940s, after which it would be demoted or relegated to the periphery of "development agendas" in light of the rise of more economic views of development.

UNESCO entered the field of copyright norm-setting with the formation of the UCC in 1952, and it did so with a different mandate and agenda of development than that of the Berne Union – one focused on contributing "to peace and security by promoting collaboration among

[16] *Convention Concerning the Creation of an International Union for the Protection of Literary and Artistic Works (Berne Convention).* Berne: Office of the International Union for the Protection of Literary and Artistic Works, September 9, 1886, Arts. 1 and 17.

[17] Ibid., Art. 17. [18] Anghie, "Finding the Peripheries," 31.

[19] These three were accompanied by occasional references to the development of education, domestic law, and creative works themselves.

the nations through education, science and culture."[20] As a result, it placed the third "development agenda" just mentioned as its foremost development concern. Emphasis was placed not primarily on the "development" of international institutions, nor of countries or industries, but rather on the development of culture, literature, and the arts.

A fourth "development agenda" – the one coinciding with Truman's vision, focusing the efforts of international institutions on economic or industrial "development," or the "development" of countries in general – was not established in the field of copyright until after 1952. There were very few references to "developing countries" and the like even at the formation of the UCC in 1952.[21] While the UCC was aimed at the inclusion of "developing" countries in a system of multilateral copyright, such countries were not granted differential treatment under the UCC; its provisions originally applied uniformly to all its member states.

There are several possible reasons that explain why, prior to the 1960s, the fourth "development agenda" was not strongly taken up in multilateral copyright institutions. First, it took time for it to spread throughout the UN system, and to organizations outside of the UN. Second, it took time for concepts, typologies, categories, techniques, strategies, institutional programs, and so on to develop. Third, in the case of copyright in particular, copyright was primarily seen as a driver of cultural development and less as a driver of the economic and industrial development of countries as a whole. Many common programs to use copyright policies to drive economic or national development, such as by allowing free translation or reprinting of foreign works, were generally prohibited rather than encouraged by the Berne system of international copyright. Fourth, efforts to encompass additional countries in multilateral copyright systems were not focused exclusively on developing countries; the United States was itself only just entering the field of copyright multilateralism, and arguments pertaining to the benefits of multilateral copyright systems were designed to appeal to all countries, industrialized or developing, rather than specifically focused on the development dimension.

This would all change following the postwar phase of decolonization. The fourth "development agenda" would become primary, and would rise, by 1967, to be almost the sole "development agenda" with which international copyright negotiations were concerned, dwarfing all other development concerns. At the same time, views were polarized on the

[20] United Nations. *UNESCO Constitution*, Art. 1(1).

[21] Nielsen, *Classifications of Countries*, 16.

question of how the international copyright system should take into account economic and national development.

By the 1960s views were polarized between "developed" and developing countries on the appropriate standards of international copyright; the former were reluctant to permit the lower standards of copyright protection required by the latter. This divide led to the failure of the 1967 Stockholm revision of the *Berne Convention*, at which a compromise Stockholm Protocol for developing countries had been drawn up. The reduced levels of copyright protection that were written into the Stockholm Protocol represented, according to the Indian delegate, "a concerted step forward in the diffusion of knowledge and culture in areas long deprived of them."[22] However, the Stockholm Protocol never came into effect as a result of widespread rejection by "developed" countries.

This led to a crisis in international copyright; fears arose that the Berne system of international copyright would disintegrate as both developing and "developed" countries threatened to leave the Union.[23] However, a new settlement was reached in 1971, establishing an Appendix to the *Berne Convention*, which provided a more modest set of concessions to developing countries. It has been widely believed that, following what had threatened to be the "complete breakdown of the international copyright system," the *Berne Convention* could never again be opened to revision.[24]

The view that developing countries had interests different from those of "developed" countries prevailed at WIPO through the decades to follow, but with few concrete outcomes. During the negotiation of the WIPO Internet Treaties in 1996, concerns about technological developments prevailed over concerns that developing countries "were barely at the threshold of the digital revolution."[25]

Intellectual property came increasingly to be seen at WIPO as "*A Power Tool for Economic Growth*" that was "not yet being used to optimal effect in all countries, particularly in the developing world."[26] WIPO's vision of development saw intellectual property protection "an essential component of economic strategy for all countries, regardless of their state of

[22] *Records of the Intellectual Property Conference of Stockholm June 11 to July 14, 1967*, Vol. 2, p. 810, item 202.4.

[23] Ricketson and Ginsburg, *International Copyright*, 913–916. [24] Ibid., 136.

[25] WIPO, Diplomatic Conference on Certain Copyright and Neighbouring Rights Questions: Summary Minutes, Plenary. CRNR/DC/101 (Geneva: WIPO, 1996), 53, item 420.

[26] Kamil Idris, *Intellectual Property: A Power Tool for Economic Growth* (Geneva: WIPO, 2003), 1.

economic development."[27] WIPO's approach to development was therefore "to raise awareness – at all levels – of the value of IP and of the potential positive impact that it can bring to society."[28]

WIPO, holding the increasingly maximalist legislative models of the West up as "power tools," provided the institutional resources to propagate such models throughout the world through assistance to developing countries.[29] However, alternative visions of development, and concrete models by which they could be realized, were simultaneously forming. These would be promoted under what would come to be known as the A2K movement.

From access to medicine to access to knowledge and the development agenda

The A2K movement came about in reaction to increasing intellectual property maximalism at both WIPO and the WTO.[30] It followed on the heels of the access to medicine movement, which arose after the negotiation of the *TRIPs Agreement* in 1994, led by AIDS activists; NGOs such as *médecins sans frontières*, Oxfam, the Third World Network; and the African Group of countries.[31] Citing a public health crisis sparked by the high cost of patented medicines, especially for the treatment of HIV and AIDS, the access to medicine movement had been successful in moderating the WTO and American approaches to patents in medicines and developing countries. That movement's work led to the 1998 WTO *Doha Declaration on TRIPs and Public Health*, the conclusion of disputes with South Africa and Brazil over their policies on access to medicine, the American declaration in 2000 that countries availing themselves of WTO TRIPs flexibilities to address a health-care crisis would raise no objection from the United States, and increased access to medicine, especially for HIV and AIDS, in developing countries like South Africa, facilitated by eased patent laws.[32] At the same time, the successes achieved continue to

[27] Ibid., 16. [28] Ibid., 33. [29] See Chapter 7.

[30] See further Chapter 9. Peter Drahos, "'IP World' – Made by TNC Inc.," in *Access to Knowledge in the Age of Intellectual Property*, eds. Gaëlle Krikorian and Amy Kapczynski (New York: Zone Books, 2010), 197–216.

[31] Amy Kapczynski, "The Access to Knowledge Mobilization and the New Politics of Intellectual Property," *Yale Law Journal* 117, 804 (2008), 804–885.

[32] Sean Flynn, "Special 301 and Global Administrative Law," in *Balancing Wealth and Health: The Battle over Intellectual Property and Access to Medicines in Latin America*, eds. Rochelle Dreyfuss and César Rodriguez-Garavito (Oxford: Oxford University Press, 2014), 231;

be under threat from new agreements that seek to raise patent protection for pharmaceuticals.[33]

Following on the successes of the access to medicine movement, some developing country and NGO representatives suggested that advocacy should go beyond a focus on access to medicine to address, as well, a broader range of issues in intellectual property, including access to educational and scientific material.[34] This would build on international mobilizations in the 1990s against copyright protection in databases, the Free and Open Source Software movement, the Creative Commons movement, and the Free Culture movement.[35]

A questioning of intellectual property's role in stimulating innovation and economic development, perhaps partly in response to the types of claims being made in Idris' publication, grew and attracted high-profile thinkers.[36] Three Nobel Prize winners: Joseph Stiglitz, John Sulston, and Harold Varmus, along with a broader group of public intellectuals, wrote a letter to WIPO in 2003 calling on WIPO to examine open models of IP licensing such as open academic journals. WIPO's negative response to this letter contributed to a growing view that WIPO's perspective was focused exclusively on the benefits rather than the potential costs of intellectual property, and on the protection of intellectual property rather than on the broader public policy goals toward which IP policies should be directed. By the end of 2003, a greater number of NGOs, along with the Consumer Project on Technology (CPTech, now known as Knowledge Ecology International, or KEI), began to attend to and participate more actively in WIPO meetings.[37] In 2004 at a meeting in New York organized by CPTech, Ahmed Abdel Latif advocated the exclusive use of the term "access to knowledge" for the movement, and shortly thereafter James Love coined the term "A2K."[38] A movement was born.

Increased efforts by NGOs and by developing country delegates led to the proposal of a Development Agenda for WIPO. This also led to a

Sangeeta Shashikant, "The Doha Declaration on TRIPS and Public Health: An Impetus for Access to Medicines," in *Access to Knowledge in the Age of Intellectual Property*, eds. Gaëlle Krikorian and Amy Kapczynski (New York: Zone Books, 2010), 146; Kapczynski, "The Access to Knowledge Mobilization."

33 *Médecins sans frontières*, *Trans-Pacific Partnership*, www.msf.caen/trans-pacific-partnership (accessed March 12, 2015).

34 Abdel Latif, "The Emergence of the A2K Movement."

35 Kapczynski, "The Access to Knowledge Mobilization," 821–830.

36 Also see Story, "Burn Berne," 763–803.

37 Abdel Latif, "The Emergence of the A2K Movement," 108–109.

38 Ibid. 110–112.

2004 *Geneva Declaration on the Future of the World Intellectual Property Organization*, which declared that "humanity faces a global crisis in the governance of knowledge, technology and culture" and called on WIPO to take alternative approaches to knowledge governance; to the development of the draft *Treaty on Access to Knowledge* in 2005, to the signing of a new *Marrakesh Treaty to Facilitate Access to Published Works for Persons Who Are Blind, Visually Impaired, or Otherwise Print Disabled* in 2013, and to additional initiatives relating to copyright exceptions and limitations that are, at this writing, still underway.[39]

The A2K movement formed on the common ground between A2K activists, based mainly in the United States and Europe, with the involvement of representatives from countries of the South.[40] Its initiatives, driven mainly by activist NGOs, were taken forward, on another front, with countries of the South in the lead.

In 2004, a group of developing countries that would later call themselves the "Friends of Development," led by Argentina and Brazil, presented a proposal for a development agenda for WIPO to the WIPO General Assembly.[41] This proposal questioned both the fourth "development agenda" itself – the basic assumption that IP protection contributes positively and in a systematic manner to international development, and WIPO's core mandate, which is "to promote the protection of intellectual property throughout the world through cooperation among States."[42]

This proposal led to a series of high-profile international meetings at WIPO in which WIPO's mandate, impartiality, transparency, and core activities, as well as intellectual property's contribution to international

39 CPTech, *Access to Knowledge*, www.cptech.orga2k/a2k-debate.html; www.futureofwipo.org/ (accessed March 27, 2015).

40 Alan Story, Colin Darch, and Debora Halbert, *The Copy/South Dossier: Issues in the Economics, Politics, and Ideology of Copyright in the Global South* (Canterbury, UK: Copy/South Research Group, 2006), 161.

41 Argentina and Brazil, Proposal by Argentina and Brazil for the Establishment of a Development Agenda for WIPO. WO/GA/31/11 (Geneva: WIPO, 2004); WIPO, Proposal to Establish a Development Agenda for the World Intellectual Property Organization (WIPO): An Elaboration of Issues Raised in Document. WO/GA/31/11. Submission by the Group of Friends of Development IIM/1/4 Annex (Geneva: WIPO, 2005). www.wipo.int/meetings/en/ (accessed March 12, 2015). The Friends of Development included Argentina, Bolivia, Brazil, Cuba, the Dominican Republic, Ecuador, Egypt, Iran, Kenya, Peru, Sierra Leone, South Africa, the Republic of Tanzania, and Venezuela.

42 WIPO, *Convention Establishing the World Intellectual Property Organization, Signed at Stockholm on July 14, 1967, and as Amended on September 28, 1979.*

development, were broadly questioned. As Christopher May notes, "[a]t the centre of the Development Agenda is a critique of the WIPO that suggests it represents a narrowly focused set of political economic interests that seek to expand the realm of commodified knowledge and information for their own commercial advantage."[43]

The proposal of Friends of Development set in motion a series of debates centering on WIPO's mandate and the role of the IP system in promoting development objectives and "the public interest." "Such a debate," argued the delegation from Brazil, "was necessary for the sake of WIPO, for its legitimacy and credibility as an institution."[44]

Discussions of the proposed development agenda were highly polarized. The Friends of Development questioned the exclusive emphasis placed in WIPO's mandate on intellectual property *protection*, arguing that there should be a corresponding emphasis on *development* in WIPO's mandate and activities. Such a mandate would require WIPO to engage more fully on the question of whether, how, and if intellectual property contributes to economic and national development. As Christopher May notes, "this attempt to shift the WIPO's priorities [was] underpinned by the argument that as the WIPO is a specialized agency of the UN it should share the UN's focus on global developmental issues rather than a more technical focus on the governance and protection of IPRs."[45] To ensure that issues of development were included, a reformulation of WIPO's mandate was felt to be necessary. The Friends of Development also argued for increased participation from NGOs that represented the public interest. In this, they addressed concerns that WIPO was being dominated by intellectual-property-rights-holder interests.

In the debates about a development agenda for WIPO, a number of groups staked out positions. First among these were the Friends of Development. Others included the African group, the group of least developed countries (LDCs), the Asian group, the industrialized countries (referred to as "Group B"), the European Community, the group of Middle-Eastern countries, and the United States. While the first four groups supported the proposals for a development agenda, the latter three did not. In

[43] Christopher May, *The World Intellectual Property Organization: Resurgence and the Development Agenda* (Abingdon, UK: Routledge, 2007), 4.

[44] WIPO, *Report from the Thirty-First (15th Extraordinary) Session of the WIPO General Assembly*. WO/GA/31/15, Item 153 (Geneva: WIPO, 2004).

[45] May, *The World Intellectual Property Organization*, 4.

particular, Group B and the European Community opposed any major reforms such as changes to WIPO's mandate or structure, the addition of any new bodies at WIPO, or any new treaties.[46]

Eventually, while some country delegates still bristled at the idea that intellectual property could be anything but beneficial to development, proposals that WIPO should take into account "a balance between costs and benefits" of IP protection were allowed to go forward.[47] However, the call for recognition that development was at the core of WIPO's mandate was ultimately set aside, allowing the negotiations, which had been stuck on this point, to proceed. In a sense, the Friends of Development traded the "card" of WIPO's mandate in the negotiations in exchange for the adoption of the development agenda recommendations.[48] Developing countries noted, however, that if development agenda proposals were sidetracked over claims that WIPO's mandate did not encompass development, the issue of the mandate would be raised again. In this, they achieved a victory. Development was raised to an important, if not central, concern at WIPO following the establishment of forty-five agreed recommendations as the Development Agenda for WIPO in 2007.[49] Nevertheless, as I shall discuss in Chapter 7, the dominant vision of development that is being taken forward under the Development Agenda may not be what the Friends of Development or the A2K movement originally intended.

Conclusion

The concept of "development" once had a broad variety of usages in the WIPO context, signifying a number of different "development agendas": the building of treaty norms, treaty membership, IP institutions, and a sense of international community. At WIPO, in part as a result of the Development Agenda established in 2007, the idea of "development" has narrowed in ways that, on one hand, allow greater attention to be paid to

[46] For more details on the specific positions, see Sara Bannerman, "The Development Agenda at WIPO: Where Is Canada?" in *Innovation, Science and Environment: Canadian Policies and Performance 2008–2009*, eds Glen Toner (Montreal and Kingston: McGill-Queen's University Press, 2008), 190–208.

[47] WIPO, *Provisional Committee on Proposals Related to a WIPO Development Agenda (PCDA)*. PCDA/3/3 Prov., Annex I, Items 10 and 18 (Geneva: WIPO, 2007).

[48] The question of WIPO's mandate continues to arise, including at the CDIP meeting held in 2014.

[49] WIPO, *The 45 Adopted Recommendations under the WIPO Development Agenda* www.wipo.int/ip-development/en/agenda/recommendations.html (accessed March 27, 2015).

crucial questions of public health, education, wealth, and employment, while, on the other hand, obscuring types of development that had previously played a larger role, such as the development of culture, or of a sense of common cause and international community. The Development Agenda will be further evaluated below in Chapter 9.

The history of the concept of "development" in international copyright reveals that the development of markets – particularly transnational ones – has taken priority over the development of either the political community or the institutional mechanisms to respond to transnational publics concerned with various forms of development. The "development agenda" of market interests, as opposed to state and civil society interests, has come to be dominant.

The development of a sense of common cause or international community is currently inhibited by the strong ideological divides currently manifested in WIPO in debates about the links between economic development and intellectual property and WIPO's mandate in general. Divisions over the links between intellectual property and development have always existed, but have come to the forefront during WIPO debates over the formation and implementation (further discussed in Chapter 9) of a Development Agenda for WIPO. While there are also competing visions of development within the A2K movement itself, including the competing visions of states and NGOs, and of "developed" and developing countries, these visions are tied together by the theme of A2K, and this has proven to be a powerful collective action frame.[50] The political, cultural, and social dangers and potentials of new technologies have led new technology companies, NGOs, and A2K advocates to engage with and contest dominant concepts of development that arose after 1949 and that are still salient at WIPO.

[50] Kapczynski, "The Access to Knowledge Mobilization."

3

Access to scientific knowledge

On January 6, 2010, internet activist Aaron Swartz was arrested on two counts of breaking and entering with intent to commit a felony.[1] Swartz had surreptitiously entered a network closet at the Massachusetts Institute of Technology (MIT), attached a laptop and hard drive to the MIT network, and installed a script to download millions of articles from JSTOR, a database housing scientific and scholarly research publications to which most Western universities subscribe.[2] Swartz, had he been successful in downloading the JSTOR repository and posting it freely online (if that, indeed, was his intent), would have made an enormous repository of research publications available not only to university faculty and students, but to the rest of the public of Internet users. Swartz had previously downloaded and made publicly available millions of records from the American Public Access to Court Electronic Records (PACER) system – documents that, unlike most JSTOR articles, were in the public domain. In the PACER case, the FBI had concluded that no laws were violated.[3] JSTOR was different.

Swartz's actions appear to have been a form of civil disobedience arising from a philosophical and moral objection to the increasing private ownership of scientific and cultural works. Swartz wrote, in his 2008 *Guerrilla Open Access Manifesto*:

> Information is power. But like all power, there are those who want to keep it for themselves. The world's entire scientific and cultural heritage, published over centuries in books and journals, is increasingly being digitized and locked up by a handful of private corporations. . . .

[1] Trial Court of Massachusetts District Court Department Statement of Facts In Support of Application for Criminal Complaint, http://mitcrimeclub.org/SwartzFilings-state.pdf.

[2] JSTOR stands for "journal storage."

[3] Harold Abelson, Peter A. Diamond, Andrew Grosso, and Douglas W. Pfeiffer (support), *Report to the President: MIT and the Prosecution of Aaron Swartz* (Cambridge, MA: Massachusetts Institute of Technology, 2013), 32.

> Those with access to these resources – students, librarians, scientists – you have been given a privilege. You get to feed at this banquet of knowledge while the rest of the world is locked out. But you need not – indeed, morally, you cannot – keep this privilege for yourselves. You have a duty to share it with the world. . . .
>
> But all of this action goes on in the dark, hidden underground. It's called stealing or piracy, as if sharing a wealth of knowledge were the moral equivalent of plundering a ship and murdering its crew. But sharing isn't immoral – it's a moral imperative. Only those blinded by greed would refuse to let a friend make a copy. . . .
>
> There is no justice in following unjust laws. It's time to come into the light and, in the grand tradition of civil disobedience, declare our opposition to this private theft of public culture.
>
> We need to take information, wherever it is stored, make our copies and share them with the world. . . . We need to download scientific journals and upload them to file sharing networks. We need to fight for Guerilla Open Access.
>
> With enough of us, around the world, we'll not just send a strong message opposing the privatization of knowledge – we'll make it a thing of the past. Will you join us?[4]

Following his arrest, Swartz was charged with multiple felony offenses, including wire fraud and violations of the *Computer Fraud and Abuse Act*, which carried maximum penalties of $1 million in fines and thirty-five years in prison.[5] Swartz declined a plea bargain, and took his own life on January 11, 2013.

Activists like Swartz, and many scientists and academics, have grown increasingly concerned about the fate of science as globalization, privatization, and commercialization change the environment within which scientific and academic work is conducted. In the past, most "developed" countries provided extensive public funding of scientific and academic work, ensuring, to some degree, widespread access to its findings. Since the 1980s, however, increasing privatization of university and scientific research has led to increased pressures for broader intellectual property rights over research findings and for protection of the databases in which they are contained.[6]

[4] Aaron Swartz, *Guerilla Open Access Manifesto*, July 2008, https://ia600808.us.archive.org/17/items/GuerillaOpenAccessManifesto/Goamjuly2008.pdf.

[5] Abelson et al. *Report to the President*, 38–40 and fn. 40.

[6] Audrey R. Chapman, "A Human Rights Perspective on Intellectual Property, Scientific Progress, and Access to the Benefits of Science," Paper presented at *WIPO Panel Discussion on Intellectual Property and Human Rights*, November 8, 1998 (Geneva: WIPO, 1998), 3–4.

The Berne Union has been central in defining and entrenching particular ideas about how scientific, academic, and medical knowledge should be treated: whether such works should be subject to copyright regulation, and what principles of access should govern their use. This chapter explores the history of how the *Berne Convention* has treated scientific knowledge, broadly defined to include knowledge in the sciences, social sciences, and humanities. Copyright in scientific works has been tempered by principles of access to scientific works, although access provisions have been reduced over time. This evolution has unfolded largely according to the ideological principles and commercial interests of dominant "developed" country states, although, as this chapter demonstrates, a number of less powerful actors have also contributed to this history.

Debates about this issue have been ongoing since the nineteenth century and have continued into the twenty-first century; the dominant principle of protection of scientific works that is inscribed in the *Berne Convention* has been recently subject to challenge by the A2K movement and the open access movement. While these movements have not shifted the dominance of ideologies of proprietary knowledge within WIPO, they have begun to nestle in to the periphery of WIPO's operations, bringing alternative visions of development to bear on the future of international copyright by attempting to inscribe a vision of more open access to scientific knowledge in new international norms.

Access to scientific knowledge: a history

1884–1948

The *Berne Convention* has always deemed "scientific" works to be works to which copyright applied. The 1886 text of the *Berne Convention*, whose purpose was defined as protecting "the rights of authors over their literary and artistic works,"[7] defined "literary and artistic works" as "every production whatsoever in the literary, *scientific*, or artistic domain which can be published by any mode of impression or reproduction."[8] Scientific works continue to form an important part of the subject matter of the *Berne Convention*.[9] As such, no member state of the Berne Union is free to withhold copyright in scientific works.

[7] *Berne Convention*, 1886, Article 1. [8] Ibid., Article 4, emphasis added.

[9] The most recent 1971 revision of the *Berne Convention* defines "literary and artistic works" as "every production in the literary, scientific and artistic domain, whatever may be the mode or form of its expression." *Berne Convention*, 1971, Article 2(1).

At the same time, tension surrounds the copyright-default status of scientific works. While it did apply to scientific works, the original 1886 *Berne Convention* also included several significant exceptions allowing liberal reproduction of scientific works. First, the *Berne Convention*'s provisions allowing the republication of newspaper and periodical articles originally applied equally to scientific articles, placing them, by default, in the public domain.[10] Only by a positive declaration of the author or publisher would newspaper and periodical articles be protected by copyright from reproduction.[11]

Second, the *Berne Convention* originally gave explicit permission to member states to put in place legislation allowing extracts of portions of copyright works to be made "for use in publications destined for . . . scientific purposes."[12] This exception would allow, for example, countries to permit the free reproduction of scientific articles from one scientific journal in another. It also granted permission to member states to make "special arrangements" between each other to allow such extracts to be made.[13]

These provisions were, in part, the result of advocacy by Haiti's delegate, Louis-Joseph Janvier, during the negotiations. Representatives of Argentina, Costa Rica, El Salvador, Haiti, Honduras, Liberia, and Paraguay were present at the first meetings at which the *Berne Convention* was founded.[14] However, in approximately 120 pages of recorded minutes from the meetings in 1884, 1885, and 1886 at which the *Berne Convention* was founded, there were only two instances in 1884, three instances in 1885, and none at all in 1886 when a representative of one of these less powerful countries was recorded as having spoken on the matters under negotiation.[15] Haiti was the only one of these countries recorded as having an independent representative speaking substantively on the issues under

[10] Here, I draw on Greenleaf and Bond's conceptualization of the public domain as a continuum that includes not only works in which there is no intellectual property, but also those works in which there is intellectual property but in which there are also certain defined "public rights" or in which only limited rights are reserved. Graham Greenleaf and Catherine Bond. "'Public Rights' in Copyright: What Makes Up Australia's Public Domain?" *Australian Intellectual Property Journal* 23 (2013): 111–138; *Berne Convention*, 1886, Article 7.

[11] *Berne Convention*, 1886, Article 7. [12] Ibid., Art. 8.

[13] Ibid. [14] See Chapter 7.

[15] Excluding Louis Renault who, while officially listed as the delegate for Tunisia, was also a delegate for France. Actes 1884, 31 and 52–54. Actes de la première conférénce internationalle pour la protection des œuvres littéraires et artistiques du 8 septembre 1884 à Berne, 9; Ricketson and Ginsburg, *International Copyright*, 52–59; Kampelman, "The United States and International Copyright," 411; Francis Adams and J.H.G. Bergne to the Earl of Iddelsleigh. *Report on the Third International Copyright Conference at Berne*,

negotiation. Janvier put forward more strongly and more passionately than any other country a principle of access to knowledge.

Janvier, a foremost Haitian intellectual, journalist, diplomat, and writer, is considered by some to be a founder of the Haitian nationalist movement.[16] He had moved to France to finish his education and commented on affairs at home from afar, studying medicine, law, and diplomacy, and writing on racism and Haitian politics. In 1884 he had begun to take on diplomatic responsibilities for Haiti, and would later become a Haitian representative in London.[17] Janvier attended all of the meetings to negotiate the *Berne Convention*, signed the convention on behalf of Haiti, and would also attend the conference to revise the *Berne Convention* in 1896.

Just as he is considered by some to be a founder of the Haitian nationalist movement, he might also be considered to be the earliest access to knowledge activist in international copyright – a founder, of sorts, of the A2K movement before it became a movement. At the negotiations in 1884, Janvier argued that the reproduction of scientific articles should be permitted in the interests of the dissemination of scientific information throughout the world.

Such provisions regarding free reproduction are best understood in the context of the time. The advancement of science was beginning to have, in the 1880s, a tremendous impact on the human condition. Louis Pasteur, the French chemist, had recently invented vaccines against rabies and anthrax, offering hope that the scourge of rabies that traversed the world might be mitigated.[18] Pasteur, at the time of the Berne conferences, was a media sensation, executing public experiments demonstrating the life-saving possibilities of vaccines.[19] His inventions and discoveries would save countless lives around the world.

September 10, 1886, in Library and Archives Canada, RG6 A3, Vol. 214, file: "Copyright Conference at Berne, 1886."

16 Karen Isaksen Leonard, *Immigrant Faiths: Transforming Religious Life in America* (Walnut Creek: AltaMira Press, 2005), 171.

17 Isabella Löhr, "Louis Joseph Janvier," *Lehman College, Île en île*, www.lehman.cuny.edu/ile.en.ile/paroles/janvier.html (accessed March 1, 2015); see also Joan Dayan, *Haiti, History and the Gods* (Berkeley and Los Angeles, Calif.: University of California Press, 1995), 6.

18 James H. Steele and Peter J. Fernandez, "History of Rabies and Global Aspects," Chapter 1 in *The Natural History of Rabies* 2nd edition, ed. George M. Baer (Boca Raton, Fla.: CRC Press, 1991).

19 Pasteur was the founder of not only the principles of vaccination and immunology but also the microbial theory of infectious disease, epidemiology and the basic rules of hygiene, preventive medicine, and the processes of pasteurization and fermentation. Maxime Schwartz, "The Life and Works of Louis Pasteur," *Journal of Applied Microbiology*, 91, 4 (2001), 597–601.

Not only was the importance of the dissemination of life-saving knowledge increasingly obvious, but copyright was also seen as less important in scientific journal publications because journals were seen as resistant to piracy; as Willinsky notes, "before a journal issue could be pirated, a new issue of the journal would already be out."[20]

While other country representatives negotiated actively throughout the meetings on a variety of topics, Janvier primarily focused his efforts on an attempt to establish just one principle: access to articles published in periodicals – especially articles in science and medicine. Placing himself as speaking on behalf not just of Haiti, but of many nations, Janvier explained that

> A number of the nations that are going to join the Union and of those that will be joining it later have as yet no real science and practically no art. [. . . Moreover,] new nations set little store by articles of pure art and literature, because for them those articles are not of immediate, topical, absolute interest. The same is not true, for them, of an article on science, . . . the discoveries and processes of which, as they become daily more numerous and more ingenious, must be brought to the attention of all peoples of the globe for the greater benefit of each one of them, in as short a time as possible.[21]

Janvier argued that the prestige of European science and scientists rested on the ready access, translation, and dissemination of such life-saving science:

> Would it not be a real blow to French science if the work of Mr. Pasteur, which is better known through magazine articles that have summarized and condensed it than through the original works of the scientist himself, had not been translated into all languages or reproduced immediately in the press of the most diverse countries?
>
> It is restricting science, indeed denigrating it, to think of material interests before moral interests, which are the fundamental, vital interests.[22]

Janvier's argument in favor of free reproduction and translation of scientific works, however, was initially rejected in a vote of eight vs. one (Haiti).[23]

When the matter was reopened in 1885, Janvier gave a second, equally passionate speech.[24] This time, his position was aided by the more active

[20] John Willinsky, *The Access Principle: The Case for Open Access to Research and Scholarship* (Cambridge: Massachusetts Institute of Technology Press, 2006), 194.

[21] Actes 1884, 52–54 (translation from the French quoted from Ricketson and Ginsburg, *International Copyright*, Appendix 22); also see Ricketson and Ginsburg, *International Copyright*, 69.

[22] Ibid. [23] Ibid., 55. [24] Ibid., 30–31.

participation of the British delegates, who argued for the deletion of the article on exceptions for the reproduction of news and periodical articles altogether.[25]

What then transpired was a major concession to Janvier, and to others around the world with a silent interest in access to scientific works. The British position was rooted in fears of upsetting colonial copyright relations, and an agreement that dealt with generalities rather than specifics aligned with Haiti's interests in creating a more general principle of access to periodical articles. The result was a compromise that Haiti, Great Britain, and the rest of the negotiating states found acceptable. The *Berne Convention* would permit the reproduction of all newspaper or periodical articles, except where expressly prohibited by the author or publisher, and this included the reproduction of scientific periodical articles.[26]

Ultimately, Janvier, supported by a confluence of interests with the British, fought for and won an important principle of access to knowledge, which placed news and periodical articles, including scientific articles, by default, in the public domain, while allowing such articles to be withdrawn from the public domain by a positive act of the author or publisher.[27] Importantly, this principle was a positive right of reproduction rather than an optional provision.

Second, the right of countries to create laws that would allow excerpting of portions of literary and artistic works for use in publications destined for scientific purposes was established.[28] In this case, Janvier was not the main advocate; it was the German government who broached the subject through a questionnaire that framed much of the 1884 debates.[29] The German delegation, originally "not opposed" to guaranteeing rights of reproduction in scientific works, later advocated instead that the right to make excerpts for use in publications destined for scientific purposes be left up to national legislation. This formulation was ultimately adopted under the *Convention*.[30]

25 Ibid., 32.

26 Ibid., 75 (Article 7); See also Ricketson and Ginsburg, *International Copyright*, 78. The reproduction of the news of the day, articles of political discussion, or miscellaneous information could not, as noted in Chapter 3, be prohibited.

27 As noted earlier, I draw here on Greenleaf and Bond's concept of the public domain. Greenleaf and Bond, "'Public Rights' in Copyright: What makes up Australia's public domain?" *Australian Intellectual Property Journal* 23 (2013), 111–138; *Berne Convention*, 1886, Article 7.

28 Ibid., Article 8. 29 Actes 1884, p. 31.

30 Ibid.; Actes 1885, 29–30. *Berne Convention*, 1886, Article 8.

The provisions established in 1886 on the reproduction of articles and excerpts would be narrowed and eroded over the years to follow. Leading up to the revision of 1908, various press, editors', and writers' associations, including representatives of the medical publishing industry, had called for greater copyright protection of scientific and medical articles.[31] In 1908, the exceptions originally put in place for serial publications (including both news articles and scientific and medical articles) were narrowed to apply only to newspaper articles, thus removing scientific articles from the public domain.[32] Since most scientific articles were not considered to be newspaper articles, this exception, in most cases, would not apply, and copyright, rather than free reproduction, became the default for scientific works under the *Berne Convention.*[33] Haiti's work to establish a default of open access to scientific articles was now largely lost, except where these could be considered to be newspaper articles. The provisions would be narrowed still further in 1928, when they were changed to apply only to "articles on current economic, political or religious topics," excluding scientific articles altogether.[34] This narrowing was done at the proposal of the host Italian government and the International Office of the Berne Union, supported by Hungary, as well as by the French government, and faced little opposition.[35]

While scientific articles would be excluded from the public domain, countries continued to have the freedom to put in place legislation pertaining to extracting of portions of "literary or artistic works for use in publications destined for educational purposes, or having a scientific character, or for chrestomathies."[36] This freedom, while more narrowly restricted, would remain part of the *Berne Convention* up to 1948.

In 1948, further limits on access to scientific works were introduced when the *Berne Convention*'s provision regarding quotation was

[31] These included the *Congrès international de la presse*, formed in 1896; the *Congrès international de la presse médicale*, formed in 1900; the *Congrès international des délégués d'Association de presse médicale, the Association allemande des éditeurs de journaux*, the *Congrès international des éditeurs*, and the *Association général des écrivains, Berlin.* Actes 1908, 79–128.

[32] *Berne Convention*, 1908, Article 9.

[33] Actes 1928, 73 and 248.

[34] *Berne Convention*, 1928, Article 9.

[35] Denmark, Finland, Greece, Norway, the Netherlands, Romania, and Sweden, which had joined the 1908 revision on the reservation that they would continue to apply the more permissive earlier revisions of the *Berne Convention*, were willing to abandon these reservations if a looser provision than the strict narrowing proposed by France was adopted, and this was done. Actes 1928, 73.

[36] *Berne Convention*, 1908, Article 10.

narrowed: "the right to include excerpts from literary or artistic works in educational or scientific publications, or in chrestomathies" would be permitted in national legislation only "in so far as this inclusion is justified by its purpose," and a requirement to acknowledge the source of the excerpt and the name of the author.[37] These changes were minor compared with more radical changes that had been proposed by the French delegation, who proposed treating quotations and excerpts separately, placing short quotations affirmatively in the public domain, while leaving to national legislation the treatment of excerpts for teaching and scientific publications, as well as in critical and polemical publications.[38]

Most delegations, however, had felt that France's proposal went too far. The Belgian host of the conference, for instance, had rejected calls to narrow the convention's provisions relating to borrowing, noting the importance of such borrowing to scientific and academic work.[39] The delegation of Denmark, for its part, had observed that sometimes it may be necessary to quote a whole work if it is very short.

The resulting debate saw a contest between France alone on one side, forced to moderate its position in light of more moderate view of the host Belgian administration, the UK, Austria, Hungary, Czechoslovakia, and Denmark, on the other. The result was that short quotations of newspaper and periodical articles, including those taking the form of press summaries, were placed affirmatively in the public domain. The requirement that the source and name of author be indicated was also added.[40]

1952

Overall, it had come to be a form of common sense within the Berne Union that "scientific" works would be treated in the same way as "literary and artistic" works. Scientific works were seen as valuable works worthy of full copyright protection, more than they were viewed as subjects of public interest requirements. However, the establishment of the *Universal Copyright Convention* (UCC) under UNESCO in 1952 challenged this notion to a certain extent. During the initial negotiation of the UCC,

[37] *Berne Convention*, 1948, Article 10(2) and (3).

[38] See Chapter 5 above. Various chapters of ALAI had also proposed narrowing the exceptions for scientific publications, and mandatory payment for the inclusion of short excerpts in scientific publications. Actes 1948, 447.

[39] Actes 1948, 244–245 and 248–249.

[40] *Berne Convention*, 1948, Article 10.

it was taken for granted that scientific works would be covered by the convention, but not necessarily that they would be treated in a uniform manner with other types of works.

So commonsense was it that scientific works would be covered by the new UCC that the Canadian delegate, along with several others, questioned whether it was even necessary, in the statement of purpose of the convention ("to assure in all countries copyright protection of literary, scientific and artistic works"), to include the word "scientific."[41] While the word was retained, it was deemed important to make it clear, in the convention, that copyright applied not to the information or facts contained in a work, but to their expression.[42]

While it was agreed that scientific works would be covered by the convention, it was not taken for granted that they would be treated in the same way as other types of works. Many delegations noted that, because scientific works went out of date more quickly than other types of works, they should receive a shorter period of exclusive translation rights than other types of works.[43] The delegates of Argentina,[44] Chile,[45] El Salvador,[46] India,[47] and Liberia,[48] along with France,[49] Greece,[50] Italy,[51] and Spain[52] supported this proposal. Spain's delegation, however, withdrew its support of special treatment of scientific works following discussions.[53] The Chilean government, for its part, staked its ratification of the UCC on the maintenance of a distinction between scientific and literary works as regards the translation right.[54]

Some delegates, including the American and Spanish delegates,[55] noted the difficulties that would be entailed in defining "scientific works" and distinguishing them in practice from other types of works.[56] Even the Indian delegate, Bhimji Narayanarao Lokur (a government minister and, later, a judge), conceded that the term "work in a scientific field" might be

[41] *UCC Records* 1952, 74; 134, item 111; 137, items 142–145.

[42] See also the remarks of the Chilean delegation, 274, item 2007: "On no account should scientific works be confused with scientific discoveries"; *UCC Records* 1952, 186, item 548.

[43] *UCC Records* 1952, 81.

[44] Ibid., 279, item 2033; 282, item 2066.

[45] Ibid., 168, item 393.

[46] Ibid., 279, item 2032; El Salvador argued that educational works should also be given special treatment.

[47] Ibid., 164, item 381; 2080, item 2056.

[48] Ibid., 167, item 389; 279, item 2037.

[49] Ibid., 173, item 417; 275, item 2009.

[50] Ibid., 171, item 409.

[51] Ibid., 278, item 2031.

[52] Ibid., 169, item 405; 274, item 2006.

[53] Ibid., 279, item 2038.

[54] Ibid., 281, item 2060.

[55] Ibid., 274, items 2005 and 2006.

[56] Ibid., 81.

confusing, and suggested therefore that provisions allowing translation should also apply to literary and artistic works.[57]

Nevertheless, some delegations felt that these difficulties could be overcome; the Canadian delegation was a strong proponent of providing a shorter term of exclusive translation rights in scientific works, proposing to grant compulsory licensing of translations, and allowing such licenses to be granted sooner in the case of scientific works than in the case of other types of works.[58]

The French delegate, Henri Puget (a councilor of state and university professor), declared that his government was prepared to accept a shorter term of translation for scientific works,[59] and argued that "a distinction between literary and scientific works seemed possible if the contents of scientific works were defined: works of the physical, mathematical and social sciences."[60] Other delegations were also willing to accept a broad definition of "scientific works," including the delegation from the Netherlands,[61] and the delegation from Mexico.[62]

However, the delegations of West Germany,[63] Japan,[64] and the United Kingdom[65] opposed the special treatment of scientific works and, ultimately, the provisions that were adopted on translation (see Chapter 6 below) did not distinguish between scientific works and other works.[66] So, despite widespread support among developing and certain "developed" countries that special provisions should be in place to ensure access to scientific works in translation, no such measures were adopted under the UCC.

The establishment, in 1952, of a new copyright convention under UNESCO may be seen as a critical juncture during which it was possible to imagine the different treatment of scientific works in international copyright. However, the moment quickly passed. It is possible that, because states had been required to protect scientific works as all other works under the *Berne Convention*, there were few alternative models to work from available in national legislation. In the "battle of models," few, if any, legislative models permitting different or freer dissemination of scientific works were available, making such provisions more difficult for delegates to imagine or adopt as an international principle of access.[67]

[57] Ibid., 276, item 2014.
[58] Ibid., 169, item 403; 318, DA/116; 284, item 2088; 216, item 873.
[59] Ibid., 165, item 383.
[60] Ibid., 275, item 2009; 279, item 2040; 283, item 2084.
[61] Ibid., 276, item 2016.
[62] Ibid., 209, item 2041.
[63] Ibid., 277, item 2020.
[64] Ibid., 278, item 2026.
[65] Ibid., 279, item 2034.
[66] UCC 1952, Art. 5.
[67] On the importance of modeling, see Braithwaite and Drahos, *Global Business Regulation*, Chapter 25.

1967–1971

The treatment of scientific works continued to be discussed in the 1967 and 1971 conferences to revise the *Berne Convention* and (in 1971) the *Universal Copyright Convention*, but the provisions that were ultimately adopted did little to establish principles pertaining to access to scientific knowledge. When the *Berne Convention* was revised in 1967 and 1971, the general right of all countries to put in place legislation granting "the right to include excerpts from literary or artistic works in educational or scientific publications, or in chrestomathies," disappeared. It was replaced by provisions that allowed countries of the Union to put in place more limited measures allowing quotation and utilization "by way of illustration" under certain limited conditions.[68] While the provisions that applied to all countries were narrowed and eliminated, discussions took place about the establishment of special provisions for developing countries.

The delegations of Congo-Brazzaville, Congo-Kinshasa, Gabon, Côte d'Ivoire, India, Madagascar, Morocco, Niger, Senegal, and Tunisia proposed in 1967 that developing countries should be allowed to restrict copyright protection while requiring, in general, equitable remuneration to authors – except in cases of use for *scientific*, educational, or scholastic purposes, where they proposed that no obligation of equitable remuneration should be required.[69] This proposal, and the prospect that no payment would be required for the use of scientific and other works, sparked heated debate at the conference and was ultimately rejected.[70] A French delegate, the diplomat Yves Mas, argued that the proposal "could deprive the Berne Convention of its substance and jeopardize the Union."[71] France, along with the UK, Italy, Japan, and the Netherlands, objected to these broad provisions, which were ultimately not adopted.[72]

The 1967 *Stockholm Protocol* did include provisions allowing a shorter term of copyright and a loosening of the translation right for developing countries that were encompassing of all works, including scientific works, but the *Stockholm Protocol* failed to enter into effect. The provisions of *Berne Appendix* that took their place, though they could be applied only for the purposes of teaching, scholarship, and research, were seldom implemented.[73] The end result was that the 1971 revisions did

[68] *Berne Convention*, 1971 Article 10(2).
[69] 1967 Records Vol. 1, 702 S/160 Art 1(e).
[70] 1967 Records Vol. 2, 960–963; 976–985.
[71] Ibid., 961, item 2083.
[72] Ibid., 960–963.
[73] *Berne Convention*, 1971 Appendix, Article 2(5). The UCC's 1971 text echoed these provisions. UCC 1971, Article Vter and Vquater; Ricketson and Ginsburg, *International*

little to address the "information famine" in access to scientific and medical works.

After 1971

Following 1971, some of the questions that arose surrounding the appropriate levels of protection of scientific information surfaced again in the context of emerging technologies and the increasing use of databases and information repositories. While intellectual property protection of traditional scientific works had tightened in many respects, it remained an open question how the provisions of the *Berne Convention* would apply in the case of these new technologies, and in particular, as to whether databases constituted "original" works.[74]

Such questions were answered under new provisions put in place under the *TRIPs Agreement* and the *WIPO Copyright Treaty* (WCT). These mandate that databases must be protected as "intellectual creations."[75] According to the *TRIPs Agreement:*

> Compilations of data or other material, whether in machine readable or other form, which by reason of the selection or arrangement of their contents constitute intellectual creations shall be protected as such. Such protection, which shall not extend to the data or material itself, shall be without prejudice to any copyright subsisting in the data or material itself.[76]

At the time the WCT was negotiated, there were proposals for a treaty to protect databases. However, a number of American NGOs, including the National Academy of Sciences, the National Academy of Engineering, and the National Institute of Medicine, expressed strong concern that protection of databases "would seriously undermine the ability of researchers and educators to access and use scientific data, and would have a deleterious long-term impact on our nation's research capabilities," sparking media interest in the WIPO negotiations.[77] A delegate from UNESCO echoed the concerns of many in the scientific community,

Copyright, 957 and see generally *Berne Convention Notifications*, www.wipo.int/treaties/en/ip/berne/.

74 Ricketson and Ginsburg, *International Copyright*, s. 8.88–8.103.

75 Ibid., 514–515, s. 8.120.

76 *TRIPs Agreement* Article 10(2). The *WIPO Copyright Treaty* provides similar protection in Article 5.

77 As quoted in Pamela Samuelson, "The U.S. Digital Agenda at WIPO," *Vanderbilt Journal of International Law* 37 (1996), 424.

saying he feared that the draft proposals would give rise to a monopoly in information that had habitually been free for use – one that was potentially permanent, rather than limited. Only through greater consultation with the scientific community, he argued, should the international information infrastructure be constructed.[78]

Since then, questions have continued to be raised about the compatibility of the international intellectual property regime adopted under the *TRIPs Agreement* with the human right, established under Article 27 of the *Universal Declaration of Human Rights*, to enjoy the benefits of scientific progress. In 2012 Farida Shaheed, UN Special Rapporteur in the field of Cultural Rights, noted that legal scholars:

> have increasingly questioned the economic effectiveness of intellectual property regimes in promoting scientific and cultural innovation. Scholars have found no evidence to support the assumption that scientific creativity is only galvanized by legal protection or that the short-term costs of limiting dissemination are lower than the long-term gain of additional incentives.[79]

She therefore stressed "the need to guard against promoting the privatization of knowledge to an extent that deprives individuals of opportunities to take part in cultural life and to enjoy the fruits of scientific progress, which would also impoverish society as whole."[80] In 2014, she further recommended that

> Copyright laws should place no limitations upon the right to science and culture, unless the State can demonstrate that the limitation pursues a legitimate aim, is compatible with the nature of this right and is strictly necessary for the promotion of general welfare in a democratic society.[81]

Summary

While the *Berne Convention* originally placed scientific articles by default in the public domain, by 1948 scientific works would be protected as all other works. The right of countries to make legislation allowing the use of

78 Records 1996, CRNR/DC/101, 60–62.

79 Farida Shaheed, *Report of the Special Rapporteur in the Field of Cultural Rights: The Right to Enjoy the Benefits of Scientific Progress and Its Applications*, A/HRC/20/26 (New York: United Nations, 2012), 17.

80 Ibid., 18.

81 Farida Shaheed, *Report of the Special Rapporteur in the Field of Cultural Rights: Copyright Policy and the Right to Science and Culture*, A/HRC/28/57 (New York: United Nations, 2014), 20.

excerpts was deleted and replaced with a provision allowing quotation and utilization "by way of illustration" under certain limited conditions.[82] The provisions of the 1971 *Berne Appendix* pertaining to reproduction do not, except as a part of systematic instructional activities, allow the reproduction of scientific works under compulsory license.[83] Developing countries including Congo-Brazzaville, Congo-Kinshasa, Gabon, Côte d'Ivoire, India, Madagascar, Morocco, Niger, Senegal, and Tunisia proposed the restriction of copyright protection in the cases of use for scientific, as well as other, purposes, but failed to see such provisions adopted.[84]

Problems of Access Today

More recently, the copyright protection of databases, and the licenses under which access to scientific and scholarly databases is provided, have tended to further reduce the scope of user rights that copyright would normally entail.[85] For example, JSTOR, which does not own the copyright in the articles in its database (though it may have copyright in the compilation thereof), licensed MIT's access to its database on the condition that "copy[ing], download[ing], or attempt[ing] to download an entire issue or issues of a journal from the Database" is prohibited. However, JSTOR contains many articles and journal issues in which copyright has expired and that are now in the public domain. JSTOR's licensing provisions, therefore, limit access to these works beyond what American copyright provides, providing one more means of limiting access to scientific knowledge.

While the internet has made access to some scientific and medical information more widely available today than in the past, access to many academic and medical journals continues to be highly restricted. Gaps remain between "developed" and developing countries, in terms both of access to scientific works, and in terms of production and publication. Further, access is not a problem that concerns developing countries alone.

A tremendous gap has been observed both between "developed" and developing countries' access to academic and scientific publication and

[82] *Berne Convention*, 1971 Article 10(2). [83] Ibid., Appendix, Article 3.

[84] 1967 Records Vol.1, 702 S/160 Art 1(e).

[85] Tomas Lipinski, "The Incursion of Contract Law (Licensing) in the Library: Concerns, Challenges, Opportunities and Risks." Paper presented at the *80th General Conference and Assembly of the International Federation of Library Associations and Institutions*, August 16–22, 2014.

between "developed" and developing countries' published research outputs. Chan, Kirsop and Arunachalam have referred to developing countries' lack of access to research literature as an "information famine," noting that

> researchers in these regions often have little or no access to the published research literature due to the high cost of journal subscriptions and inadequate and expensive distribution mechanisms. According to a recent survey conducted by the World Health Organization (WHO), in the 75 countries with an annual GNP per capita of less than US$1000 some 56 per cent of medical institutions had no subscriptions to journals over the previous five years; in countries with a GNP between US$1000 and US$3000 34 per cent had no subscriptions and a further 34 per cent had an average of two subscriptions per year.[86]

King shows that there is also a tremendous discrepancy between developing and "developed" countries as represented in research literature:

> [t]he [United States, together with the EU, UK, Germany, Japan, France, Canada, Italy] produced about 84.5% of the top 1% most cited publications between 1993 and 2001. . . . Moreover, although my analysis includes only 31 of the world's 193 countries, these produce 97.5% of the world's most cited papers.
>
> The political implications of this last comparison are difficult to exaggerate. South Africa, at 29th place in my rank ordering, is the only African country on the list. The Islamic countries are only represented by Iran at 30th, despite the high GDP of many of them and the prominence of some individuals, such as Nobel prizewinners Abdus Salam (physics, 1979) and Ahmed Zewail (chemistry, 1999).[87]

Lack of access to scientific and medical publications is not a problem that concerns those in developing countries alone. Medical students, patients, families, social workers, business owners, and others in "developed" countries do not always – and in some cases, rarely – have access to scientific and academic journal databases.

Tim Anderson, while a third-year medical student at Case Western Reserve University, experienced the following situation:

> I had a patient who had developed gastrointestinal (GI) bleeding but was on medications to thin his blood due to heart problems. This is a risky

[86] Barbara Kirsop and Subbiah Arunachalam, *Open Access Archiving: The Fast Track to Building Research Capacity in Developing Countries* (London: Science and Development Network, 2005), 2.

[87] David A. King, "The Scientific Impact of Nations," *Nature* 430, 6997 (July 15, 2004), 314.

> but very common medical situation. So I began looking up papers on the topic as the management is very controversial. . . . I found the perfect paper which looked at outcomes of stopping vs. continuing blood thinners after a GI bleed. It had just been published 1 month ago, and in fact the authors are faculty at my medical school . . . and yet I was unable to access the article.[88]

Anderson argues that open access publishing is the answer, not only for doctors themselves, but also for the sake of patients and patients' families, to provide them with reliable information that is scarcely available through the mixed assortment of online sources currently available.[89]

The principle of open access was defined at a 2001 meeting convened by the Open Society Institute to launch the Budapest Open Access Initiative in 2001:

> [b]y "open access" to this literature, we mean its free availability on the public internet . . . and the only role for copyright in this domain, should be to give authors control over the integrity of their work and the right to be properly acknowledged and cited.[90]

Recent trends have begun to challenge the closed proprietary model of access to scientific works, based on the open access model. A rising number of granting agencies now request or require that publicly funded research be published under open access regimes.[91]

Open access has been proposed not only as a way of ensuring access to scientific publications that arise from publicly funded research but also as a way of decreasing the North to South knowledge gap (increasing access to "developed" country publications by developing countries),[92] the South to North knowledge gap (increasing the ability of developing countries'

88 Tim Anderson, *6 Reasons Open Access Matters to the Medical Community* (Washington, DC: The Right to Research Coalition, 2011).

89 Ibid.

90 "Budapest Open Access Initiative," www.soros.org/openaccess/read.shtml (accessed July 5, 2007).

91 For example, see United States, National Institutes of Health, *Policy on Enhancing Public Access to Archived Publications Resulting from NIH-Funded Research*, http://grants.nih.gov/grants/guide/notice-files/NOT-OD-05–22.html (accessed March 1, 2015).

92 As a way of increasing the accessibility of academic literature to developing countries, the Commission on Intellectual Property Rights recommended expansion of free open access initiatives for academic journals, Commission on Intellectual Property Rights, *Integrating Intellectual Property Rights and Development Policy: Report of the Commission on Intellectual Property Rights* (London: WIPO/WTO/TRIPS, 2002), 102, www.iprcommission.org/graphic/documents/final_report.htm (accessed May 22, 2007).

researchers to get their work published in ways that are accessible to "developed" countries), and the South to South knowledge gap (assisting developing countries in sharing their research with neighboring countries facing similar problems).[93] Open access is seen as a way to establish a more equitable world information order.[94]

As John Willinsky argues, while "open access obviously represents a break with the past," open access "also speaks to the spirit of that past, to the long-term aspects of the access principle."[95] Willinsky places the open access movement in a line of revolutions in access to knowledge that go back to the rise of the printing press and the Great Library at Alexandria.[96] The printing press, Willinsky notes, "had its greatest scientific impact on those working outside of the universities, rather than on the scholars within," who were satisfied with the accessibility of manuscripts already available.[97]

The open access movement is highly political; it is based on an optimistic vision that current regimes of knowledge production can and should be changed. "Open access," says Willinsky, "is ultimately about people deciding that there may be a way to extend the circulation of knowledge."[98]

While a multilateral treaty on open access to basic science and technology has been proposed by scholars, WIPO's approach has been much more modest.[99] WIPO, while not a cheerleader of the open access movement, has taken on certain initiatives related to access to scientific information and open access, partly at the prompting of the Development Agenda.[100] For example, in 2009 WIPO launched an Access to Research for Development and Innovation (ARDI) program, which provides free online access to some scientific and technical journals to not-for-profit institutions in least developed countries, and reduced prices for access by industrial property offices in developing countries. The program is run by

[93] Christine Deschamps, Kay Raseroka, Barbara Kirsop, Jean-Jacques Pierrat, Georges Malamoud, Barbara Aronson, and Manfred Spiesberger, "Round Table: Open Access Issues for Developing Countries," *Information Services and Use* 23, 2–3 (2003), 150–152.

[94] Willinsky, *The Access Principle*, 94. [95] Willinsky, *The Access Principle*, 190.

[96] Ibid., Chapter 1 "Opening" and Chapter 13: "History."

[97] Ibid., 192. [98] Ibid., 190.

[99] John H. Barton and Keith E. Maskus, "Economic Perspectives on a Multilateral Agreement on Open Access to Basic Science and Technology," *SCRIPT-Ed* 1, 3 (September 2004), 369–387.

[100] Gavin Baker, *Open Access and the New WIPO Director*, www.gavinbaker.com/blog/2008/09/23/open-access-and-the-new-wipo-director/ (accessed March 27, 2015).

WIPO with twelve major publishers.[101] As well, under the Development Agenda, WIPO has initiated a number of studies, workshops, and web site initiatives to explore, create taxonomies of, evaluate, and highlight open collaborative projects.[102] Such initiatives may provide windows of access into an edifice of increasing copyright protection that has developed over the past century, but they also represent a highly tentative, limited, and incremental approach that may assist a limited number of institutions in least developed countries and developing countries, but their contribution is minor in the face of the scale of the "information famine" and the potentials of widespread access to knowledge that new technologies might offer.[103]

The A2K movement has inspired a more ambitious initiative. WIPO's Standing Committee on Copyright and Related Rights (SCCR) is, as of this writing, discussing a possible international instrument on limitations and exceptions for educational, teaching, and research institutions and persons with other disabilities.[104] Many of the proposals made have been submitted by the African Group of countries.[105] These include proposals that publicly funded research should be made available to the public free of charge within twelve months of its fixation, that use of copyright works for scientific research, including use or reuse of compilations of data, data-mining, linking, and data manipulation – subject to reasonable attribution requirements – should not be an infringement of copyright.[106] Further, they include proposals that would eliminate the contractual overrideability of the limitations and exceptions proposed.[107] Should such proposals be adopted, the A2K movement will have achieved the most significant victory in its history. However, this vision, developed

[101] This includes: The American Association for the Advancement of Science; the American Institute of Physics; Elsevier; the Institute of Physics; John Wiley & Sons; Oxford University Press; the National Academy of Sciences; Nature Publishing Group; the Royal Society of Chemistry; Sage Publications; Springer Science+Business Media; and Taylor & Francis (www.wipo.int/ardi/en/about.html).

[102] WIPO, *Progress Reports* CDIP/8/2 Annex XVIII (Geneva: WIPO, 2011).

[103] Abdel Latif, "Change and Continuity in the International Intellectual Property System: A Turbulent Decade in Perspective," *WIPO Journal* 3, 1 (2011), 53.

[104] WIPO, Standing Committee on Copyright and Related Rights, Twenty-Eighth Session, Chair's Conclusions SCCR/28/REF (Geneva: WIPO, 2014).

[105] WIPO, Standing Committee on Copyright and Related Rights, *Provisional Working Document Towards an Appropriate International Legal Instrument (in Whatever Form) on Limitations and Exceptions for Educational, Teaching and Research Institutions and Persons with Other Disabilities Containing Comments and Textual Suggestions* SCCR/26/4 Prov. (Geneva: WIPO, 2013).

[106] Ibid., 31 and 33. [107] Ibid., 53.

by the A2K movement among both "developed" and developing country representatives, must, to be successful, be adopted by "developed" country states and dominant groups in industry as well as by NGOs and the developing country representatives that have proposed it. Given the extent to which visions of more narrow economic development through property in scientific knowledge are entrenched, this may be an uphill battle.

Conclusion

The history of the Berne model of copyright has tended on a path that assimilates scientific, medical, and research works to all other types of material, treating all under the same copyright umbrella, allowing monopolies in such works to create an "information famine" not only in developing countries but also in "developed" countries for those who do not have institutional access to scientific databases and works. Scientific works were, over time, taken out of the realm of established exceptions on the premise that they were more valuable, and thus deserved greater protection, than, for example, some works of fiction. This path toward increasing protection of scientific works was reinforced by entrenched actors and institutional dynamics, to be discussed in the two later parts of this book.

Recently, the A2K movement and the open access movement have begun to challenge, and to provide alternatives to, the copyright status for scientific works and other types of works. WIPO's role in these initiatives has been peripheral. The adoption of new international norms on limitations and exceptions for research institutions could change that.

Following the initial success of Louis-Joseph Janvier, supported by Great Britain, in pressing for the inclusion of scientific works in the category of articles for which free reproduction would be permitted by default, developing countries won few battles in the fight for access to scientific, medical, and research works, despite the efforts of delegations from Congo-Brazzaville, Senegal, and others. Although the commonsense notion that scientific works should be treated as other literary and artistic works was opened to questioning under UNESCO's UCC negotiations in what was a critical juncture in the history of international copyright that saw many country representatives express willingness to treat scientific works differently, the end result was that principles of more open access to scientific works were not broadly established. However, a new challenge to establish more open access to scientific works has recently been launched.

The regulation of ownership of scientific knowledge has been, recently, the subject of intervention by private open access norms and projects, rather than by initiatives at the level of international copyright. The open access movement has been able to accomplish what the negotiation of complex rules under the Berne and Universal copyright conventions had failed to secure: fuller access to scientific works. Open access initiatives have been able to go forward on the initiative of individuals and institutions, and, where necessary, to work around states that resist the principle of access to scientific works in the interests of copyright owners in scientific works. At the same time, initiatives to establish principles of access relating to scientific research have returned to the international level, led by developing country delegations and especially the African Group.[108] It is imperative, for these initiatives' success, that the states of "developed" countries also adopt a new and more open vision of the future of access to scientific knowledge.

[108] WIPO, Standing Committee on Copyright and Related Rights, Twenty-Eighth Session, Chair's Conclusions SCCR/28/REF.

4

Access to education, libraries, and traditional knowledge

> So here I stand, one girl, among many. I speak not for myself, but so those without a voice can be heard. Those who have fought for their rights. Their right to live in peace. Their right to be treated with dignity. Their right to equality of opportunity. Their right to be educated.[1]

These are the words of Malala Yousafzai on her sixteenth birthday as she addressed the United Nations General Assembly on July 12, 2013. July 12 would be known as "Malala day" in honor of Malala's strength in campaigning for girls' education. Malala continued her courageous campaign even after she was shot in the head by a member of the Taliban in retribution for her prior campaign for girls' access to education, which had been severely curtailed by the Taliban in her region. Just over a year later, Malala would also be honored with the Nobel Peace Prize.[2]

Malala, in her speech to the UN General Assembly, called on children to unite in empowering themselves for education, and on world leaders to fight fear and ignorance by prioritizing access to education:

> So let us wage, so let us wage a glorious struggle against illiteracy, poverty and terrorism, let us pick up our books and our pens, they are the most powerful weapons. One child, one teacher, one book and one pen can change the world. Education is the only solution. Education first.[3]

Malala's bravery in campaigning for access to education has been well heralded. She is, for many, a symbol of access to education and access to knowledge for all. In her speech, she pointed to the legacies of Martin Luther King Jr., Nelson Mandela, and Mohammed Ali Jinnah – to the strong legacies of heroic leaders who have fought for human rights and

[1] Malala Yousafzai, *Address on Education to the United Nations General Assembly*, July 12, 2013, www.theguardian.com/commentisfree/2013/jul/12/malala-yousafzai-united-nations-education-speech-text.

[2] She shared the prize with Indian child rights campaigner Kailash Satyarthi.

[3] Yousafzai, *Address on Education*.

civil rights, and, in so doing, she placed access to education and knowledge among human and civil rights.[4] Her work builds on approaches to development that highlight the importance of education.[5]

At the same time, Malala is not an uncontroversial figure. She first rose to the height of prominence in Western media when, following her shooting, she was transported to the UK for reconstructive surgery. Freelance journalist Assed Baig noted that, for some, Malala is a symbol of Western imperialism and secular education who, unwittingly, through her UK surgery following her shooting, became part of a false narrative of Western benevolence and superiority to the East:

> This is a story of a native girl being saved by the white man. Flown to the UK, the Western world can feel good about itself as they save the native woman from the savage men of her home nation. It is a historic racist narrative that has been institutionalised. Journalists and politicians were falling over themselves to report and comment on the case. The story of an innocent brown child that was shot by savages for demanding an education and along comes the knight in shining armour to save her.[6]

There are thousands of "other Malalas," argues Baig, who, as a result of the military interventions of the West, also do not have access to education or the security that makes education possible.[7]

Malala's case thus reveals an important truth about education more generally in a globalized world – far from being a neutral and apolitical right, education is a politically charged issue, not least of all in the relationship between "developed" and developing countries. In this, international institutions are also often implicated in the dual narratives of access to education on one hand, and Western superiority and the dependency of developing countries on the other.

WIPO is no different. These dual narratives rose to prominence in the international copyright system during the 1960s, when state representatives began to grapple with the question, raised by newly independent developing-country representatives, of how the international copyright system should facilitate access to educational materials in developing countries. After all, the international copyright system is responsible for

4 "This the legacy of change I have inherited from Martin Luther King, Nelson Mandela and Mohammed Ali Jinnah." Yousafzai, *Address on Education*.

5 Margaret Chon, "Intellectual Property 'From Below': Copyright and Capability for Education," *UC Davis Law Review* 40, 3 (2007), 818–819.

6 Assed Baig, "Malala Yousafzai and the White Saviour Complex," *Huffington Post*, July 15, 2013.

7 Baig, "Malala Yousafzai."

placing limits and conditions on the flow and reproduction of educational materials in developing countries; and in contrast to the UN's Millennium Development Goal to ensure universal access to primary education, the principle of access to education has not been a prominent or founding principle of the Berne/WIPO system of international copyright in the past seventy-five years.[8] Still, BIRPI in the 1960s posed as a "white knight," attempting to find a copyright solution that might encourage access to educational materials in developing countries, while operating largely on the principle that educational materials would flow from the North to the South. When access to educational materials was discussed, it was posed as a problem of access in developing countries, rather than as a principle that should be applied in all countries.

Education should not be seen as something provided by the West to developing countries, as many postcolonial theorists have noted. At the same time, it must be acknowledged that there are tremendous international divides pertaining to access to education in matters of copyright and beyond – divides that go beyond simple questions of access in the first sense outlined in Chapter 1; there are barriers to access to the institutional processes of the creation, circulation, and regulation of knowledge; and barriers to access to processes and norms that recognize sources of knowledge as residing outside those habitually recognized under Western norms.[9] As Malala's story shows, barriers to access to education are much more complicated than a matter of copyright alone. It also reminds us that education is political, for more than just copyright owners.

Today, as Malala works to reaffirm education as an international issue and to raise its priority at international institutions, some states have undertaken initiatives at WIPO that are intended to mitigate extremist copyright policies as they relate to educational institutions and libraries. We can ask whether the Berne/WIPO system of international copyright is up to the challenge of tackling the difficult questions surrounding education and copyright.

A history of international copyright and access to education

Outside of the international copyright system, the history of Western copyright is strongly tied to the principle of access to education. The

[8] Chon, "Intellectual Property," 818–819; United Nations, The Millennium Development Goals, www.undp.org/mdg/? (accessed March 1, 2015).

[9] See Chapter 2.

first British copyright act, from 1710, was titled *An Act for the Encouragement of Learning by Vesting the Copies of Printed Books in the Authors or Purchasers of Such Copies, during the Times Therein Mentioned*, otherwise known as the *Statute of Anne*.[10] The American Constitution vests Congress with authority over copyright.[11] Myra Tawfik notes that the copyright clause appeared, when it was originally recommended, in direct succession with other education-related clauses, including the powers to establish a university and to encourage the advancement of useful knowledge and discoveries.[12] Such early laws were rooted in eighteenth-century Enlightenment ideals concerning the dissemination of knowledge for the sake of the public good. These concerns were manifested in other ways too, such as in the founding of learned societies and universities, as well as public elementary education.[13]

At the same time, postcolonial theory points to links between Enlightenment, education, libraries, and colonial subjectification. Enlightenment's legacy – "the sense that European rationality holds out the possibility of improvement for all humanity" – was a powerful driver of colonialism.[14] This mindset was reflected in ideas like Kipling's "White Man's Burden," or the French *mission civilisatrice* – the perceived duty to "civilize" colonized peoples, which served as a justification for empire. "Education," Ashcroft et al. note, "was a massive cannon in the artillery of empire."[15] To that end:

> Domination by consent is achieved through what is taught to the colonised, how it is taught, and the subsequent emplacement of the educated subject as a part of the continuing imperial apparatus . . . it is the foundation of colonialist power. . . .
>
> Education becomes a technology of colonialist subjectification in two other important and intrinsically interwoven ways. It establishes the locally English or British as normative through critical claims to 'universality' of the values embodied in English literary texts, and it represents the colonised to themselves as inherently inferior beings – 'wild', 'barbarous', 'uncivilised.'[16]

[10] 8 Anne, c. 19 (1710). [11] *U.S. Constitution*, art. 1, sec. 8, cl. 8.

[12] Myra Tawfik, "History in the Balance: Copyright and Access to Knowledge," in *In the Public Interest: The Future of Canadian Copyright Law*, ed. Michael Geist (Toronto: Irwin Law, 2005), 78.

[13] Tawfik, "History in the Balance," 73.

[14] Leela Gandhi, *Postcolonial Theory: A Critical Introduction* (New York: Columbia University Press, 1998), 33.

[15] Bill Ashcroft, Gareth Griffiths, and Helen Tiffin, eds. *The Post-Colonial Studies Reader* (London: Routledge, 1985), 425.

[16] Ibid., 425–426.

They also note that,

> [i]mperial education systems . . . also paved the way for subversive education. . . . Education thus remains one of the most powerful discourses within the complex of colonialism and neo-colonialism. A powerful technology of social control, it also offers one of the most potentially fruitful routes to a dis/mantling of that old authority.[17]

Education systems, as part of the legacy of colonialism, often remained as a structural remnant of colonization – whether to be maintained as before, reoriented, or abandoned by new political leaders. Education systems can continue to perform "cognitive imperialism."[18]

Many libraries in the Global South are also connected historically to both a legacy of colonialism and, potentially, to its dismantling. Many libraries in the South were established in the tradition of European librarianship, often perpetuating the dominance of European culture and literature. They often served limited elite populations and were, and sometimes still are, ill-equipped to serve local populations or local culture; in many cases, they continue to be symbols of European colonialism. At the same time, traditions of anti-imperial librarianship have begun to take hold and challenge the colonial model by serving local languages, rooting their programs in local needs, taking into account situations of poverty, and encompassing oral traditions rather than focusing exclusively on the written word.[19] Libraries have also become engaged in efforts to preserve, manage, and maintain the integrity of traditional knowledge.[20]

The Berne Convention and technologies of knowledge

While the history of Western copyright is strongly tied to "the encouragement of learning," the history of *international* copyright is not. The *Berne Convention* does not, and never has, identified the advancement of learning, science, or progress as among its goals or purposes. Instead,

[17] Ibid., 426.

[18] Marie Battiste, "Post-colonial Remedies for Protecting Indigenous Knowledge and Heritage," Chapter 15 in *Teaching as Activism: Equity Meets Environmentalism* (Montreal and Kingston: McGill-Queens University Press, 2005), 224–232.

[19] Natalia Taylor Poppeliers, "Cultural Rights and Library Development and Discourse in Sub-Saharan Africa: Is the Colonial Legacy Still Alive?" in *Beyond Article 19: Libraries and Social and Cultural Rights*, eds. J. B. Edwards and S. P. Edwards (Duluth, MN: Library Juice Press, 2010), 41–84.

[20] Terri Janke, "Managing Indigenous Knowledge and Indigenous Cultural and Intellectual Property," Chapter 8 in *Australian Indigenous Knowledge and Libraries*, eds. Martin Nakata and Marcia Langton (Sydney: Sydney University Press, 2005), 83–93.

its goal is "the protection of the rights of authors over their literary and artistic works."[21]

While the encouragement of education was not a central component of the *Berne Convention*, the convention did originally contain an important and fairly broad provision that allowed countries to put in place legislation that would permit the extracting of portions of copyright works "for use in publications destined for educational . . . purposes, or for chrestomathies [educational anthologies]."[22]

Books and educational anthologies were central learning materials in public schools in the West at the time that the *Berne Convention* was founded, and still are. The book, Tawfik emphasizes, came to be viewed as the primary vehicle for both storing and disseminating knowledge.[23] Textbooks remain central in education systems today, both in "developed" countries and in developing countries.[24] This occurred, as Poppeliers notes, as libraries established according to European models proliferated in Africa through colonial expansion.[25] Through them, both European material and the printed word in general were granted precedence over indigenous knowledge systems.[26]

Significantly, the Western library system discounted oral tradition:

> The focus on the preservation of books and "knowledge" in archives ran counter to already existing African systems of information and communication networking and the highly developed oral tradition. Oral tradition was one of the widespread elements of African culture that came under attack during the colonial period. The labeling by Western colonials and neo-colonials of the oral tradition as a "problem" ignored the social, historical, and literary relevance of the tradition. Similarly, it severely limited the understanding of African cosmology, knowledge, and the intricate and rich communication systems which had developed over thousands of years.[27]

While failing to recognize and strengthen the full diversity of important knowledge systems, many governments, and the international system, have also failed to ensure access to Western textbooks. Most governments of developing countries do not provide textbooks (or are unable to due

21 *Berne Convention*, 1886, Article 1. 22 Ibid., Article 8.
23 Tawfik, "History in the Balance," 74.
24 Chris Armstrong, Chris, Jeremy de Beer, Dick Kawooya, Achal Prabhala, and Tobias Schonwetter, eds. *Access to Knowledge in Africa: The Role of Copyright* (Cape Town: University of Cape Town Press, 2010), 2–3.
25 Poppeliers, "Cultural Rights and Library Development," 57–58.
26 Ibid. 27 Ibid., 59–60.

to public spending rules attached to Structural Adjustment Programs), so they must be purchased out-of-pocket. However, due to the high cost of the texts, they are often unaffordable.[28] Altogether, this has created, in effect, a knowledge crisis – indigenous knowledge has been displaced by Western education systems, and access to textbooks is severely restricted.

As new technologies permeate the educational and library systems, some are optimistic that, while textbooks remain central, new formats of educational materials may also facilitate new forms of access to education. Armstrong et al. argue that digital materials are potentially democratizing in that they can facilitate education to marginalized groups by overcoming infrastructure and geographical challenges that previously made educational materials unobtainable.[29] Open courseware and free textbook initiatives all take advantage of these new technologies in ways that aim to create greater access to education.[30] However, it is important, as Poppeliers notes, not to get swept up in the notion that information and communication technologies are necessarily democratizing or equality-producing, since "unless existing disparities and traditions which work against equity, access, and cultural rights are addressed, the use of ICTs will only amplify current conditions."[31]

Such "existing disparities and traditions" include the international copyright system that prioritizes some forms of knowledge, fails to take into account traditional knowledge systems, fails to adequately encourage either the production or dissemination of learning materials, and – often – purports to hold the solution to such problems.

National experiences

While the *Berne Convention*'s provisions relating to educational materials were, from the beginning, very specific in that they pertained to borrowings or excerpts of works for use in educational anthologies (see this

[28] Chon, "Intellectual Property," 824.

[29] Armstrong et al., eds. *Access to Knowledge in Africa*, 2–3.

[30] Such initiatives include the Massachusetts Institute of Technology (MIT)'s Open Courseware, and similar initiatives at the United Kingdom Open University. The Indira Gandhi National Open University provides a national digital repository of open courseware, and India's National Council of Educational Research and Training (NCERT) is working towards making school textbooks available freely on the Internet. S.B. Ghosh and Anup Kumar Das, *Open Access and Institutional Repositories – a Developing Country Perspective: A Case Study of India*, in 72nd IFLA Council and General Conference, Seoul, August 20–24, 2006 [Conference Paper], 4.

[31] Poppeliers, "Cultural Rights and Library Development," 83–84.

chapter, below), some countries had in place broader provisions allowing not only borrowings or excerpts for educational purposes, but other educational uses as well. While Western copyright traditions were centrally tied to notions of education and learning, and contained specific copyright limitations and exceptions to further these ends, many of these exceptions and limitations were not internationalized.

As Ricketson notes, "[m]ost national laws recognized exceptions and limitations on the exercise of rights, for example, for educational or religious purposes."[32] Most countries' laws still do contain limitations and exceptions for educational purposes, though many countries do not make full use of the flexibility available to them under the *Berne Convention* and other international treaties to maximize these exceptions and limitations.[33]

Many of the founding member states of the *Berne Convention* viewed copyright as having some role in encouraging education and allowed some degree of freedom from copyright restrictions in the use of works in educational contexts. German legislation, for example, allowed professors to draw from all works in the interest of instruction, and British law incorporated "fair abridgment" and later "fair dealing," allowing certain free uses of work on some condition of "fairness."[34] In France, the copyright file was given to the Committee on Public Instruction, charged with establishing a system of public education.[35]

Other countries had in place copyright provisions intended to encourage access to education and library materials that were disallowed by the Berne system of international copyright. For many countries, copyright was tied to the building up of national libraries, but the practice of tying the grant of copyright to the deposit of copies of the work in national libraries or other deposit libraries was rejected and ultimately prohibited under the *Berne Convention.*[36] Such systems of legal deposit were especially emphasized in Latin American countries, and the *Berne*

[32] Sam Ricketson, "The Birth of the Berne Union," *Columbia-VLA Journal of Law and the Arts* 11, 9 (1986), 12.

[33] WIPO Standing Committee on Copyright and Related Rights, *Updated Report on the Questionnaire on Limitations and Exceptions* SCCR/21//7 (Geneva: WIPO, 2010), 16.

[34] Actes 1884, 31; Martine Courant Rife, "The Fair Use Doctrine: History, Application, and Implications for (New Media) Writing Teachers." *Computers and Composition* 24 (2007), 154–178.

[35] Tawfik, "History in the Balance," 76.

[36] *Berne Convention*, 1908, Article 4. See Bannerman, *The Struggle for Canadian Copyright*, 57–58 and 62–65.

Convention's prohibition on formalities such as legal deposit was one of the reasons why Latin American countries initially spurned the Berne Union in favor of the *Montevideo Convention.*[37]

Access to education and copyright: a history

The international copyright system established at Berne was put in place to protect the interests of Western copyright holders internationally, paving the way for the international dissemination of the sorts of "knowledge containers" and forms of production recognized by Western education, library, and legal systems. Its few provisions relating to the encouragement of education were peripheral and under constant threat throughout the history of the *Berne Convention* revisions. Efforts made by developing countries to promote the recognition of rights in other sorts of "knowledge containers," such as folklore, traditional cultural expressions, and other types of traditional knowledge within the Berne system have met, historically, with failure, or highly limited success.

Education and libraries

The *Berne Convention* originally contained a provision allowing exceptions for educational borrowing. In the revisions to follow over the next ninety years, this provision faced proposed narrowing and deletion, especially by the governments of France and Italy. However, the *Berne Convention*'s provisions relating to education were defended, and even ultimately expanded in some respects, by delegations from countries like Australia, Bulgaria, Czechoslovakia, Romania, Hungary, India, Switzerland, Japan, Norway, and Poland. Moreover, while it has dealt in a limited way with educational uses, the *Berne Convention* has never contained specific exceptions or limitations pertaining to libraries, although there are limits on the sorts of exceptions that can be put in place for libraries and educational institutions.

At its founding in 1886, the *Berne Convention* touched on education in just one respect: it would give countries the ability to create exceptions for copying portions of a work for educational or scientific purposes, or for anthologies (chrestomathies).[38] States were not required, under the

[37] Jose Bellido, "Latin American and Spanish Copyright Relations (1880–1904)," *Journal of World Intellectual Property* (2009) 12, 1: 1–39.

[38] *Berne Convention*, 1886, Article 7.

convention, to put in place such exceptions, but rather such exceptions were *permitted* in national legislation.

A draft of the convention adopted in 1884 had originally contained a positive right to publish extracts or fragments especially for teaching or in a chrestomathy. This right excluded, however, musical compositions in collections destined for schools of music, due to the fact that, for some composers, use in such schools provided a main source of income.[39]

When negotiations took place in 1885, the German delegates, supported by the Haitian delegate, Louis-Joseph Janvier, were the biggest advocates of enshrining a right to use works in educational contexts in the convention itself.[40] German delegate Reichardt argued that such borrowing was necessary to teaching and to the progress of science; it did not, as some delegates argued, harm the development of copyright.[41] Otto Dambach, also a German delegate and a professor of law at the University of Berlin, noted that national law varied in its treatment of borrowing for educational works, and argued that, therefore, the right should be enshrined in the *Berne Convention.*[42] While German support for a right of educational excerpts did not extend to musical works, Janvier sided with those who wished the exception to apply, as well, in the case of music for schools.[43]

While Germany and Haiti supported the right of educational borrowing, the British, French, Swiss, and Italian delegates argued that the provision should be deleted.[44] Ultimately, the German and Haitian delegates wavered, and the article ultimately adopted left the specifics of exceptions up to domestic legislation, without requiring a minimum set of exceptions:

> As regards the liberty of extracting portions from literary or artistic works for use in publications destined for educational or scientific purposes, or for chrestomathies, the effect of the legislation of the countries of the Union, and of special arrangements existing or to be concluded between them, is not affected by the present Convention.[45]

Even this weaker provision on educational extracts would be challenged when the *Berne Convention* was revised in the decades to follow as writers' groups, along with ALAI, called for the narrowing or elimination of the educational exceptions.[46]

[39] Actes 1884, 79, Art. 8; Actes 1885, 29. [40] Actes 1885, 29. [41] Ibid. [42] Ibid., 30.
[43] Ibid., 29. [44] Ibid., 29–30. [45] *Berne Convention*, 1886, Article 8.
[46] Actes 1908, 79–128; Actes 1948, 447.

In 1928 the Italian government and the International Office proposed replacing this exception with provisions that would have guaranteed a positive right of short quotation in critical, polemical, or educational works, but that also effectively narrowed the conditions in which quotations could be made to particular types of works.[47] However, the provisions established in 1886 were defended by the delegates of Hungary, Switzerland, Japan, Norway, and Poland and were retained in the 1928 revision of the *Berne Convention.*[48]

The provision on educational extracts remained relatively unchanged until 1948, when it was narrowed to apply only insofar as the inclusion of the extract was "justified by its purpose," with the requirement that quotations and excerpts be accompanied by a citation.[49]

That year, France had proposed that a regime of equitable payment should be required, and that, in all cases, the source of quotations and excerpts must be indicated.[50] While the requirement that the source and name of author be indicated was added to the convention,[51] France stood alone in its call for a regime of equitable remuneration for the inclusion of copyright works in anthologies; the Belgian host administration, along with delegates of the UK, Austria, Hungary, Czechoslovakia, and Denmark, once again resisted the French proposals to narrow the convention's provisions on excerpts and quotations.[52]

During the crisis in international copyright of 1967–1971, when developing and "developed" countries clashed over demands by developing countries for reduced international copyright obligations, the provision relating to the making of excerpts was narrowed in some respects and expanded in others. With regard to the existing provisions relating to education, which applied to all member states, the types of works the provision applied to, and the circumstances in which the provision might apply, were narrowed; the provision would now apply not to "educational and scientific" works, but now only to uses of works "for teaching." As well, excerpts (now "uses") of works would need not only to be justified by the purpose of their inclusion but also to be used "by way of illustration" and "compatible with fair practice."[53] On the other hand, the exception

[47] Actes 1928, 74–75. [48] *Berne Convention*, 1928, Article 10.

[49] Ricketson and Ginsburg, *International Copyright*, 790–791; *Berne Convention*, 1948, Article 10(2).

[50] Actes 1948, 246. [51] *Berne Convention*, 1948, Article 10.

[52] Actes 1948, 244–245 and 248–249.

[53] *Berne Convention*, 1967, Article 10; *Berne Convention*, 1971, Article 10.

was broadened to apply not only to the use of works in publications, but also to use in broadcasts, and in sound or visual recordings.[54]

The delegates of Bulgaria, Czechoslovakia, Poland, and Romania together had successfully proposed the extension of this exception to new media, including radio and television broadcasts, and sound and visual recordings.[55] They were supported by the Indian delegation, whose delegate, the government minister Sher Singh, commented:

> [i]n international relations the spirit of give and take should prevail. The use of the word "borrowings" was therefore very appropriate. It would be impossible to advance in education or science if countries were unable to borrow knowledge from, or the results of research done by, other countries.[56]

While the Australian delegate expressed highly qualified support for the expansion of the provision to new media, delegates from the UK, Netherlands, Japan, and France expressed opposition to the expansion. The delegate from the Netherlands (university professor Dr. Gerbrandy) noted that "commercial business and authors should not be deprived of their rightful share in the business."[57] On the other hand, the Czech legal advisor Vojtech Strnad responded that financial benefits from the production of textbooks "could not be justified." "It was essential," he said, "that many countries should be allowed to improve their educational systems."[58] Ultimately, the expansion was adopted, as was the narrowing of the types of works and the conditions under which the provision would apply.

The right of reproduction and the three-step test

The significance of the changes to the education exception was dwarfed by a larger change adopted in 1967: the introduction of a general right of reproduction to the *Berne Convention*.[59] The right of reproduction would mean that the sorts of reproduction that previously may have been routinely permitted in educational institutions and libraries – such as photocopying – would potentially come into conflict with copyright law granting a right of reproduction to copyright owners.

54 Ibid.
55 *Records*, 1967 Vol. 1, 692 (S/83); Actes, Vol. 2, 861; Ricketson and Ginsburg, *International Copyright*, 791.
56 *Records*, 1967 Vol. 2, 862. 57 Ibid. 58 Actes 1967, Vol. 2, 862.
59 *Berne Convention*, 1967, Article 9(1).

In response to such concerns, the 1967 revision of the *Berne Convention* also put in place a new broad exception known as the "three-step test."[60] The formulation of the three-step test established in 1967 is still in effect today under the 1971 revision of the *Berne Convention:*

> It shall be a matter for legislation in the countries of the Union to permit the reproduction of such works in certain special cases, provided that such reproduction does not conflict with a normal exploitation of the work and does not unreasonably prejudice the legitimate interests of the author.[61]

While the new right of reproduction potentially came into conflict with the types of reproduction done by libraries and educational institutions, the three-step test allowed the possible inclusion of other limitations and exceptions for libraries and educational institutions in national laws, so long as they met the specific terms of the test.[62] Štrba argues that this has been an unsatisfactory solution, placing restrictions on the number of copies that can be made by libraries and educational institutions; it is poorly structured to facilitate access to educational material.[63]

Developing countries and educational uses

During two meetings in Brazzaville (more below) and New Delhi in 1963 that paved the way for the negotiation of the failed Stockholm Protocol for developing countries in 1967 (see Chapter 2 above), proposals were made, respectively, for the free use of copyright works for educational and scholastic purposes, and for the compulsory licensing of copyright works for educational purposes.[64] The Study Group preparing for the Stockholm revision conference then drafted a proposal that would have permitted developing countries to put in place regulations allowing use of copyright works for educational or scholastic purposes.[65] As a result, the program of the 1967 conference proposed to allow member states to put in place regulations concerning works "used for exclusively educational or scholastic purposes."[66]

60 Ibid., Article 9(2). 61 *Berne Convention*, 1971, Article 9(2).

62 See Sam Ricketson, WIPO Study on Limitations and Exceptions of Copyright and Related Rights in the Digital Environment SCCR/9/7 (Geneva: WIPO, 2003), 75–76.

63 Susan Isiko Štrba, *International Copyright Law and Access to Education in Developing Countries: Exploring Multilateral Legal and Quasi-Legal Solutions* (Leiden: Martinus Nijhoff, 2012), 203–240.

64 Ibid., 84, citing 1967 *Records* Vol. 1 S/1 p. *137 and* citing 1967 *records* Vol. 2, p. 947 – comment by Mr. Krishinamurti of India.

65 Ibid. Citing 1967 records S/1 p. 140. 66 1967 *Records* Vol. 2, 138.

The Stockholm Protocol, though it never came into effect, did contain a number of education-related provisions intended to facilitate the reproduction of educational materials in developing countries specifically. First, the Protocol would have made it possible for countries to put in place compulsory licensing systems to produce and publish foreign works that had not been published domestically within three years after their initial foreign publication for educational purposes, although certain fairly extensive qualifications applied. Second, the Protocol also would have allowed developing country governments to restrict copyright protection in uses exclusively for teaching, study, and research in all fields of education, so long as the author was assured compensation conforming to standards of payment made to national authors.

In any case, as mentioned in Chapters 2 and 3, both "developed" and developing countries refused to implement the Stockholm Protocol. The measures that were put in place for educational and scholastic use in 1971, under the *Berne Appendix*, which attempted to replace the Stockholm Protocol for developing countries with something that all countries could accept, were significantly more restrictive. Whereas the *Stockholm Protocol* had allowed compulsory licensing of reproduction and translation "for teaching, study and research in all fields of education," the *Berne Appendix* allowed only compulsory licensing of translation (not reproduction), and "only for the purpose of teaching, scholarship, or research."[67] For reproduction and publication, compulsory licensing is available only "for systematic instructional activities," thus excluding, as Štrba observes, "private study, research and distance education."[68] The *Berne Appendix* fails in particular, she argues, because its administrative and procedural requirements make it prohibitively expensive for developing countries to operate.[69]

Summary

Education, while central to the purpose of many countries' copyright regimes, has not been a core purpose of the *Berne Convention*. While Germany and Haiti won certain education exceptions under the original 1886 *Berne Convention*, these were always contested and never constituted a positive right of access to or use of copyright works for educational purposes. At revision after revision, the education exception was challenged, until it was eventually narrowed down to allow simply the use of works

[67] Ibid., 91. [68] Ibid. [69] Ibid., 204–205.

"for illustration." The broader three-step test's applicability and usefulness in an educational context is also highly limited. Finally, Štrba observes that the provisions made available to developing countries under the *Berne Appendix* are more restrictive than those that many "developed" countries put in place under fair dealing.[70]

In sum, while a variety of models at the level of national copyright legislation were focused on encouraging education, these were not internationalized or transformed into international principles of access to knowledge. Access to education is not, and has not historically been, a core principle of the international copyright system as founded in Berne. This can be explained, in part, by examining the actors who were involved in the *Berne Convention*'s negotiation (see Part II below); representation by diplomats and rights-holder groups in the negotiations has far outweighed any representation of educational institutions. It can also be explained by the institutional structures that constructed the Berne Union and WIPO as serving the interests of intellectual property owners and as compatible with, and as continuing, the structures of colonialism (see Part III).

Traditional knowledge

While the *Berne Convention*'s provisions relating to Western-style education were on the relative margins of the convention, other traditional forms of education and knowledge fell almost completely outside the notice of those who negotiated the *Berne Convention* and who viewed themselves as representing "civilized" countries.[71] Prior to 1963, Western international IP lawmaking proceeded largely by ignoring questions of its appropriateness to and effects on traditional knowledge, loosely defined as "a living body of knowledge that is developed, sustained and passed on from generation to generation within a community, often forming part of its cultural or spiritual identity," often referring to the knowledge of indigenous peoples and traditional communities.[72] In 1910, during the British Imperial Copyright Conference – which sought to include British colonies and dominions in discussion on revision of British Imperial copyright system in light of the *Berne Convention*'s 1908 revision – Thomas

70 Ibid., 91. 71 Actes 1884, 10.

72 WIPO, *Traditional Knowledge and Intellectual Property – Background Brief*, www.wipo.int/pressroom/en/briefs/tk_ip.html (accessed March 30, 2015).

Raleigh, representative for the India Office overseeing the Provinces of British India, argued that Indian forms of knowledge were not, and should not be, encompassed by copyright law: "we must also take into account that there are indigenous forms of literature and the drama, which have never come within the purview of our laws at all, and to which it would probably not be expedient to apply the elaborate code of your European law."[73]

Imperial and international law proved, not only in India but also throughout the rest of the non-Western world, to take very little account of traditional knowledge and cultural expressions, many of which as thus considered to be part of the public domain. This has led to the appropriation of traditional knowledge as the "raw material" of Western creativity.[74] Profits flow to the Western intellectual property holders who appropriate traditional knowledge and cultural expressions as a part of their own works, while the originating traditional communities are left unrecognized.[75] As Bently has noted, this "prompts the question whether there is much substantive difference, as far as intellectual property norms are concerned, between a world dominated by colonialism, and the contemporary world of Berne, Paris, WIPO, and the WTO."[76]

Traditional knowledge was discussed for the first time in the context of the international copyright system in 1963 when BIRPI, jointly with UNESCO, organized a meeting of African countries in Brazzaville. The meeting aimed "to assist the African Member States and Associate Members of Unesco in defining the general principles applicable in their respective territories to the protection of authors, notably writers, composers, and artists, with regard to their literary, musical and dramatic works or works of the plastic arts."[77]

The Brazzaville meeting, to which only African states were invited,[78] was expected to be a forum for teaching Africans about copyright: "to give African countries a series of lectures on copyright and connected

[73] United Kingdom, *Minutes of Proceeding of the Imperial Copyright Conference, 1910,* in Library and Archives Canada, Microfilm reels B-2392 to B-2393 26.

[74] Sunder, "The Invention of Traditional Knowledge." [75] Ibid.

[76] Ibid., 1240; see also Bannerman, *The Struggle for Canadian Copyright.*

[77] *G.H.C. Bodenhausen and René Maheu,* circular, undated, received May 1960, in Library and Archives Canada, RG25, Vol. 5169, file 5582-U-2–40.

[78] Except South Africa, which was not a member of UNESCO, having withdrawn in 1956, claiming UNESCO "interference in South Africa's racial problems." UNESCO. Executive Board, 42nd Session. (1955). *Report of the Director-General on the Activities of the Organization* (March–November 1955). Paris, November 9, 1955. 42 EX/43. Part I Relations with Member States, paragraph 3. A South African delegation did attend the Committee

legislation."[79] UNESCO also proposed to establish "a national association of authors for Africa, which will actively follow up on any governmental measure" following the meeting.[80] However, instead of this, Brazzaville unexpectedly became a key vehicle for placing the concerns of African countries on the agenda of revision of the *Berne Convention* – one that highlighted the exclusion of a whole class of creators and works from the framework of international copyright. In one of the three recommendations arising out of the conference, the Brazzaville meeting called for the "inclusion of provisions safeguarding the interests of African countries in their folklore."[81] During the meeting itself, the need to address folklore was mentioned by the representatives of Niger, Mali, and the Central African Republic, while Guinea's representative, Fodé Lamine Touré, spoke of the importance of "cultural patrimony."[82] Such a concern is perhaps natural, since Touré was a key figure promoting education in Senegal both before and after independence, as well as being a noted author.[83] This emphasis resulted in a commission on folklore being formed to draft recommendations and led Charles Johnson to conclude that the "problem of the protection of African folklore appeared to be the greatest concern to the delegates."[84]

The 1967 and 1971 revisions of the *Berne Convention* did not ultimately, however, provide protection for folklore directly or explicitly, but did provide for the protection of unpublished anonymous works (which could

of Experts of July 5–14, 1965, and, though delegates were concerned about objections to their attendance on the part of other African states, no objections were raised and the delegation found "majority support for all our points of view." The objective of the delegation, which took the view that South Africa was "mainly a user country of copyright material and not a substantial producer," "was to ensure that our users were not unduly restricted in the use of copyright material." *Report on the Copyright Conference at Geneva by Registrar of Copyright*, July 22, 1965, in National Archives of South Africa, National Archives Repository (public records of central government since 1910) (SAB) BTS System 01 Reference 38/6 Part 7 *International Copyright Convention.*

79 Lionel V.J. Roy to Under-Secretary of State for External Affairs, July 26, 1963, in Library and Archives Canada, RG25, Vol. 5169, file 5582-U-2–40.

80 Roy to Under-Secretary of State for External Affairs, Ibid.

81 WIPO, Records of the Intellectual Property Conference of Stockholm June 11 to July 14, 1967, 137.

82 Jean-Baptiste Ntahokaja, "Rapport présenté par M. l'Abbé Ntahokaja (Burundi) Rapporteur général" *Droit d'Auteur* 76, 10 (October 1963), 250–259. The CAR also noted the importance of addressing illiteracy, and the representative for Tanganyika also spoke about the need to develop education on a national level.

83 He is best known for his autobiographical story *Une Enfance Africaine.*

84 C.F. Johnson, "The Origins of the Stockholm Protocol," *Bulletin of the Copyright Society of the USA* 18 (1970), 106–107.

include folklore).[85] These provisions, inspired by Czechoslovakia, were intended to grant ownership rights in unpublished works with unknown authors to a competent authority empowered to represent the author and to assert the author's rights throughout the countries members of the *Berne Convention*.[86] However, such powers disappear on the publication of a work.

While little was achieved in terms of the *Berne Convention*'s protection of traditional knowledge, much was achieved by those who were interested in maintaining and expanding the geographical reach of the *Convention*. Eugen Ulmer, Munich professor of law, had introduced the Brazzaville seminar with a lecture in which he emphasized the importance of intellectual property to African states and, in particular, the importance of protecting national music and folklore.[87] Peukert calls this a "brilliant maneuver"; in so doing, Ulmer had "offered a deal: If you, developing countries, join the global copyright club and protect our cultural products, we will protect your 'folklore'."[88] However, the deal fell through. While developing countries met their half of this bargain, the other side of the deal would not be fulfilled.[89] Folklore, once published, or folklore that did not meet the definition of a "work," would not be protected by the *Berne Convention*.

Outside of the *Berne Convention*, various projects relating to traditional knowledge would be taken forward in the years to follow, mainly in the form of model laws that created offenses that included the failure to mention the source of the expression, the use of an expression without necessary authorization, misleading the public by falsely presenting an object as being an expression of folklore as originating from a community, and deforming an expression in a way prejudicial to the cultural interests of the community concerned.[90] Some of these included a variety of exceptions, including uses for teaching, illustration within the limits

85 Ricketson and Ginsburg, *International Copyright*, 127–28 (n. 26); *Berne Convention for the Protection of Literary and Artistic Works, Stockholm Act of 14 July 1967* (GENEVA: WIPO, 1967), Art. 15(4).

86 *Berne Convention*, 1967 and 1971, Article 15(4).

87 Alexander Peukert, "Intellectual Property: The Global Spread of a Legal Concept," *Goethe Universität Faculty of Law Research Paper No. 2/2013* (Forthcoming in *Legal Cultures, Legal Transfer, and Legal Pluralism*), 14.

88 Ibid., 14–15. 89 Ibid.

90 Von Lewinski, *Indigenous Heritage and Intellectual Property: Genetic Resources, Traditional Knowledge and Folklore*, 2nd edition. Alphen aan den Rijn: Kluwer Law International, 2008, 445–447; WIPO, *Tunis Model Law on Copyright for Developing Countries* (UNESCO and WIPO, 1976).

of fair use, borrowing for the creation of an original work, and incidental uses.[91]

Recently, in response to the entry of what might be seen as competing international organizations into the field of international intellectual property norm-setting, WIPO has expanded upon this work. Following the establishment of the *Convention on Biological Diversity* (CBD) in 1992 and the negotiation of the WTO *TRIPs Agreement* in 1994, suggestions were made that WIPO could expand its role in the area of traditional knowledge.[92]

For instance, the Centre for International Environmental Law (CIEL) prepared a paper in 1997 suggesting that WIPO should contribute to efforts to develop *sui generis* systems, should consult with and survey indigenous peoples on how certain products might benefit from protection as trademarks and geographical indications, should play a role in the development of registries of traditional knowledge, should play a role in studying disclosure of origin in patent applications, and should examine the ways that traditional knowledge might be protected using moral rights.[93]

In response, WIPO began to give issues of "culture" a higher profile in order to remain relevant within the international intellectual property system.[94] The General Assembly of WIPO in 2000 created an Intergovernmental Committee on Intellectual Property and Genetic Resources, Traditional Knowledge, and Folklore (IGC).[95] The IGC was established and met for the first time in 2001 as WIPO's main body dealing with traditional knowledge. The Development Agenda, beginning in 2004 (see Chapter 2), helped to spark increased momentum within the IGC toward negotiation of an international instrument for the protection

[91] Von Lewinski, *Indigenous Heritage and Intellectual Property*, 447–450.

[92] *Convention on Biological Diversity*, adopted June 5, 1992, 1760 UNTS 79; *Final Act Embodying the Results of the Uruguay Round of Multilateral Trade Negotiations*, Annex IC: *Agreement on Trade-Related Aspects of Intellectual Property Rights* (Geneva: World Trade Organization, 1994); David Downes, "Using Intellectual Property as a Tool to Protect Traditional Knowledge: Recommendations for Next Steps," Center for International Environmental Law (CIEL) Discussion Paper. Madrid: CIEL, 1997.

[93] David Downes, "Using Intellectual Property as a Tool to Protect Traditional Knowledge: Recommendations for Next Steps."

[94] Kathy Bowrey and Jane Anderson, "The Politics of Global Information Sharing: Whose Cultural Agendas are Being Advanced?" *Social & Legal Studies* 18 (December 2009), 490.

[95] Von Lewinski, *Indigenous Heritage and Intellectual Property*, 461; WIPO, Matters Concerning Intellectual Property and Genetic Resources, Traditional Knowledge and Folklore – An Overview IGC/01/03 (Geneva: WIPO, 2001), 10.

of traditional knowledge, traditional cultural expressions/folklore, and genetic resources.[96]

The desire to maintain and extend WIPO's role, along with its "mission" to "spread, inculcate, and enforce global values and norms," may be seen as playing a part in the institution's willingness to play a role in the field of traditional knowledge.[97] WIPO has, as a result, undertaken massive projects and fact-finding missions relating to traditional knowledge.[98] These would give WIPO greater authority, expertise, and relevance to stake a claim in an emerging field of intellectual property.

The situation today

Traditional knowledge

Since at least 2002, WIPO has offered, on request, technical assistance to governments, indigenous peoples, and others on traditional knowledge, traditional cultural expressions, and genetic resources.[99] WIPO organizes workshops and seminars, disseminates information and resources, and provides legislative advice, education, and training.[100] As a part of its Creative Heritage Project, launched in 2006, WIPO established a training program focused on teaching communities how to record and archive their heritage, manage access to their cultural documentation, and to protect their intellectual property. This program is offered in partnership with the American Folklife Center at the United States Library of Congress and the Center for Documentary Studies at Duke University. WIPO also partners with the Pacific Islands Forum Secretariat (PIFS) to help implement a *Traditional Knowledge Action Plan* for the Pacific Island countries of Cook Islands, Fiji, Kiribati, Palau, Papua New Guinea, and Vanuatu. A similar project is being established in the Caribbean, and by

[96] WIPO, *Intergovernmental Committee*, www.wipo.int/tk/en/igc/ (accessed January 29, 2013).

[97] Finnemore and Barnett, "The Politics, Power and Pathologies," 229 (n. 24).

[98] See Chapter 9; Von Lewinski, *Indigenous Heritage and Intellectual Property*, 65 and 461; WIPO, WIPO Report on Fact-Finding Missions on Intellectual Property and Traditional Knowledge (1998–1999) (WIPO, 2001).

[99] United Nations Economic and Social Council, *Information Received from Entities of the United Nations System and other Intergovernmental Organizations: World Intellectual Property Organization E/C.19/2012/5 23 February 2012* (United Nations Economic and Social Council, 2012), 7–8.

[100] WIPO, *Intellectual Property and Genetic Resources, Traditional Knowledge and Traditional Cultural Expressions: An Overview* (Geneva: WIPO, 2012), 35–36.

involving PIFS in the Caribbean project, WIPO facilitates South–South cooperation.[101] In 2007, the IGC formulated a set of draft recommendations for patent offices dealing with traditional knowledge, encouraging them to prioritize and recognize relevant traditional knowledge in patent search and examination, and to systematically incorporate traditional knowledge in search procedures and staff training.[102]

The WIPO Indigenous Intellectual Property Law Fellowship Program was inaugurated in 2008, which, each year, appoints one member of an indigenous community to, among other things, "assist in the conceptualization, development and organization of outreach and awareness-raising activities with indigenous peoples and local communities related to intellectual property and genetic resources, traditional knowledge and traditional cultural expressions."[103] Drawing on its massive efforts to construct frames of knowledge about traditional knowledge, traditional cultural expressions, and genetic resources, WIPO "teaches" indigenous communities about "the law," thus spreading and establishing Western-style intellectual property law and its acquired expertise and frameworks of knowledge about indigenous needs, interests, and norms in indigenous and local communities around the world. Through its Fellowship Program it solicits indigenous elites to take part in this project.

Ulmer's "deal" of 1963 may still hang in the air as developing countries continue to press for international protection of traditional knowledge. The IGC is, as of this writing, "undertaking text-based negotiations with the objective of reaching agreement on a text(s) of an international legal instrument(s), which will ensure the effective protection of traditional knowledge (TK), traditional cultural expressions (TCEs), and genetic resources (GRs)."[104] Such discussions have been ongoing for over a decade. However, it remains to be decided what groups will be the beneficiaries of the instrument, how such groups will be identified, the criteria to be used, and who should apply such criteria.[105] Neither the scope of the

[101] Ibid. [102] Von Lewinski, *Indigenous Heritage and Intellectual Property*, 105.

[103] WIPO, WIPO Indigenous Fellow: One Year Fellowship (2013), Renewable for One Further Year (2014): Call for Expressions of Interest (WIPO, 2012), www.wipo.int/export/sites/www/tken/training/fellowship/pdf/call_ind_fellowship_2013-2014_final.pdf (accessed January 29, 2013).

[104] WIPO, *Intergovernmental Committee*, www.wipo.int/tk/en/igc/ (accessed January 29, 2013).

[105] Von Lewinski, *Indigenous Heritage and Intellectual Property*, 71, notes that "Self-identification is arguably an element of self-determination, and some have essentially called for communities to have the capacity to determine their own eligibility – an essentially subjective test. In practice, it is difficult to imagine a fully international approach

possible instrument, nor the rights it will put in place, are yet determined. Furthermore, it is not certain whether the negotiations have the support of indigenous peoples, or whether indigenous peoples recognize WIPO as a legitimate forum for norm-setting on traditional knowledge, traditional cultural expressions, and genetic resources (see Chapter 9 below).[106]

Bowrey and Anderson argue that the operations of imperialism continue through the sorts of knowledge constructed by WIPO. WIPO's knowledge frames construct a class of "aboriginal" or "indigenous" that, in reality, includes hundreds of different groups and positions. They argue that by continuing to divide "indigenous" and "non-indigenous," "developed" and "developing," "Western" and "non-Western," WIPO continues to create and bolster a sense of "otherness" that designates indigenous people as "special" or "particular," and that continues to exclude and marginalize indigenous peoples.[107] Boateng argues that the terms "folklore" and "indigenous knowledge" naturalize Western cultural production, conferring a second-class status on different kinds of knowledge and cultural production.[108] Bowrey and Anderson argue that, in its relatively late efforts to include and take account of traditional knowledge, WIPO continues to employ categories of knowledge that subjugate aboriginal peoples, reproducing in WIPO literature an idea of "traditional" that continues to situate indigenous peoples as existing somewhere outside of "modernity."[109] Such categories tend to assume a shared identity, shared artistic practices, shared interests, and the appropriateness of a shared form of intellectual property.[110]

Overall, in the history of international copyright, developing country and aboriginal representatives have pressed for, to limited effect, greater provisions relating to education and traditional knowledge. However, they were most successful when supported by an outside actor, such as in cases where a core country like Germany supported the bid for education-related provisions, or when WIPO had an institutional interest in staking

to this question, and a case-by-case determination under national law, perhaps guided by international rules or guidelines, may be inevitable."

106 See *Recommendations of the North American Indigenous Peoples' Caucus to the Eleventh Session of the United Nations Permanent Forum on Indigenous Issues* (United Nations Permanent Forum on Indigenous Issues, 2012), 9–10.

107 Bowrey and Anderson, "The Politics of Global Information Sharing," 487 and 490.

108 Boatema Boateng, *The Copyright Thing Doesn't Work Here: Adinkra and Kente Cloth and Intellectual Property in Ghana* (Minneapolis: University of Minnesota Press 2011), 12–13.

109 Bowrey and Anderson, "The Politics of Global Information Sharing," 491.

110 Ibid., 493–494.

out territory in the subject-matter of traditional knowledge. Even so, a formal treaty on traditional knowledge has yet to be achieved.

Educational institutions and libraries

While the international copyright system does not mandate many specific exceptions or limitations to copyright in an educational context, it does leave flexibility for member states to make such exceptions and limitations in their domestic laws. However, while most countries have some limitations and exceptions pertaining to education, including, for example, fair use and fair dealing provisions, many countries do not take full advantage of the flexibilities available under international law, possibly due in part to the technical assistance provided by WIPO, which has not historically advised maximum use of the flexibilities available.[111]

Most countries also have a copyright exception relating to libraries, often permitting libraries or their patrons to reproduce copyrighted works for private research and study, to preserve and replace library materials, and to undertake interlibrary lending.[112] However, the library exceptions available in some countries are not sufficient. Armstrong et al. note that library photocopying plays an important role in facilitating access to works in some of the African countries:

> the law library at the Université de Cheikh Anta Diop (UCAD) in Dakar has book stacks full of photocopies rather than printed textbooks because students vandalise the originals through 'page-tearing' in order to secure access to portions of the books. Signs posted next to photocopiers at a UCAD library instruct students to photocopy rather than tear pages out of books, while at the same time informing students that photocopying could be an infringing activity.[113]

They found in 2010 that library exceptions did not permit either the copying of entire works by libraries or the digitization of library collection material. This, they argued, was a concern:

[111] Consumers International, *Copyright and Access to Knowledge: Policy Recommendations on Flexibilities in Copyright Laws* (Kuala Lumpur: Consumers International Asia Pacific Office, 2006); Armstrong et al., eds. *Access to Knowledge in Africa*, 318; WIPO Standing Committee on Copyright and Related Rights, Updated Report on the Questionnaire on Limitations and Exceptions, 16.

[112] WIPO, Study on Copyright Limitations and Exceptions for Libraries and Archives SCCR/29/3 (Geneva: WIPO, 2014), 4.

[113] Armstrong et al., eds. *Access to Knowledge in Africa*, 335–336.

> [l]ibraries and archives are among the most important institutions for enabling access to learning materials and creating a literate and well educated population. . . . Though libraries and archives do not expect to be completely free from ordinary copyright rules and in fact appreciate the need to protect authors and their publishers, some additional freedoms could be created without unduly impacting upon copyright-owners' legitimate interests.[114]

Only 34 of 186 countries examined in a 2014 WIPO study had in place a general exception for library copying, while more (100) had in place an exception permitting the preservation of works or (93) copying for research or private study, still leaving significant numbers of countries without such exceptions.[115] At least twenty-one countries did not have any statutory library exception.[116]

The International Federation of Library Associations and Institutions (IFLA), the International Council on Archives (ICA), and other associations and NGOs have noted that libraries face a number of problems as they attempt to provide both traditional and new services to their users – many related to new technologies. Digitization, license agreements imposed by publishers of electronic journals and books, and Technological Protection Measures (TPMs) all introduce problems of access, preservation, and maintaining copyright exceptions. Moreover, the globalized possibilities of resource sharing, which take place increasingly across borders, are undermined by the territoriality of copyright law.[117] IFLA, the ICA, and others suggest that a treaty is the best way to ensure that a minimum set of limitations and exceptions for libraries and archives exist, and that they apply in cross-border environments.[118]

It is in this context that WIPO's Standing Committee on Copyright and Related Rights (SCCR) is, as of this writing, examining two possible international instruments: the first on limitations and exceptions for libraries and archives, the second on limitations and exceptions for educational, teaching, and research institutions and for persons with other disabilities. The work on these international instruments originates in a proposal made by Chile in 2004 that "the subject of exceptions and limitations to

[114] Ibid., 324. [115] WIPO, *Study on Copyright Limitations and Exceptions*, 5–6.

[116] Ibid., 7; WIPO, The Case for a Treaty on Exceptions and Limitations for Libraries and Archives: Background Paper by IFLA, ICA, EIFL and Innovarte SCCR/23/3 (Geneva: WIPO, 2011).

[117] WIPO, *The Case for a Treaty on Exceptions and Limitations for Libraries and Archives*, 3.

[118] Ibid.

copyright and related rights for the purposes of education, libraries and disabled persons" be added to the agenda of the SCCR.[119] The specific format of such instruments – whether binding or non-binding, and whether formulated as a set of principles or in specific treaty language outlining specific required exceptions and limitations – is not yet agreed. Neither the United States nor the European Union currently support binding treaties, while the Latin American and Caribbean Group of countries and the African Group of countries are more in favor.[120]

Significantly, the proposed international instrument would apply to all countries rather than only to developing countries. The African Group, which has taken a lead in making proposals for the language of the new instrument, has proposed that it should include much broader principles of access to facilitate teaching, scholarship, and research than those inscribed in the *Berne Convention* and its Appendix, including the right of any educational institution or research organization to "make copies of books and other works used by students and teachers, when the prices charged for the works are unaffordable by the education institution or by the students" and "to make copies of works no longer available from publishers, and/or for which the owner of the work cannot be found, if a good faith effort fails to identify and locate the owner of the work," with "reasonable and fair compensation" to be awarded by the state in which the use takes place.[121] Such provisions, should they be established, would give to states far greater tools to achieve public policy objectives, and they would establish WIPO as a fruitful forum for the establishment of minimum standards of access to educational materials.[122] However, "developed" country governments, as well as developing country states, must be convinced to support a new vision of access to educational materials for such provisions to be adopted as mandatory norms in the international copyright system, and such is not currently the case.

[119] Chile Proposal by Chile on the Subject "Exceptions and Limitations to Copyright and Related Rights." SCCR/12/3 (Geneva: WIPO, 2004). See also section "L&E work" in DA chapter above.

[120] WIPO, Standing Committee on Copyright and Related Rights, Twenty-Seventh Session, Provisional Report SCCR/27/9prov (Geneva: WIPO, 2014), 36–37.

[121] WIPO, Standing Committee on Copyright and Related Rights, Provisional Working Document Towards an Appropriate International Legal Instrument (in Whatever Form) on Limitations and Exceptions for Educational, Teaching and Research Institutions and Persons with Other Disabilities Containing Comments and Textual Suggestions SCCR/26/4 Prov, 18.

[122] Štrba, *International Copyright Law and Access to Education*, 7 and 206–208.

Conclusion

The relationship between the A2K movement and efforts to gain recognition for traditional knowledge is uneasy. Many supporters of access to knowledge principles view new forms of protection, whether of traditional knowledge or other subject matter, as prohibiting, rather than promoting, access to knowledge and culture. Others see alternative models of governing knowledge, such as those based on indigenous peoples' models of knowledge governance, as rich alternatives to the Western models of private property that currently dominate the norms of international intellectual property. Debora Halbert, for example, argues that indigenous peoples' struggles at local, national, and international levels to disrupt traditional ideas about intellectual property offer "a catalyst for others who are also interested in a future for creativity that is more flexible than that advocated by the culture industry."[123] Here, competing visions of development conflict: the visions of proponents of protection for traditional knowledge, and those of the A2K movement, both offer alternative visions of development to those inscribed by copyright owners and dominant states.

WIPO activities in the field of traditional knowledge, traditional cultural expressions, and genetic resources form a continuous part of a long history where international law and institutions have come to define the terms and methods by which non-Western norms might be admitted and assimilated into the Western legal framework. This is done in such a way as to maintain and extend the marginal position of indigenous peoples and customary laws. The goal of encouraging education, which has been central to copyright law at domestic levels, has also long been kept at the periphery of the Berne system of international copyright. Minimum standards of limitations and exceptions to copyright in an educational context have never been established under the *Berne Convention*. Today, however, both proponents of the recognition of traditional knowledge, and the A2K movement, aim to bring alternative visions of education and knowledge governance to a more central position in the WIPO system of international copyright by establishing such minimum standards for copyright, and by establishing a treaty on traditional knowledge.

It should be acknowledged that WIPO's relative transparency and openness to observers, as compared to other international institutions

[123] Debora J. Halbert, *The State of Copyright: The Complex Relationships of Cultural Creation in a Globalized World*. London and New York: Routledge, 2014, 144.

(see Chapter 10), allows WIPO to adapt and respond to new trends and requirements, to extend its practices to allow new voices to be heard, and to encompass, to a greater extent, its margins. The opportunities that this flexibility provides are, on the other hand, limited. It remains possible that indigenous peoples may be able to make use of WIPO's flexibility and contradictions to introduce conflict, debate, norms, and possibilities to the organization that could be of benefit to indigenous peoples and, perhaps, to effect limited or incremental institutional change at WIPO itself. The efforts of the A2K movement, until the states of "developed" countries are brought on board in the initiative to establish minimum standards of access to educational materials under international copyright law, are also likely to see highly limited success. WIPO's ability to encompass its margins allows it to continue to act as a gatekeeper to the "realm of legality," enshrining particular visions of development in international law while consigning others to the periphery.[124] It is thus crucial to the future of education that all states engage to establish an inclusive vision of both what constitutes educational materials, and of access to educational materials, allowing states and communities, rather than intellectual property owners, to act as the gatekeepers of education.

[124] Anghie, "Finding the Peripheries," 31 (n. 21).

5

Access to news

Since the turn of the millennium, sparked by the proliferation of free and advertising-supported news-aggregating web sites, new questions have been raised about whether there is or should be copyright in the headlines and snippets of news reproduced by aggregators such as *Google News*. This is not an issue that is confined to developing country access to news; rather, it is an issue of access to knowledge that has equally arisen in countries considered to be "developed." In Belgium, Brazil, Germany, Ireland, Spain, and the United States, news aggregators and news producers have clashed over the question of whether copyright subsists in short snippets of news displayed as summaries, or in the links that some aggregators provide to news items from other online sources.[1] Such clashes have been resolved differently in different national contexts.

The role of copyright in facilitating, or inhibiting, access to news is a policy issue that has been raised from the founding days of the *Berne Convention* and that continues to be a live issue into the new millennium, sparking polarized visions of free, diverse, and plentiful sources of news on one hand, and of the rise of "content kleptomaniacs" on the other:

> The [news] aggregators and the plagiarists will soon have to pay a price for the co-opting of our content. But if we do not take advantage of the current movement toward paid-for content, it will be the content creators,

[1] Sam Schechner, "Google Settles with Belgian Newspapers amid European Copyright Fights." *Dow Jones Institutional News*, December 13, 2012; Frank Jordans, "German Publishers Opt to Stay on Google News for Now, as New Copyright Law Comes into Effect." *Associated Press Newswires*, August 1, 2013; John Burns, "Media Player," *SundayTimes.co.uk*, November 16, 2013; Emma Pinedo, "Spain to Force Search Engines to Pay to Display Some Content." *Reuters News*, February 14, 2014; Heidi Tworek and Christopher Buschow, "History Lessons: Why Germany's 'Google Tax' Won't Work," *Nieman Reports*, October 3, 2014, http://niemanreports.org/articles/history-lessons-why-germanys-google-tax-wont-work/ (accessed March 7, 2015).

> the people in this hall, who will pay the ultimate price and the content kleptomaniacs will triumph.[2]

These are the words of Australian media mogul Rupert Murdoch to the World Media Summit at Beijing in 2009, as he encouraged China to open "the digital door" to foreign media while protecting foreign media content. He called on China to own up to its "global responsibility," back freer trade, and emerge as a global superpower on side with Murdoch's vision of a new digital landscape that allows "access to news and information and entertainment on an unprecedented scale" – to those willing to pay for it.[3] Indeed, international copyright in news can be linked to agendas of media dominance, media imperialism, and liberalism in international trade.

However, it is not only giant media conglomerates that have raised concerns about the free use of news by news aggregators; Brazil was one of the first countries to examine the problems of news aggregation and copyright. In 2012, 154 Brazilian newspapers, making up ninety percent of Brazilian newspaper circulation, opted out of Google News. Brazilian newspapers noted that circulation did not decline greatly as a result.[4]

Some newspapers choose to opt out of Google News because they wish to protect their news content. However, international copyright offers no clear answers, at present, on the question of whether news aggregation by third-party aggregators is legitimate. International copyright, in fact, was once closer married to a vision of news as a public service, rather than as property.

Some thinkers suggest that a key to a better world lies in the ability of people, using the Internet, to circumvent traditional property relations in communication and culture in order to create, communicate, and share more freely.[5] However, the real picture may be more complex. Property in news might be placed on one end of a continuum whose opposite end is the absence of property in news, or the "free flow of information"; and neither extreme necessarily serves the ideals of diversity, quality, and balance in news content or flow. Political economists of communications have noted

2 Rupert Murdoch, *Speech at the World Media Summit*, Beijing, October 9, 2009, www.bloomberg.com/apps/news?pid=newsarchive&sid=afMeMv0ZHo1I (accessed March 5, 2015).

3 Ibid.

4 S. B. Ghoshand Anup Kumar Das, "Googling the News; European Publishers Want to Fleece Their Online Middleman," *The Wall Street Journal Online*, November 7, 2012.

5 Yochai Benkler, *The Wealth of Networks: How Social Production Transforms Markets and Freedom* (New Haven: Yale University Press, 2007).

that the absence of ownership or content regulation can tend to shore up dominant (Western) sources of news, crowding out local sources, the former being relatively less expensive to access when compared to the costs of local production.[6] Absence of copyright could therefore exacerbate inequalities by reducing the price of the reproduction of dominant news sources to zero and reducing, simultaneously, the incentive to produce local or alternative news. In other words, both arrangements (strong intellectual property and its absence) can facilitate monopolies or the dominance of a few providers in news.

International copyright is a key structuring factor in the creation and dissemination of news transnationally. Thus, struggles over international copyright in news are also struggles over the construction of public spheres, and over the question of whose infrastructure and voices public spheres will contain. Rupert Murdoch's media empire has, for example, exerted tremendous power over public debate by taking up a "privileged position to decide which issues and actors are included and excluded from the space of communication" – in part, through its ability to own, control, and profit from news content.[7]

One strategy for increasing the diversity of voices in the public sphere, and of ensuring that news of important events reaches the widest possible public, has been to allow local and more peripheral news publications to access and republish facts or even stories from larger corporate news enterprises.[8] However, it is now a global giant – Google – that appropriates and aggregates sometimes more local and peripheral news sources in its aggregation service, with mixed effects on the success and profitability of those sources. While news aggregators make news increasingly accessible to users, they also raise fears, among news publishers, of "brutal information capitalism" that would make Germany, Brazil, and other countries "digital colonies" that are "ruled by Silicon Valley."[9]

Questions around imperialism and copyright in news did not arise simply with *Google News* but have existed throughout the history of copyright

[6] Herbert Schiller, "Genesis of the Free Flow of Information Principles," in *Communication and Class Struggle*, Volume I: Capitalism, Imperialism, eds. Armand Mattelart and Seth Siegelaub (New York: International General, 1979), 345–353.

[7] Amelia Arsenault and Manuel Castells, "Switching Power: Rupert Murdoch and the Global Business of Media Politics," *International Sociology*, 23, 4 (2008), 505.

[8] Tworek and Buschow, "History Lessons: Why Germany's 'Google Tax' Won't Work."

[9] Juliette Garside, "From Google to Amazon: EU Goes to War Against Power of US Digital Giants," *The Guardian* July 6, 2014, www.theguardian.com/technology/2014/jul/06/google-amazon-europe-goes-to-war-power-digital-giants (accessed March 7, 2015).

laws as they relate to news and periodicals. For example, Read notes the important role that Reuters played in serving British imperialism and in circulating news and acting as the "nerve center of the Empire."[10] News, as well as other literature, played, and continues to play, an important role in colonialism and postcolonialism.

The questions surrounding news aggregators' use of short snippets of news are reminiscent of debates in the nineteenth and early twentieth centuries about whether copyright existed in short telegrams carrying news from abroad.[11] Today's debates can be illuminated by an examination of the lines originally drawn around news' commodification, and of the historically shifting conceptualizations of copyright in news.[12] Past settlements, along with the particular copyright laws and institutions in which those settlements were embedded, continue to mediate processes of commodification, decommodification, and recommodification of news today, illustrating the continuities and changes that exist among the relevant actors and principles.

Is there copyright in news?

Today's international copyright system operates on the general principle that, while there is copyright in a particular *expression* of news, such as the actual text of a news article, there is no copyright in the information and facts contained in such articles; the information and facts found in news articles may be used and expressed in different words by other news agencies or other actors.[13] However, the distinction between fact and expression can be difficult to draw, especially when the facts are contained in very short sections of text, such as the headlines and "snippets" displayed by news aggregators. This distinction is particularly blurred if there are relatively few ways of expressing a particular set of facts.

[10] Donald Read, "Reuters: News Agency of the British Empire," *Contemporary Record* 8, 2 (2008), 197.

[11] Peter Putnis, "The Struggle over Copyright in News Telegrams in Australia, 1869–1912," In *When Journalism Meets History 2003*, 58–68. Edited by Sybil Nolan. Melbourne: RMIT Publishing, 2004.

[12] As Allen notes, news' commodification also occurred through the commodification of memberships in newswires such as the Associated Press. Gene Allen, "News as Property: The Case of Associated Press, 1942–1945," Paper presented at the *Annual Meeting of the International Communication Association*, May 25, 2014, Seattle.

[13] Ricketson and Ginsburg, *International Copyright*, 497–501.

In most countries, news aggregators have been considered not to infringe copyright. One reason is because linking is deemed not to infringe any right, such as reproduction, translation, or telecommunication rights, enumerated in copyright legislation. Another reason is that headlines may lack the originality required for copyright. Third, whereas lead sentences or short snippets may be copyrightable works, their use by news aggregators may constitute, at least in the United States, fair use because readers would not find lead sentences a substitute for viewing the original work.[14]

The tensions between ownership of and access to news, and between local and the multinational, are rooted in, and have been shaped by, both the Berne system of copyright protection and the overall international political economy of communications. However, whereas the *Berne Convention* originally was once more so interpreted as *prohibiting* copyright in short snippets of news, this may no longer be the case.[15]

Access to news: a history

The 1880s

Newspapers in the nineteenth century commonly copied articles from one another. Thirty percent of articles in American newspapers, for example, were extracted from other papers.[16] The *Berne Convention* supported this practice; under the original *Berne Convention*, the reproduction of the news of the day, articles of political discussion, or miscellaneous information could not be prohibited.[17] Rather, the *Berne Convention* permitted the reproduction of all newspaper or periodical articles, except where expressly prohibited by the author or publisher. The main proponent of these access principles was Louis-Joseph Janvier, the Haitian delegate, whose position was supported by Great Britain.

When the *Berne Convention* was originally negotiated in the 1880s, it was generally agreed by all delegates that newspaper articles should be available for copying, and the draft articles permitted, in the public

[14] Allen, "News as Property," 954–960.

[15] *International News Service v. The Associated Press* 248 US 215; 39 S. Ct. 68 at 264–265.

[16] Heidi Tworek, "Protecting News before the Internet," Chapter 8 in *Making News: Historical Perspectives on the Political Economy of the Press in Great Britain and the United States since 1688*, eds. Richard R. John and Jonathan Silberstein Loeb (forthcoming, Oxford University Press, 2015).

[17] *Berne Convention*, 1886, Article 7.

interest, the reproduction of articles extracted from newspapers either in the original language or in translation. However, the breadth of this principle was was a matter of dispute; the draft articles did not permit the reproduction of serial novels, articles on art, or articles on science.

Haiti had in place copyright legislation from 1835 and adopted a new copyright act in 1885.[18] Under this act, Haitian newspapers would reprint articles from the foreign press without permission into at least the mid-twentieth century – as was the case in many countries at the time.[19]

At the negotiations in 1884, Janvier is recorded as having spoken twice. Under discussion on both occasions were draft articles concerning the reproduction of articles in newspapers and periodicals. Janvier argued for a broader principle of access, and that especially the reproduction of scientific articles should be permitted in the interests of the dissemination of knowledge throughout the world. He gave an impassioned and lengthy speech on the subject, but his argument was rejected in a vote of eight vs. one (Haiti).[20] When the matter was again discussed in 1885, Janvier gave a second, equally passionate speech. This time, his position was aided by the more active participation of the British delegates, who argued for the deletion of the article on exceptions for the reproduction of news and periodical articles altogether.[21]

The British government, for its part, hoping to reduce the burden of obligations it would be required to implement throughout the British Empire, wished to negotiate an agreement that dealt with generalities rather than specifics. This desire to remove specific requirements, such as exceptions for the reproduction of news and periodical articles, from the treaty aligned with Haiti's interests in creating a more general principle of access to periodical articles, and the result was a compromise that both Haiti and Great Britain found acceptable. The article that was ultimately adopted stated:

> Articles from newspapers or periodicals published in any of the countries of the Union may be reproduced in original or in translation in the other countries of the Union, unless the authors or publishers have expressly forbidden it. For periodicals it shall be sufficient if the prohibition is indicated in general terms at the beginning of each number of the periodical.[22]

[18] Richard Rogers Bowker, *Copyright: Its History and Its Law* (Boston and New York: Houghton Mifflin, 1912), 424.

[19] Department of State Memorandum: "Copyright in Haiti," January 31, 1945, in United States National Archives and Records Administration, RG59 150–68–32–1 Box 1.

[20] See also Chapter 2. [21] Actes 1885, 32. [22] *Berne Convention*, 1886, Article 7.

Articles of political discussion, the news of the day, and miscellaneous information, moreover, were entirely excluded from copyright.[23] As a result, Janvier, aided by the British, fought for and saw established a broad and significant principle of access to knowledge.

1896–1908

The provisions of the *Berne Convention* that applied to newspaper and periodical articles would prove to be some of the most contentious provisions of the agreement, and would undergo fundamental changes at every revision of the *Berne Convention.*[24] As discussed further in Chapter 7, a perennial problem in sustaining principles of access was the loss, from the negotiations, of their key proponents. The Haitian government sent no representative to the negotiations to revise the *Berne Convention* in 1896 or the revisions to follow and, while the provisions of the *Berne Convention* permitting the reproduction of news survived through several revisions, that would not last.[25]

Articles of political discussion, the news of the day, and miscellaneous information (but not necessarily scientific articles) continued to be *required* to be left in the public domain at the 1896 revision. However, at the revision conference of 1908 "articles of political discussion" were removed from the *Berne Convention*'s provision that excluded such articles from copyright protection. Articles of political discussion would thus no longer form a part of the public domain. The term "miscellaneous information" was also narrowed to apply only to items that were "simply of the nature of items of news," narrowing still further the public domain.[26]

Reservations were permitted on the provisions on the reproduction of serial articles, allowing for some flexibility in application. A number of countries would take advantage of this capability.[27]

[23] Ibid. [24] Actes 1928, 71.

[25] Actes 1908, 86 and 213: Haiti, though listed as a delegate, was not present at the conference; *Berne Convention*, 1897, revision of article 7. As noted earlier, I draw here on Greenleaf and Bond's concept of the public domain. Greenleaf and Bond, "'Public Rights' in Copyright: What makes up Australia's public domain?".

[26] Ibid. See also Tworek, "Protecting News before the Internet."

[27] Including Denmark, Finland, Greece, Norway, the Netherlands, Romania, and Sweden (See Actes 1928, 11–12). Also see Ricketson and Ginsburg, *International Copyright*, 105.

1928

In 1928, the host Italian government and the International Office, supported by Hungary, proposed that the exception allowing newspaper articles to be reproduced by another newspaper be narrowed to apply only to articles on certain subjects.[28] They proposed that only articles of political, economic, or religious discussion, and "other works of that genre," would be open for free reproduction periodical-to-periodical if not prohibited, and this formulation was accepted after a modification insisted on by the French delegation. The French delegates, seeking to narrow the provision still further, insisted that it be narrowed to include *only* articles of political, economic, and religious discussion – removing "works of that genre" from the list. The provision was also changed to include reproduction "by the press."[29]

The allowance for the reproduction of newspaper articles by another newspaper, then, was narrowed to apply only to articles on certain topics ("current economic, political, or religious topics"), yet also expanded to pertain not only to newspaper articles, but to any newspaper or periodical article. The allowance, however, would apply to reproduction by "the press" rather than by "other newspapers," meaning that non-journalistic newspapers or publications would no longer be able to make use of it, and that journalistic magazines or serials would, although this still left room for different interpretations.[30] Thus, free reproduction was narrowed in terms of subject matter, but widened to apply to "the press" rather than only newspapers. In response, Sweden and Finland declared that they intended to interpret "by the press" in the same sense as the word "periodical," and on these terms accepted the new formulation.[31] The *Berne Convention* would continue to positively define the public domain as including the news of the day and miscellaneous information in the nature of items of news.

In the heated debates that took place on this topic between country delegations, the host Italian government, along with the International Office and Hungary, sought to narrow the principle of access to news, while the French sought to narrow it still further. The delegates of Denmark, Holland, and Sweden pressed for an article closer to the lesser narrowing proposed by the host, and the Scandinavian countries, along

[28] Actes 1928, 73. [29] Ibid., 72–73; 247.
[30] Ibid., 248. See, for instance, the positions of Sweden and Finland. [31] Actes 1928, 248.

with Romania and Greece, expressed willingness to abandon their reservations in relation to article 9 if a looser provision, closer to the more permissive International Office/Italian/Hungarian proposal, were adopted.[32]

In Haiti's continuing absence, no country advocated for the *status quo* on the free reproduction of newspaper articles.[33] At the same time, the retention of some provisions on access to news, as opposed to the assimilation of news to other forms of copyright works, can be explained by the fact that, in many countries, including the UK and the United States (not yet a member of the Union), news was not treated as protected by copyright.[34] The Pan American copyright system also excluded news from copyright.[35] The Berne provisions, thus, reflected the dominant model around the world. News agencies' strategy, at the time, facing the view inscribed in many countries' copyright legislation that news was not the subject of copyright, was to attempt to have news protected as industrial property, rather than as intellectual property.[36]

1948–1967

Facts and news of the day

In 1967, the program of the conference to revise the *Berne Convention* proposed a change in wording to the clause excluding the news of the day from the convention, although this proposal was not intended to change the substance of the provision.[37] The correct interpretation of this provision was considered to be that it excluded from protection articles containing news of the day or miscellaneous information, provided that such articles have the character of mere items of news, since news of this nature does not fulfill the conditions required for admission to the category of literary or artistic works.[38]

The British delegate, William Wallace from the Board of Trade, attempted to narrow the public domain still further by expanding copyright in news. The British delegation proposed the following language:

[32] Ibid. [33] Actes 1928, 247–248. See also Tworek, "Protecting News before the Internet."

[34] Tworek, "Protecting News before the Internet."

[35] *Convention de Buenos Aires peur la protection de la propriété littéraire et artistique, révisé par la sixième conférence international americane*, 1928, Art. 11.

[36] Actes 1928, 34; Tworek, "Protecting News before the Internet."

[37] Actes 1967, Vol. 1, 89 (S/1); see pp. 115–116 (of S/1) for commentary.

[38] Ibid., 115 (S/1).

> [t]he protection of this convention shall not apply to the facts constituting news of the day or having the character of mere news items.[39]

The French delegate Charles Rohmer, who was the head of France's Copyright Office, spoke in favor of this proposal, observing that there were cases where a journalist's personality shone through in a mere news report – sometimes even in reports of relatively minor events – and that, therefore, even such news reports were deserving of protection.[40] However, the delegates of Japan, Monaco, Czechoslovakia, Bulgaria, Belgium, and India, all preferred the proposal included in the program, which was seen as retaining the status quo in the protection of news.[41] The latter countries prevailed in a vote of thirty votes to two, with three abstentions.[42] This was a case where a group of less powerful countries fought and won to maintain an existing principle of access.

In the end, the program wording was adopted, and the term "miscellaneous information" was replaced by "miscellaneous facts," and "mere items of news" was replaced by "mere items of information," wording that was not seen as effecting any substantial change.[43]

Reproduction of articles by the press

Whereas, in 1928, the host Italian government had attempted to pare back the exception that allowed reproduction of articles by the press, in 1967, the host Swedish government proposed to eliminate this exception entirely.[44] The conference program, composed by the Swedish government with BIRPI, proposed to delete the exception for the press – one of the few mandatory copyright exceptions in the *Berne Convention* – and to replace it with a new and broad-reaching right of reproduction for copyright holders.[45]

The delegations of Hungary, Poland, Japan, Portugal, and Czechoslovakia objected strongly to the deletion of the exception for the press.

[39] Actes 1967, Vol. 2, 883 and Vol. 1, 704 (S/171). [40] Ibid., 883 (1053).

[41] Ibid., 883. [42] Ibid., 883 (1057).

[43] 1967 act art. 2(8): "The protection of this Convention shall not apply to news of the day nor to miscellaneous facts having the character of mere items of press information."

[44] Actes 1967, Vol. 2, 859.

[45] Only two mandatory limitations and exceptions remain under the *Berne Convention*: the limitation that prevents copyright from extending to the news of the day or to "miscellaneous facts having the character of mere items of press information." (Art 2(8), 1971 version); and the exception allowing quotation (Art. 10(1), 1971 version). Ricketson and Ginsburg, *International Copyright*, 848–849. The proposal for a general right of reproduction had originally been made by Austria in 1948 but had been rejected. A right of reproduction would be added in 1967. See Actes 1967, Vol. 2, 851.

Czechoslovakia, Hungary, and Poland together submitted a proposal not to delete, but instead to extend the exception to reproductions in translation and by broadcast.[46] The Hungarian delegate, István Timár, the director-general of Hungary's copyright-protection office, also stressed the importance of the exception for reproduction by the press, and the importance of the free flow of information to "promoting a spirit of peaceful coexistence in international relations," emphasizing in particular the need to "keep the public informed of trends in the world press."[47] The Polish delegate (Edward Drabienko, a government counselor) argued that compulsory licenses should form a part of the exceptions and made it clear that reproduction should be permissible in translation as well as in the original language,[48] which a Japanese delegate (likely Kenji Adachi, a director in Japan's Ministry of Education) also supported.[49] The delegation from Czechoslovakia also argued that it was sometimes necessary to reproduce full articles, and not just quotations from articles, which some delegations argued was sufficient. Strnad, Czechoslovakia's delegate, also noted that it was often difficult to obtain the necessary permission to reproduce an article. Therefore solutions requiring permission were seen as inadequate.[50]

The proposals of Czechoslovakia, Hungary, and Poland arose out of their socialist approach to copyright, which, consistent with those countries' approaches on property rights generally, and intellectual property rights in particular, placed restrictions on intellectual property in news reports, while granting freedom for other noncommercial uses "for the benefit of the general public."[51] A greater emphasis was placed on "free use" rather than on notions of private property.[52]

On the other hand, several delegations, alongside the Swedish government and BIRPI, were in favor of the deletion of the exception for the press, such as Denmark, France, and Monaco.[53] However, in a vote of twenty-four to eight, with seven abstentions, the exception was retained in Article 10*bis*, where it remains.[54]

Although the exception was retained, it was also transformed from a mandatory exception, which all member countries had no choice but to recognize, to an optional exception that could be implemented through

[46] Actes 1967, Vol. 1, 688, S/51. [47] Actes 1967, Vol. 2, 859.

[48] Ibid. [49] Ibid.; Actes 1967, Vol. 1, 691, S/80. [50] Actes 1967, Vol. 2, 859.

[51] Silke von Lewinski, "Copyright in Central and Eastern Europe: An Intellectual Property Metamorphosis," *Fordham Intellectual Property Media & Entertainment Law Journal* 8, 1 (1997), 39–61.

[52] Halbert, The State of Copyright, 99. [53] Ibid. [54] Ibid.

national legislation. Whereas previously, the convention had declared that "articles on current economic, political or religious topics *may be reproduced by the press* unless the reproduction thereof is expressly reserved," the new article left it as a "matter for legislation in the countries of the Union to permit" broadcasting, communication to the public by wire, or reproduction by the press of articles on current economic, political, or religious topics.[55] The results of these revisions demonstrates the steady erosion of the provisions on access to news, but also the active engagement by less powerful countries in maintaining, and attempting to extend, principles of access.

The right of quotation

An important aspect of the right to reproduce news and periodicals is the limited right of quotation, which was added to the *Berne Convention* in 1948 ("It shall be permissible in all the countries of the Union to make short quotations from newspaper articles and periodicals, as well as to include them in press summaries."[56]). This proposal arose out of a broader French proposal that would have limited the right previously granted to allow the making of excerpts, such as the sort that might be included in anthologies, to a more limited right to make short quotations; longer excerpts would require a system of equitable remuneration.[57] While the host Belgian government, Denmark, and the UK, among others, disagreed with the more restrictive elements of France's proposal, which were not retained, the positive right of quotation that had formed part of the French delegation's proposal was adopted.[58]

In 1967, however, the hosting Swiss administration proposed to set conditions on this right. First, Switzerland proposed that quotations be "short," that quotations be compatible with fair practice, and that they serve "as explanation, reference, or illustration in the context in which they occur."[59]

Delegates from the UK, the Federal Republic of Germany, Austria, Sweden, Monaco, Tunisia, India, Ireland, and Czechoslovakia objected to the inclusion of the word "short" and the conditions proposed by Switzerland, arguing that, in some cases, long quotations might be

[55] *Berne Convention*, 1948, Article 9(2), emphasis added; *Berne Convention*, 1967, Article 10*bis*(1).

[56] Ibid., Article 10(1).

[57] *Berne Convention*, 1928, Article 10.

[58] Actes 1948, 245–249.

[59] Actes 1967, Vol. 1, 690 (S/68).

considered to be fair.[60] France, Hungary, Italy, and the Netherlands supported Switzerland's formulation of conditions on the right of quotation.[61]

In the end, a formulation that had been proposed in the conference program was adopted, which extended the right of quotation to apply to all works (as opposed to allowing quotations only from newspaper articles and periodicals), and did not contain the requirement that quotations be "short," but restricted the right of quotation to situations "compatible with fair practice" and to the extent that the quotation "does not exceed that justified by the purpose."[62]

The resulting formulation was therefore a compromise solution between two groups of countries, neither of which was made up of developing countries alone, but where those objecting to greater restrictions on the right of quotation did include a number of former colonies that were now independently represented.[63] Tunisia and Monaco, now represented by independent, rather than French, delegates, parted ways with France on this issue, joining the UK alongside two of its former colonies (India and Ireland) in objecting to further restrictions on the right of quotation.[64] Here too, former colonies, with the backing of some of the core countries, did not entirely prevent the narrowing of the right of quotation but did stand in the way of France's proposal to narrow it even further.

Telegraphic news

In its early days, the *Berne Convention* was used to prohibit copyright in news and in short telegraphed news messages. Between 1869 and 1912, for instance, a number of key battles were fought in Australia over copyright in telegraphic news.[65] Peter Putnis notes that, while many countries limit copyright in news for the purpose of encouraging the transmission of news and the free flow of information, each country's particular balancing of property in news and openness is ultimately a product of the unique domestic institutions (political, economic, and social structures) at play. In Australia, this balance was struck differently than in any other country

60 Actes 1967, Vol. 2, 860–861. 61 Ibid. 62 *Berne Convention*, 1967, Article 10.

63 For further on the rising influence of developing countries after decolonization, see Chapter 7 below.

64 Actes 1967, Vol. 2, 860–861.

65 Putnis, "The Struggle over Copyright in News Telegrams in Australia, 1869–1912." See also Lionel Bently, "Copyright and the Victorian Internet: Telegraphic Property Laws in Colonial Australia," *Loyola of Los Angeles Law Review* 38 (2004–2005), 71–176.

between 1869 and 1912, when some of the British colonies that would eventually make up Australia recognized copyright in telegraphic news. Provisions granting short twenty-four- to seventy-eight-hour copyright in news telegraphs were put in place in Victoria in 1871, South Australia in 1872, Tasmania in 1891, and Western Australia in 1895.[66]

These provisions, as Putnis notes, were out of sync with the *Berne Convention.*[67] Australia was, under Great Britain, a member of the *Berne Convention.* Eventually, after Australian federation in 1901, this inconsistency with the *Berne Convention* was resolved; the 1905 *Commonwealth Copyright Act* dropped the colonial provisions for copyright in telegraphic news.[68] German efforts to establish copyright in news telegrams for 24 hours after publication also failed.[69] The failure to establish copyright in telegraphic news is one where local (colonial or national) regulatory power was ultimately usurped by the *Berne Convention.* The *Berne Convention* was, in this case, a force for openness and access to foreign telegraphic news.

Other news companies, including *The Times* of London, Reuters, and the Associated Press (AP), all sought various forms of protection for the news of the day. Reuters was particularly concerned about the reproduction of Reuters news in Indian vernacular newspapers and in Transvaal newspapers.[70] However, news companies encountered resistance to the recognition of copyright in news. Such resistance was bolstered by the exclusion of news of the day from copyright under the *Berne Convention.*[71] Delegates in 1908 rejected calls from the Belgian government to inscribe the protection of telegraphic news under an unfair competition provision in the *Berne Convention.*[72]

Although the *Berne Convention* stood in the way of telegraphic news legislation in Australia, it did not do so elsewhere. The concept of copyright in telegraphic news was influential and, despite rejection in the context of the *Berne Convention* revisions, became a model for legislation

66 Putnis, "The Struggle over Copyright in News Telegrams in Australia, 1869–1912."
67 Ibid. 68 Ibid.
69 Tworek and Buschow, "History Lessons: Why Germany's 'Google Tax' Won't Work."
70 Tworek, "Protecting News before the Internet"; Letter, October 14, 1902 in National Archives of South Africa, National Archives Repository (TAB), CS Vol. 154 Ref. 13027/02: Newspapers Using Reuter's Telegraphic News Without Authority or Payment; correspondence November 17, 1902 to September 26, 1902 in National Archives of South Africa, National Archives Repository (TAB), LD Vol. 411 Ref. AG1881/03 Part 1: Admission into the Transvaal of British Copyright Works.
71 Tworek, "Protecting News before the Internet."
72 Actes 1908, 44, 88, 179, 206–207, and 215.

elsewhere, especially in other British colonies.[73] Legislation establishing copyright in telegraphic news was established in the Cape of Good Hope in 1880, New Zealand in 1882, Natal in 1895, Sri Lanka in 1898, the Torres Straits in 1902, Transvaal in 1902, the Orange River Colony in 1904, the Federated Malay States in 1911, the Union of South Africa in 1917, Mandate Palestine in 1932, and Kenya in 1934.[74] As Birnhack shows, such legislation was a form of colonial copyright modeled from the bottom up, rather than from the top down, generated locally rather than being imposed by either international treaties or imperial law.[75]

Copyright in telegraphic news was put in place in British colonies to protect the interests of British Reuters and the local news organizations that carried Reuters. Such legislation reflected the interests of colonial and imperial governments in controlling the flow of information, as it could be used by newspapers carrying Reuters news from the British Empire to challenge more local, anti-imperial, or nationalistic publications that copied telegraphic news without authorization.[76] It could also be used to protect local news agencies' relationships with Reuters, and to discourage their use of other competing news sources, such as those from central Europe.[77] Thus, while the fact/expression dichotomy ruled in the metropole and was enshrined in the *Berne Convention*, a stricter control of the flow of news, using copyright, was implemented in the colonies, and the *Berne Convention* rarely stood in the way of that.

Elsewhere in the world, some dominant news companies attempted to achieve protection of news through non-copyright means. Attempts to establish new forms of protection of news were made, unsuccessfully, under the League of Nations, the *Paris Convention for the Protection of Industrial Property*, and, successfully, through the tort of unfair competition under the American common law doctrine of "hot news."[78]

Media imperialism, increasingly a concern for newly independent countries following the postwar phase of decolonization given the "flood of American media material and the usurpation of national media systems that were required to disseminate it," eventually led to a focus, within the UN and UNESCO, on "reorganizing the global flow of

[73] Bently, "Copyright and the Victorian Internet," 167–168; Birnhack, *Colonial Copyright*, 213.
[74] Ibid. [75] Birnhack, *Colonial Copyright*, 213.
[76] Ibid., Chapter 9. [77] Ibid., 223–224.
[78] Tworek, "Protecting News before the Internet"; Tworek and Buschow, "History Lessons: Why Germany's 'Google Tax' Won't Work."

news."[79] Discussions of a New World Information and Communication Order (NWICO), begun in the Non Aligned Movement, led eventually to the establishment of UNESCO's International Commission for the Study of Communication Problems and its controversial 1980 report *Many Voices, One World* (the MacBride Report), which issued recommendations intended to address international inequalities in access to information and communication. The Commission did not recommend strategies relating to property in news but, rather, focused on non-profit models of news provision.[80] This model of development, in attempting to construct a New World Information and Communication Order, was strongly condemned by the United States and the United Kingdom, leading to their withdrawal from UNESCO in 1984.[81]

Access to knowledge and access to news today

Unlike the early days of the *Berne Convention*, the existence of copyright in news articles today goes relatively unchallenged, even as the sharing of news articles through social media becomes increasingly the norm. Rupert Murdoch's speech to the World Media Summit at Beijing and, on the other hand, new models of open source journalism, participatory journalism, and open data, as well as mass data leaks such as those of Wikileaks, represent conflicting models for and visions of the development of journalism and news. News industries, and models of news production and consumption, are developing in new directions, and visions of the future development of news are hotly contested.[82]

The key battles over the future of journalism are not currently being fought at WIPO but form part of a broader rethinking of the practices of journalism and open access. Nevertheless, a few of the proposals made

[79] Schiller, "Genesis of the Free Flow of Information Principles," 351; Tworek, "Protecting the News before the Internet."

[80] Tworek, "Protecting the News Before the Internet"; Ulla Carlsson, "The Rise and Fall of NWICO – and Then? From a Vision of International Regulation to a Reality of Multilevel Governance," from *EURICOM Colloquium in Venice – Information Society: Visions and Governance*, May 5–7, 2003; Sean MacBride. *Many Voices, One World: Communication and Society, Today and Tomorrow: the MacBride Report* (Paris: UNESCO, 1980).

[81] Braithwaite and Drahos, *Global Business Regulation*, 568–569.

[82] Robert McChesney, "Will the Last Reporter Please Turn out the Lights?", in *News 2.0. Can Journalism Survive the Internet?* eds. Martin Hirst (Crows Nest, N.S.W.: Allen & Unwin, 2011); Benkler, Wealth of Networks, 176–211.

under the rubric of the proposed new international instruments on limitations and exceptions are relevant to journalism, including proposals made by the African Group and Brazil intended to reaffirm the right to quote from copyright works in newspapers and magazines.[83] These proposals, in light of the other proposals related to access to knowledge in science and research, and in light of the NWICO proposals made decades earlier under, seem incremental. At the same time, many of the other proposed limitations and exceptions relating to research and access to knowledge and data could have a significant effect in news and journalism.

Conclusion

In its early days, the *Berne Convention* was often an instrument used by those who were invested in a more open environment in access to news. Today, however, neither the *Berne Convention* nor other WIPO treaties stand in the way of copyright in short excerpts of news. WIPO Director General Francis Gurry argues that news aggregators, for example, "are exploiting holes in the system" and profiting from the work of others in gathering the news.[84]

Despite the fact that the *Berne Convention* continues to declare that it "shall not apply to news of the day or to miscellaneous facts having the character of mere items of press information," this provision is now seen as applying to facts and not to news articles themselves.[85] Many countries, including France, Germany, Belgium, Spain, and Ireland have contemplated or implemented the granting of rights of remuneration or "ancillary copyright" in news "snippets" and/or in the right to provide links to news stories.[86]

[83] WIPO, Standing Committee on Copyright and Related Rights, Provisional Working Document Towards an Appropriate International Legal Instrument (in Whatever Form) on Limitations and Exceptions for Educational, Teaching and Research Institutions and Persons with Other Disabilities Containing Comments and Textual Suggestions SCCR/26/4 Prov, 14, 22.

[84] As quoted in James Eyers, "Facing up to the IP Tsunami," *Australian Financial Review*, August 11, 2009.

[85] *Berne Convention*, 1971, Article 2(8).

[86] Gerrit Wiesmann, "Axel Springer Expects Google Fee for Web Content," *Financial Times* Asian edition, March 7, 2013, 16; Jordans, "German Publishers Opt to Stay"; Schechner, "Google Settles with Belgian Newspapers"; Pinedo, "Spain to Force Search Engines to Pay"; Burns, "Media Player"; Vanessa Fuhrmans, "New German Bill is Key Win for Google," *Wall Street Journal Europe*, March 4, 2013, 21.

Currently it is left up to countries themselves whether they opt to allow reproduction by the press of articles of news, while significant room for flexibility remains in the interpretation of the *Berne Convention*'s provisions on news. There is ongoing debate on both the national and international levels surrounding how – and how much – news can be reproduced, combining longstanding tensions between copyright protection and access to information with issues generated by new technological innovations.

In the original negotiation of the 1886 *Berne Convention*, Haiti's delegate played a significant role, and this influenced in very significant ways the shape of the original *Berne Convention* and its provisions regarding news. Between 1928 and 1967, however, these original provisions were eroded. Throughout this period, other less powerful states also participated in the revision of the *Berne Convention* and, although they did not entirely prevent the principle of access to news' erosion, they did prevent the still further erosions proposed by France. International copyright was one of the mechanisms that allowed news agencies to profit multinationally. As such, the convention has been one of the foundation stones shaping the history of international news agencies, news empires, colonialism, and neocolonialism. At the same time, firm provisions on international copyright have, to a significant extent, been set aside both as tools of colonialism and decolonization in favor of other mechanisms, such as unfair competition law and non-profit mechanisms of news provision.

Whereas the *Berne Convention*, as a product, in part, of Haiti's influence, originally played a strong role in excluding news articles and facts from copyright, today it no longer plays that role. "Border struggles" lost have led to the strengthening of copyright ownership of news.[87] Rather than continuing to act as a force for access to news by preventing its ownership, the *Berne Convention* has left a certain degree of flexibility, especially in the treatment of news, for nation states to adopt provisions relating to news – including in short snippets and headlines. As a result, it is at the national level that battles over copyright in news currently play out, whether in the interests of dominant actors or in the interests of more marginal news producers. This leaves, at present, greater scope for differences, diversity, and experimentation in the regulation of ownership of and access to news, as well as greater scope for privately generated policies, such as those of Google, to regulate access to news.

87 Nancy Fraser, "Behind Marx's Hidden Abode: For an Expanded Conception of Capitalism," *New Left Review* 86 (March 2014), 55–72.

Whereas the *Berne Convention* once inscribed access to news as an international norm that was connected to visions of press freedom, WIPO has stepped out of the fray as guarding the border between property and news. Industry visions of development, including those of dominant news corporations like Reuters or Fox, have inscribed in international copyright one vision of the development of the news industry: for them, the news is a multinational business that depends on property and paywalls enforced around the world. Google presents a slightly different vision of development from the perspective of a dominant multinational news aggregator. Civil society visions of development associated with open source journalism, participatory journalism, and open data, associated loosely with the A2K movement, present additional alternatives and models that compete, from the bottom up, with proprietary visions of property in news. WIPO and the Berne system of international copyright, while guarding the greying border between facts and expression, so far sit this battle out.

6

Access to translations

In January 2015 Google launched an update to its *Google Translate* smartphone app. Delighting tourists, the app allowed users for the first time to point their smart phone camera at foreign-language text, such as text on a street sign, and see, on the phone's screen, the sign with translated text. The app also brought to smart phone users the capability of translating spoken language live, a feature whose usefulness was proven when two Irish ambulance attendants made the news by delivering a healthy baby girl on the side of the road in southern Ireland to a mother who spoke only Swahili.[1]

Translation heightens the possibility of access to knowledge – in the sense of access to ideas, interests, and institutions – in all languages. Today, automated or machine translation brings this possibility to new levels. At the same time, copyright laws allow copyright owners to regulate who can translate copyright works, and on what terms, placing copyright owners in the drivers' seat in deciding which works will flow across linguistic barriers.

While translation offers the reward of access, the possibilities of translation also come with unique postcolonial baggage. Translation is never simply about access; it creates the possibilities of dominance, remote governance, and neocolonialism; it involves translation of ways of thought and ways of life, while also opening possibilities for hybridity and subversion.[2] The opportunities and possibilities associated with translation are accompanied by fears about the dominance of a single language, or that the widespread availability of translation may replace the need

[1] Jason Mick, "Quick Note: Google Translate Helps Irish Paramedics Deliver a Baby," *DailyTech.com*, February 12, 2015, www.dailytech.com/Quick+Note+Google+Translate+Helps+Irish+Paramedics+Deliver+a+Baby/article37155.htm (accessed March 27, 2015).

[2] Salah Basalamah, "Compulsory Licensing for Translation: An Instrument of Development," *IDEA* 40 (2000), 503.

to learn other languages, thus contributing to nondominant languages' decline.[3]

Such concerns apply not only in the realms of governance and power, but also in markets. Translation, if widely available and especially if automated, can facilitate the expansion and globalization of businesses and the dominance of foreign markets in a variety of languages.[4] Currently, the international dominance of the English language affords English-language businesses, web sites, cultural products, and software international reach. On one hand, translation facilitates the localization of originally English-language software into a greater number of local languages. On the other hand, it also (to a lesser extent) facilitates access to broader markets for software developed in nondominant languages.

Whereas absent or limited translation rights under the international copyright regime once facilitated the local production of foreign works in translation, with profits often flowing to local cultural producers, the translation right in international copyright facilitates the reaping of profits in peripheral countries by a dominant centralized core of copyright owners. Political struggles between copyright owners in core countries and translators, publishers of translations, and users of works in translation on the periphery of international system have a history of contention.

Access to works in translation: a history

The grant of translation rights to copyright holders was an early source of conflict in the history of the international copyright system. In adopting a model that viewed translated works as derivative works, the regime would privilege the author of the original work by granting the original author the right to authorize translations, while threatening to impose liability on translators and publishers of translations. This was especially problematic in countries where translation was an important source of access to knowledge and literature from foreign sources, and also in countries with multiple local languages.[5] The negotiations that established the *Berne Convention* in 1886 made clear a gulf between Great Britain and France – major exporters of books and novels – and countries that were

[3] Erik Ketzan, "Rebuilding Babel: Copyright and the Future of Machine Translation Online," *Tulane Journal of Technology and Intellectual Property* 9 (Spring 2007), 206–207.

[4] Ketzan, "Rebuilding Babel," 225.

[5] Salah Basalamah, *Le droit de traduire: une politique culturelle pour la mondialisation* (Ottawa: Les Presses de l'Université d'Ottawa, 2008).

net importers and translators of such works – including most prominently the Scandinavian countries and Japan – that was severe enough to cause concern that it might undermine the establishment of the *Berne Convention.*[6]

The original text of the *Berne Convention* required the grant of translation rights for a ten-year term from the publication of the work in a country of the Union. This was the end result of a highly contentious battle over translation rights. Three main proposals were discussed during the initial negotiations: first, a translation right lasting for ten years but expiring if not used within the first three years (proposed by the Norwegian delegate);[7] a translation right limited to ten years (the proposal that was ultimately adopted);[8] and full assimilation of the translation right to the full term of copyright (the position supported by the delegates of France, Haiti, and Switzerland).[9] The first proposal, granting a translation right of ten years, but expiring after three years if not used, was adopted by the conference in 1884 but was revisited in 1885.

In 1885, the French position in favor of the full assimilation of the translation right was strengthened by the fact that one of the French delegates was also the sole member of the delegation from Tunisia, effectively giving France two votes.[10] The delegates of Germany, Honduras, Spain, Sweden, and Norway all preferred the 1884 draft, under which the translation right would expire if not used after three years;[11] and the British delegation, for its part, wished the term of translation rights to be left to national legislation.[12] However, the extra vote of the Tunisian delegate was a deciding vote in favor of France on the question of translation rights, defeating the previously agreed provision.[13] The Haitian delegate also voted with France on this question, as did those of Belgium, Italy, and Switzerland.[14]

While the question of translation rights did not prove to be the death blow to the Union that some negotiators had feared, it did prove to be an issue that excluded a number of countries from the initial Union.[15] As a result of the defeat of the Norwegian proposal, the Scandinavian countries

[6] Eva Hemmungs Wirtén, *Cosmopolitan Copyright: Law and Language in the Translation Zone* (Uppsala: Uppsala University Press, 2011), 17–27.

[7] Actes 1884, 46. [8] *Berne Convention*, 1886, Article 5.

[9] Actes 1884, 47–48; Hemmungs Wirtén, "Cosmopolitan Copyright," 8.

[10] Actes 1885, 8. Note the absence of Tunisa in 1884: Actes 1884, 16.

[11] Ibid., 129. [12] Ibid., 128.

[13] In rejecting the 1884 draft of the article on translation rights. Actes 1885, 44.

[14] Ibid. [15] Hemmungs Wirtén, *Cosmopolitan Copyright*, 27.

(Norway and Sweden) did not ultimately sign the 1886 agreement.[16] The Scandinavian countries were lost until 1896, 1903, and 1904, when Norway, Denmark, and Sweden, respectively, joined the Union, having adjusted their domestic copyright legislation.[17] Ultimately, a ten-year term was adopted for the right of translation in order to ensure Great Britain's signature of the 1886 Convention.[18]

In 1896, the original ten-year term of translation rights was replaced by a translation right running the full term of copyright but expiring if not used in the first 10 years.[19] Then in 1908, a full translation right with no early expiry or usage requirement was adopted, and France won what it had sought since the 1880s: full assimilation of the translation right.[20] The limitations on translation rights that had been earlier won under leadership of the Scandinavian countries were now lost, leaving other "user countries" who joined the Union later with little chance of concession on translation of foreign works.

The translation right was one of the earliest principles of access to be tied to the question of development and access to foreign works. In 1908 a Japanese delegate (likely Horiguchi Kumaichi) argued that, as a country that was mainly a "user" of foreign intellectual property, Japan should be granted access to foreign knowledge through permissive provisions on translation.[21] Ricketson and Ginsburg have pointed to this moment in 1908 as prefacing future divides between developing and "developed" countries in international copyright.[22]

In 1908 the Japanese delegate, attending, for the first time, a *Berne Convention* revision conference, attempted to press for completely free translation into Japanese. In debating the question, the Japanese delegate took note that, while there was a great deal of interest in translating European works into Japanese, there was little interest on the part of other countries in translating Japanese works; he was aware that it was often

16 Berne 1886 Art. 5; Hemmungs Wirtén, *Cosmopolitan Copyright*, 29–31.

17 Hemmungs Wirtén, *Cosmopolitan Copyright*, 12; www.wipo.int/treaties; see also "Pays scandinaves," *Le Droit D' Auteur* 5, 9 (September 1892), 115–118.

18 Lionel Bently, "Copyright, Translations, and Relations between Britain and India in the Nineteenth and Early Twentieth Centuries," *Chicago-Kent Law Review* 82, 3 (2007), 1181–1240.

19 *Berne Convention*, 1896, Article 5.

20 *Berne Convention*, 1908, Article 8.

21 Ricketson and Ginsburg, *International Copyright*, 102. Interestingly, Hiriguchi's son, Horiguchi Daigaku, would become a famous poet and translator of works from French into Japanese.

22 Ibid.

considered by those in the West that "Orientals have no literature."[23] As a compromise to the Japanese position (and to the Russians and Dutch delegates, who also objected to full assimilation), the 1908 revision allowed countries to make reservations to the translation right, and many, including Japan, did just that.[24]

As mentioned, Norway, Denmark, and Sweden had eventually joined the convention in 1896, 1903, and 1904, respectively. Partly, the change to the Scandinavian position resulted from successful lobbying by domestic authors and publishers whose works sold well abroad.[25] Swedish law had contained provisions that barred Sweden from joining the *Berne Convention*, but these were removed through legislative revisions that followed lobbying in 1897 and 1904, at which point Sweden joined the Berne Union.[26]

Other "user countries" who might have had an interest in resisting the full assimilation of the translation right were, as colonies, not yet present at the negotiating table. Two are worthy of particular mention: Australia and India, both British colonies.

Australia had adopted the shorter term of protection of translation rights under its 1905 *Copyright Act*. The Act allowed a person to apply to the government for a license to translate a book if the author had not exercised the translation right within ten years of publication.[27] The Australian right of translation was assimilated to the full term of copyright in Australia in 1912 under its adoption of the 1911 British *Imperial Copyright Act*.[28]

India, a colony of the British Empire until 1947, was also one of the "user countries" particularly affected by the full assimilation of the translation right. India, because of its colonial status, was also not directly represented at the diplomatic conferences to found or revise the *Berne Convention* until 1928; instead, India was "represented" by British delegations, which, in

[23] Hemmungs Wirtén, *Cosmopolitan Copyright*, 39, quoting Actes 1908, 202.

[24] Including Estonia, Greece, the Irish Free State, Italy, Japan, and the Netherlands. Actes 1928, 11–12. Also see Ricketson and Ginsburg, *International Copyright*, 105; WIPO, Treaties and Contracting Parties: Berne Convention: Japan, www.wipo.int/treaties/en/remarks.jsp?cnty_id=975C (accessed March 27, 2015).

[25] Regarding Sweden, see Hemmungs Wirtén, *Cosmopolitan Copyright*, 33.

[26] Hemmungs Wirtén, *Cosmopolitan Copyright*, 32–33.

[27] Atkinson, *The True History of Copyright* 22; Australia *An Act Relating to Copyright No. 25 of 1905*, Section 30–31. See also drafting of the copyright regulations 1906–1907 in Australian National Archives Series A2863 Control 1912/20 Part 2 F Copyright Act 1912.

[28] Atkinson, *The True History of Copyright* 109. *An Act Relating to Copyright No. 20 of 1912*; *Copyright Act* 1&2 Geo. 5 Ch. 46 (1911), Section 1 (2).

the early years, had resisted strong translation rights on the idea that the translation of British works into local languages in India was an effective tool of colonialism, as bringing "civilization" and progress to the indigenous people of India, and that translations represented "precursors of original literature."[29]

Although translation was seen as having a special importance in India, following the full assimilation of the translation right under the *Berne Convention* in 1908, full assimilation was adopted in British imperial copyright legislation as well. Despite requests by the Government of India (comprising mainly Europeans) that the imperial act not be brought into effect in India, and that India be excluded from the British ratification of the *Berne Convention*, the imperial law and the full translation right was adopted in India in 1912.[30] Subsequently in 1914, the Government of India limited translation rights to ten years as it applied to Indian works, although this limitation did not go so far as to limit translation rights in foreign works, perhaps, as Bently suggests, because the Government of India did not see itself as having sufficient independence to vary from imperial and international standards.[31] This move may be seen as either a mainly symbolic move to assert independence and act on the need for access to works in translation, or a move designed to improve access to Indian works in particular.[32]

At the revision conference of 1928, additional countries with interests in weaker translation rights emerged. The Siamese and Irish delegates both requested provisions to allow the compulsory licensing of translations in cases where the copyright holder, without justification, refused to authorize a translation. The Siamese delegate, Prince Varnvaidya, who was a career diplomat and chief delegate to the League of Nations, spoke eloquently in favor of free translation for young countries that were rapidly developing.[33] While he did not convince delegates to reduce copyright control over translation, he did convince those present that it continued to be necessary for countries newly joining the Union to have the option of adhering to the 1896 level of translation rights, whereby the translation right expired if not used within ten years.[34] Greece, Iceland, Ireland, Japan, Siam, and Turkey would all make use of this reservation.[35] The Czech and Norwegian delegates, having abandoned their positions of years past, now spoke in favor of the existing text, responding to the Siamese proposal

[29] Actes 1928, 134; Bently, "Copyright, Translations, and Relations," 1218.
[30] Ibid., 1225, 1236. [31] Ibid., 1236–1237. [32] Ibid., 1237.
[33] Ibid., 246. [34] Ibid., 246. [35] UCC 1952 Actes, 234, item 1045.

by noting that the existing text allowed for the translation of works, as long as such translations did not interfere with the exclusive rights of the copyright holder (such as by publishing the translation). This interpretation, though, did not address the substance of the Siamese proposal, which was likely aimed at commercial works rather than private translations.[36]

The question of translation was also particularly important to the Irish Free State, which was concerned with ensuring the availability of material in Irish, an issue linked to administrative needs and to asserting a sense of nationhood as they achieved greater sovereignty from the UK.[37] This was "the only matter before the conference deemed by the Minister to be of importance to this country."[38] In Irish copyright law, the translation right ceased to exist ten years after first publication unless the copyright owner published an Irish translation in the Irish Free State.[39] Thus, the ability to reserve to the 1896 level of translation rights was crucial to the Irish position.

While the ability to make reservations was retained, arguments for compulsory licensing or free translation fell on a conveyor belt of "progress" that was moving in the wrong direction from a Siamese and Irish perspective, and provisions for compulsory licensing of translations were not put in place. For these new "user" countries, the battle had been lost before they became part of the discussion.

The Universal Copyright Convention and translation

In a 1947 report, following its founding in 1945, UNESCO noted that copyright created a barrier to the "free flow of culture among all the peoples of the world."[40] Under UNESCO, the *Universal Copyright Convention* would attempt to loosen some of these barriers, including the barrier of translation rights provided under the *Berne Convention*. The

[36] Actes 1928, 247.

[37] National Archives of Ireland, DFA/408/136 (66–95) and DFA/408/51 (7586–7589, 7602–7611, 7623–7665).

[38] M.M. Campbell, Secretary, Department of External Affairs Dublin, *Revision of the International Copyright Convention: Proposed Conference at Rome,* June 16, 1927, in National Archives of Ireland, DFA LN 6/5.

[39] Ibid.

[40] UNESCO, "The Administrative Obstacles to the Universal Free Flow of Culture, Deriving From the Existence of Copyright." Free Flow Com./14, October 13, 1947, 1, cited by Wirtén, *Cosmopolitan Copyright,* 46.

UCC, as a whole in 1952, was intended to be universal and to encompass all countries, including developing and least developed countries.

The UCC, when it was established in 1952, contained more lenient and flexible provisions on translation rights than those granted under the *Berne Convention* or the Pan American system.[41] While the UCC granted a translation right to copyright holders,[42] it generally required a relatively short term of protection of the life of the author plus 25 years (in contrast to the *Berne Convention*'s term of life plus 50 years). This shorter term applied to most rights granted under the UCC, including translation.[43] As well, the UCC provided the possibility of compulsory licensing for the translation of works that were not translated within seven years into a national language, subject to a variety of provisos.[44] These compulsory licensing provisions for translations applied to all contracting states; they were not restricted only to those considered to be "developing." They would serve as a basis for the 1971 Appendix to the *Berne Convention*'s provisions on translation for developing countries.

Six of the seven reservatory countries under the Berne system (Japan, Turkey, Greece, Ireland, Thailand, and Yugoslavia) once again picked up the battle for freer translation in the highly contentious negotiation of the translation provisions of the UCC, with the former three leading the charge.[45] In a new forum, less burdened by the path dependency of decisions already taken, these countries were more successful.

A Japanese delegate (likely Kenji Adachi) was the first representative at the 1952 conference to highlight the importance of translation, not only to Japan but to all African and Asian countries:

> [e]very endeavor must be made to facilitate the translation of works from the more advanced countries, with a view to attaining Unesco's aim of spreading culture and educating mankind for justice and freedom. Another reason for facilitating translations is to bring cultural assistance to the underdeveloped countries – a programme to which the Specialized Agencies are directing their efforts.[46]

[41] Nedjelko D. Suljak, "Right to Translate and International Copyright Conventions," *Law Library Journal* 62 (1969), 51–53; the Pan American conventions of 1889, 1902, 1906, 1910, and 1928 also enumerated a translation right as one of the rights granted to copyright owners.

[42] UCC 1952 Art. V(1). [43] Ibid., Art. IV(2). [44] Ibid., Art. V(2).

[45] Thailand: UCC 1952 records, 172, item 415; Ireland: 236, item 1064; UCC 1952 Actes, 43; Yugoslavia: UCC 1952 records, 172 item 413; Turkey: UCC 1952 Records, 268, item 1470. Iceland, also a reservatory country, was not in attendance. Also see Records UCC 1952, 80.

[46] UCC 1952 Actes, 123, item 62.

The delegate of Japan declared the exclusive right of translation to be "unacceptable," noting that "the high cost of translation into a difficult language was liable to place an almost insurmountable barrier between the Western and Eastern civilizations."[47]

The Japanese delegate was soon joined by the Turkish and Greek delegations in his efforts to pursue provisions for access to works in translation. All three countries were members of the *Berne Convention*, and all three had made reservations under that convention to maintain translation rights at the 1896 level, thus limiting those rights to 10 years after which the right expired and works, for the purposes of translation, entered the public domain.[48]

The Yugoslav delegate declared a limited term of translation rights to be necessary, considering his country to be "in too great a need of foreign works to contemplate any change of attitude."[49] At the same time, he supported a system of remuneration for translations, which was already the "customary procedure" in Yugoslavia.[50]

The dilemma faced by Greece, Japan, and Turkey, along with the other members of the *Berne Convention* who had made reservations at the 1896 level on the translation right, was that, although generally the UCC offered a lower level of protection than did the *Berne Convention*, on the question of translation rights, this was not the case. Whereas the *Berne Convention* 1896 translation right lasted 10 years before expiring entirely, the UCC translation right lasted for the full term of copyright (at least 25 years), with the possibility of compulsory licensing of translations after seven years.[51]

Other countries also wished to see a regime that would facilitate greater access to works in translation. Spain, though not a country that had made reservations on translation rights under the *Berne Convention*, was critical of arguments that placed authors' interests at the center of the debate. The Spanish delegate, José Forns, a law professor at Spain's Royal Academy of Fine Arts, noted that the royalties and profits from the publication of works generally went to publishers, and not to authors. It was publishers who stood in the way of the production of translations, he said, and who demanded exorbitant fees to license translations. He believed that any profits generated through compulsory licensing should go directly

[47] UCC 1952 Records, 166–167, item 388.

[48] Ibid., 234, item 1045; Iceland, Ireland, and Thailand made similar reservations.

[49] Ibid., 172 item 413. [50] Ibid.

[51] *Berne Convention*, 1896, Article 5; UCC 1952, Art. IV(2); UCC 1952, Art. V.

to the author of a work, and not to its publisher or other copyright owner.[52]

The Liberian delegate, Nathaniel V. Massaquoi, also spoke in favor of greater access to works in translation, noting that the free flow of information was essential to "underdeveloped" countries, and asking that this be considered by other "more developed" countries when provisions were decided. Massaquoi was well placed to make such arguments since, not only did he have a background in law and education, but he was also the co-founder and editor of a weekly newspaper in Liberia titled *Forward*.[53] He noted, "In the underdeveloped countries there existed neither the desire nor the means to exploit an author, since all intellectual activity came under the aegis of academic and government authorities whose funds were modest but who were inspired by the desire to spread knowledge among the people."[54]

Other countries saw limitations on the translation right as being tantamount to not granting copyright at all. "If translation was not protected," the American delegate (John Schulman, an attorney for the Authors League) noted, "a foreign author who wrote in a foreign language actually had no copyright protection in a State whose citizens used a different language."[55]

Greece, Japan, and Turkey, as "reservatory states"[56] would fail in their attempts to insert clauses into the UCC that would allow them to maintain their Berne reservations.[57] They were successful in winning a majority vote on this issue.[58] However, Italy and the United States were extremely unhappy with this result and called for a re-vote.[59] This re-vote was never held; rather, the majority passage of the proposal was effectively reversed as a result of the American objections. The American delegation declared that the reservatory countries' proposal would threaten the conclusion of the treaty.[60] Greece, Japan, and Turkey would not win a special provision in the UCC on translation rights and would have to leave it to the courts to sort out the conflict between the UCC and the *Berne Convention*.[61] The government ofTurkey, as a result, refused to sign the UCC.[62]

52 UCC 1952 Actes, 169–170, item 405.

53 UNESCO, *Candidates for election to executive board: Curriculum vitae, Professor Nathaniel V. Massaquoi 8C/NOM/9* (Paris, 1954).

54 Ibid., 172, item 412. 55 Ibid., 274, item 2005.

56 As the countries with reservations on the translation right under the *Berne Convention* came to be called, UCC 1952 Records, 221, item 904.

57 UCC 1952 Records, 218–225 and 234–236, items 887–953 and 1045–1060.

58 Ibid., 223, item 920. 59 Ibid., 223–225, items 921–953. 60 Ibid., 235, item 1054.

61 Ibid., 237, item 1078. 62 Ibid., 268, item 1470.

However, the delegations who took the position of supporting very strong translation rights, including those of Portugal,[63] Belgium,[64] and Cuba,[65] were also forced to compromise, and some countries' efforts at compromise were notable. The Cuban delegation took no position, expressing faith that the conference would come to a solution on the difficult problem of translation rights.[66] The delegates of India, the UK, Argentina, and the US also supported the ultimate compromise that was reached: allowing compulsory licensing after a period of seven years.

The UCC safeguard clause

To make matters more complicated, the UCC contained a "safeguard clause" governing its relationship to the *Berne Convention* (see Chapter 10 below). Suggested by the American delegation,[67] this clause stipulated that the UCC would not apply to relationships between Berne countries, but that copyright owners could rely on the UCC where the UCC granted more extensive rights than did the *Berne Convention* if the work were published simultaneously in a Berne and a UCC country.[68] This had the effect of binding Berne countries that had reserved 1896-level translation rights to the higher level of protection for translation rights required under the UCC, thus either forcing them to abandon their reservations under the *Berne Convention* or requiring them to apply a differential regime to Berne and UCC countries. This presented possible legal difficulties as to the priority and application of the two treaties, and would remain important in the coming years as former colonies began to adhere to one or both unions.[69]

The Berne Convention revisions of 1967 and 1971

The question of compulsory licensing of translations was one of the key issues to be negotiated when newly independent developing countries came to the table to revise the *Berne Convention* in 1967 and 1971. It may be seen as *à propos* that the 1967 revision of the *Berne Convention* was done at Stockholm, Sweden, a country that had been unable to join the *Berne Convention* in the 1880s due to its liberal stance on translation rights.[70]

[63] Ibid., 163, item 378. [64] Ibid., 170, item 406. [65] Ibid., 221–222, item 908.
[66] Ibid., 152, item 282. [67] UCC 1952 Records, 237, item 1070.
[68] UCC 1952, Article 17. [69] UCC 1952 Records, 236, item 1061; see Chapter 10 below.
[70] Hemmungs Wirtén, *Cosmopolitan Copyright*, 48.

The importance placed on access to educational materials at the negotiations of 1967 and 1971 brought with it an emphasis on access to educational materials *in translation*. Translation rights in educational materials were seen as less important than in other types of works, since educational materials were less creative, less subject to interpretation, and as such the author's control on the quality of translation appeared less justified than it did in the case of literary works.[71]

The Indian government, now independent, had a strong presence in the negotiations leading up to the diplomatic conference to revise the *Berne Convention* and took the initiative to propose that provisions on translation similar to those under the UCC be adopted under the Berne system as well.[72] Others wished to go further, proposing that compensation should disappear on a compulsory license for translation ten years following the original publication of the work.[73]

This proposal provoked heated objection. No longer restrained by colonial concerns, the UK government (represented by Roger Harben from the British Copyright Council) stood as chief objector, stating that the British delegation "regarded the proposal as a sufficiently grave departure from the established principles of the Berne Union to constitute at least the beginning of a threat to its existence."[74] The deletion of said clause was supported also by the delegates of Mexico, Argentina, and Uruguay,[75] while the delegate from Australia (Lindsay James Curtis, an important legislator and judge) proposed that a compromise might be worked out.[76]

Ultimately, the Stockholm Protocol contained a compromise option allowing developing countries to permit the translation right to expire if not used within ten years, as well as the possibility of *remunerated* compulsory licensing for translation.[77] This result faced a storm of criticism.[78] The UK, whose publishing industry projected that they would lose a quarter of total earnings annually as a result of the Stockholm Protocol, was

[71] Ibid., 61–62. [72] Ibid., 57–61.

[73] Actes 1967, Vol. 1, 718, Article 1(a)(viii): "should, however, the author not avail himself of the right under sub-paragraph (i) above during the said term of ten years, compensation under the non-exclusive license referred to above shall cease to be due for any uses made after the expiry of such term." See also developing country proposal S/160: Actes 1967, 702 and Hemmungs Wirtén, *Cosmopolitan Copyright*, 61.

[74] 1967 Records, Vol. 2, 977, item 2262. [75] Ibid., item 2263. [76] Ibid., 978, item 2265.

[77] *Berne Convention*, 1967; *Berne Convention*, 1967: *Protocol Regarding Developing Countries* Article 1.

[78] Hemmungs Wirtén, *Cosmopolitan Copyright*, 64.

the main skeptic of the Stockholm Protocol, refusing, in the end, to vote in the passage of the Stockholm Act of the *Berne Convention*, along with the delegates of Mexico and Uruguay.[79]

India threatened to withdraw from all international copyright conventions unless, within six months, the UK accepted the Stockholm Protocol.[80] However, in the end, neither did the UK sign the protocol nor did India withdraw; instead, a new compromise was reached in 1971.

When revision of the *Berne Convention* was attempted again in 1971, with a simultaneous and largely matching revision of the UCC, the 1952 compulsory licensing provisions of the UCC served as the basis for negotiations. The 1971 revision of the UCC retained the provisions on compulsory licensing of translations as they applied to all contracting states with only minor changes,[81] and added additional provisions for compulsory licensing of translations that would apply only to countries considered to be developing countries under the United Nations system.[82] Such licenses were for teaching, scholarship, or research only.[83] The additional provisions shortened the period of time before the compulsory licensing could be authorized from seven years to three years, or to one year if the translation were into a language not in general use in any "developed" country party to the convention.[84]

While the 1971 revision of the *Berne Convention* did not contain compulsory licensing provisions for translation that applied to all member states, the provisions for developing countries that were provided in the *Universal Copyright Convention* that year were replicated in the Appendix to the *Berne Convention*.[85] As with the UCC provisions, these licenses were available only for the purposes of teaching, scholarship, and research.[86]

Compulsory licensing is of little value if the capacity to translate and publish works does not exist. Therefore, a joint proposal supported by a

[79] Ibid., 57 and 64. [80] Ibid., 66.

[81] UCC 1971 Art. V. Rather than providing compulsory licensing for works not published in the "national language or languages" as had the original 1952 convention, the 1971 UCC provided compulsory licensing for works not published in "a language in general use in the Contracting State." See paragraphs a and e of the 1971 revision. This may be seen as a narrowing of the compulsory licensing provisions because, as the Director General of WIPO observed in 1971, "with regard to the comment by the Delegate of India, India had a very large number of languages, of which only a few were in general use." Actes 1971, 148. The language of "general use" was also adopted in the 1971 Appendix to the *Berne Convention*. *Berne Convention*, 1971, Appendix, Art. II(2)(a) and (3)(a).

[82] UCC 1971, Article V*bis* and V*ter*. [83] Ibid., V*ter* (3). [84] Ibid., V*ter* (1)(a).

[85] *Berne Convention*, 1971, Appendix, Articles 2, 4, and 5. [86] Ibid., Article 2(5).

group of former French colonies called for the ability to *share* licenses.[87] As the delegate from Côte d'Ivoire – Ketty-Lina Liguer-Laubhouet – pointed out, with only two publishing houses across fourteen French-speaking African states, *not* allowing shared licenses would doom the whole enterprise from the start.[88] Such cooperation was furthermore necessary, noted Senegalese delegate, the academic Saliou Kandji, to overcome the challenges imposed by colonial administration, whereby indigenous languages had been divided by political borders, and new languages imposed on people.[89]

The role of translation in copyright resonated to the very core of the linguistic impact of colonialism, and the debates over the translation right following decolonization highlighted the desire to foster cultural production in indigenous languages, while responding to the imposing presence of European languages. The consequences of this impact were present at the Brazzaville meeting, as well as at the meeting that led to the formation of the Organization of African Unity (OAU), both in 1963.[90] Here, it was recognized that the use of African languages was at the heart of the "revalidation of African culture," but the contemporary reality meant that European languages would play an important role too, requiring a balance between metropolitan languages and local ones, both within the OAU and more broadly.[91] As the Guinean president, Ahmed Sékou Touré, explained it: "[h]istory has made us – and we have no compunctions about this – use borrowed languages."[92]

Such developments help to reveal how deeply embedded issues of language and translation were in the institutions of colonialism and in the direction of postcolonial development. However, despite the tremendous diplomatic effort that resulted in the new provisions, they have had

87 This group included Congo-Brazzaville, Côte d'Ivoire, Niger, and Senegal, among other supporters.

88 *Berne Records* 1971, 152, item 411.1; see also 151, item 402.2 and 152, item 409. Liguer-Libhouet would become Deputy-General for WIPO, the first national of a developing country to hold that position. WIPO, Coordination committee, Fourteenth Session (11th Ordinary), WO/CC/XIV/5 (Geneva: WIPO, 1980).

89 Ibid., 152, item 409. Another Senegalese delegate, N'Déné N'Diaye, wrote important articles on copyright. They include: "The Influence of Copyright on Cultural Development in the Developing Countries," *RIDA* 86 (1975); and "The Berne Convention and Developing Countries," *The Columbia-VLA Journal of Law & the Arts* 47 (1986–1987).

90 Jean-Baptiste Ntahokaja, *African Study Meeting on Copyright: Report. RADA/10 Paris: UNESCO, 1963,* 5–6.

91 Michael Wolfers, *Politics in the Organization of African Unity* (London: Methuen and Co., Ltd., 1976), 31.

92 As quoted in Ibid., 31. Thanks Nicholas Must for offering these observations.

little effect. Few countries appear to have used the Paris Act Appendix, although a number have made declarations that they intended to avail themselves of its provisions and some, while not formally availing themselves of the Appendix, have put in place compulsory licensing regimes for translation.[93]

Copyright and translation today

The fully assimilated translation right has not succeeded in universalizing access to knowledge in translation, if that was ever its purpose. There continue to be tremendous barriers to access to works in translation, and imbalances in the direction and flow of translations. Both the linguistic distributions of copyright works, and the flow of translation of those works, are highly unequal, with English-language works dominating both production and as the source language of translations. In 1999, despite the fact that less than 10 percent of the world's population spoke English, approximately 80 percent of web pages were written in English.[94] More recently, the dominance of English on the Internet has declined but is still substantial, with 45 percent of web pages estimated to be in English.[95] The percentage of books published in English and box-office movies in English also far surpass the percentage of the world population that are English speakers. Alongside the dominance of the English language as the original language of many cultural products, English has also been estimated to dominate as the source language of 49 percent of translations.[96] Relatively few non-English-language works are translated into English. About 3 percent of books published in the United States, for example, are translated works.[97]

New automated translation technologies could help to bridge this divide. Since 1949 researchers and entrepreneurs have worked to develop machine translation, initially driven by Cold War military and intelligence requirements, as well as by projects on virtual diplomacy that attempted

[93] Ricketson and Ginsburg, *International Copyright*, 957; Armstrong et al., eds. *Access to Knowledge in Africa*, 326–327; and see generally *Berne Convention Notifications*, www.wipo.int/treaties/en/ip/berne/.

[94] Ketzan, "Rebuilding Babel," 215.

[95] Daniel Pimienta, Daniel Prado and Álvaro Blanco, *Twelve Years of Measuring Linguistic Diversity in the Internet: Balance and Perspectives* (Paris: UNESCO, 2009).

[96] Lawrence Venuti, *The Scandals of Translation: Towards an Ethics of Difference* (New York: Routledge, 1998), 160.

[97] Ahmed Abdel Latif, *About Three Percent*, www.rochester.edu/College/translation/threepercent/index.php?s=about (accessed on March 27, 2015).

to build policymaker dialogue across linguistic divides.[98] While some researchers have concluded since that time that the perfection of machine translation is an impossible goal to reach, recent innovations in machine translation may hold the key to the development of the technology.[99]

Machine translation is not a panacea and raises many of the problems noted at the start of this chapter, as well as additional ones. It could facilitate the continued dominance of English as a source language and the decline of other languages by making multilingualism less necessary; it could also facilitate the dominance and globalization of core states and businesses, which may have greater access to machine translation than those on the periphery. Machine translation could also facilitate, further than do existing translation services, the ability of states and international organizations to operate and extend their governance around the world.

While translation generally, and machine translation in particular, brings with it a variety of problems and cannot, alone, be equated with "access," it can facilitate some forms of access, and not only to ideas, knowledge, or copyright works; it can also facilitate dialogue among a greater diversity of interests, and access to institutions. Copyright, and the translation right in particular, however, may continue to stand in the way of some of these forms of access.

Copyright can stand in the way of translation and adaptation of software from one human language to another. Here, the translation right complicates not only economic, social, and cultural borders but also some technological developments as the potential of machine translation becomes more apparent. In such cases, two groups especially risk liability for copyright infringement: end-users and intermediaries.

The translation and adaptation of software from one language (often English) into local languages, or "software localization," is important for access to ideas, interests, and institutions. However, intellectual property rights could impede some localization efforts. The UK Commission on Intellectual Property Rights has expressed concern that the protection of software source code might prevent products from being adapted to local needs.[100]

Copyright might also be an inhibitor of the rising potential of amateur translation and, thus, a risk to end-users. While professional translators

[98] Ketzan, "Rebuilding Babel," 209–210. [99] Ibid., 211–212.

[100] Commission on Intellectual Property Rights, *Integrating Intellectual Property Rights and Development Policy*, 105.

may often be paid by the copyright holder or publisher of a work to produce a translation, many web sites afford amateur translators and end-users the ability to translate texts. Sites like Wikipedia encourage the translation of texts into new languages.[101] Other companies have turned amateur translation into a business model, crowdsourcing translation to language learners in ways that may have begun to undermine professional translation services.[102] Insofar as sites encourage the translation of factual material such as weather, locations, or recipe listings in which copyright does not subsist, then copyright liability may not arise.[103] However, sites that encourage the translation of copyright works without the copyright holders' permission may give rise to end-user liability.

It may be that fair dealing or fair use exceptions,[104] or, in the case of material made available online by the copyright holder, an implied license,[105] would apply to such translations where done for personal research or education, to simply read a work, or for other non-commercial uses. However, if fair use and fair dealing provisions did not apply or were not available in the jurisdiction in question, the end-user could be liable for copyright infringement.[106] This could be especially important in countries that do not have such fair use or fair dealing provisions.

Intermediaries providing translation services, such as software developers and internet translation service providers, could also be liable for copyright infringement in some jurisdictions. Jurisdictions requiring that a "volitional act" be undertaken for a finding of copyright infringement may not find direct infringement by such intermediaries, but intermediaries may be liable for secondary infringement for "inducing, causing, or materially contributing" to the infringing conduct of another.[107]

Ketzan argues that copyright may, in the ways just described, stand in the way of what he views as the enormous potential of machine translation. He puts it dramatically: "Technology may have put man on the moon, but machine translation has the potential to take us farther, across the gulf of comprehension that lies between people from different places."[108]

Such new global links may, Ketzan feels, be accompanied by a new localism; just as translation might decrease the need for dominant-language

[101] Ketzan, "Rebuilding Babel," 218.

[102] Victoria Livingstone, "Google, Duolingo, and the Problems of Internet Translation," *Fairobserver.com*, March 28, 2014. www.fairobserver.com/region/north˙america/google-duolingo-problems-internet-translation-67312/ (accessed March 27, 2015).

[103] Ketzan, "Rebuilding Babel," 225. [104] Ibid., 232–233. [105] Ibid., 229–231.

[106] Ibid., 232. [107] Ibid., 227–228. [108] Ibid., 206–207.

speakers to learn minority languages, so may a reduced need to learn dominant languages allow minority languages to flourish.[109] Further, automatic computerized translation of internet texts and social media "would increase social interaction across cultures and languages, possibly dramatically." "It is easy to imagine," Ketzan says, "a future in which we seamlessly surf the entirety of the Internet in our native language, with occasional (or frequent) linguistic mistakes being the only indication that we're reading [machine] translated text."[110] On the other hand, it may not be the case that machine and amateur translation does equalize the directional flow of translation. As Victoria Livingstone observes, the Duolingo crowdsourcing translation service translates primarily from English into foreign languages, reinforcing English as the dominant source language of translation.[111]

Conclusion

Translation, and the translation right, continues to be associated with a number of forms of access, and to carry with it the baggage of colonialism. Translation cannot be equated with "access" in the sense of access to ideas, knowledge, and works alone; it also facilitates dialog among interests; and the ability of institutions to operate internationally. At the same time, to the extent that translation is viewed as facilitating useful forms of access, copyright, and the translation right in particular, may continue to stand in the way.

The earliest strategy for facilitating access to works in translation was to deny a right of translation to copyright owners, thus allowing local cultural producers and states to facilitate and regulate access to works in translation. The Scandinavian countries that, at the time, considered themselves in some respects to be developing, played an important role in limiting the translation right until 1908.[112] However, domestic lobby groups eventually changed those countries' governments' ideas about what their position on translation rights should be, highlighting the interests of domestic authors who had strong sales abroad, over and above consumers' and students' interests in access to foreign works in translation.[113]

[109] Ibid., 221–222. [110] Ibid., 218–219.
[111] Livingstone, "Google, Duolingo, and the Problems of Internet Translation."
[112] Hemmungs Wirtén, *Cosmopolitan Copyright*, 24–33.
[113] Regarding Sweden, see Hemmungs Wirtén, *Cosmopolitan Copyright*, 33.

Haiti and Tunisia, both former French colonies, did not vote for weaker copyright and more open access to translation in the early days of Berne negotiations; instead, their position as contemporary or past French colonies may have been determinative. The fact that France had two votes (one for France, and one for Tunisia) prevented the right of translation from being limited further than it actually was in the original *Berne Convention.* Haiti's support of France on a stronger translation right was also crucial to this outcome.

Following the full assimilation of the translation right in 1908, the access strategy shifted to a battle to allow compulsory licensing of translations. Siam and the Irish Free State lost their battles for compulsory licensing of translations in 1928. However, India and other newly independent developing countries won battles for limited compulsory licensing provisions under both the UCC and the *Berne Convention.* They also won provisions that allowed countries to rest at earlier, more limited, versions of the *Berne Convention*'s standard of full translation rights.

The issue of access to translation has arisen, once again, in discussions toward an international instrument on limitations and exceptions for educational, teaching, and research institutions and persons with other disabilities. The delegations of the African Group, Brazil, GRULAC, and China have proposed exceptions that would allow translation of copyright works in an educational context.[114] In the light of tremendous changes in the translation industry, and the potential of machine translation, these proposals seem modest.

The translation industry is undergoing massive change. Machine translation and crowdsourced translation are more accessible than ever before, challenging notions that copyright owners can or should control the translation of their works. However, even as they become more accessible, machine translation and crowdsourced translation may exacerbate as much as rectify inequalities in the directional flow of knowledge across linguistic and geographical borders. Thus, the question of translation, and visions of its future development, may be important questions to be addressed both in international copyright regimes and the A2K movement. Access to translation is a question affecting developing

[114] CPTech. *Treaty on Access to Knowledge, Draft of 9 May 2005.* www.cptech.org/a2k/a2k_treaty_may9.pdf (accessed March 27, 2015); WIPO, Standing Committee on Copyright and Related Rights, Twenty-Eighth Session, Chair's Conclusions SCCR/28/REF (Geneva: WIPO, 2014); Argentina and Brazil, Proposal by Argentina and Brazil for the Establishment of a Development Agenda for WIPO GA/31/11 (Geneva: WIPO, 2004); WIPO, *The 45 Adopted Recommendations under the WIPO Development Agenda.*

and "developed" countries alike as linguistic frontiers and barriers are reshaped globally.

It may be that, as much as copyright facilitates or stands in the way of translation, translation has done much more to facilitate the dominance and spread of copyright around the world. WIPO operates in Arabic, Chinese, English, French, Russian, and Spanish, and also Portuguese under specific conditions, providing translation services at its meetings. Its meeting documents are made available online, in English and often in translation to multiple languages, as are many of its publications. *WIPO Lex* service has made the laws of WIPO member states available not only in local languages but also in translation to English.[115] Such services allow forms of access to member state and secretariat knowledge about copyright and dialog among those interests and representatives who are present at the WIPO table. Certainly, it facilitates access to, and the dominance of, WIPO as an institution.

[115] WIPO, About WIPO Lex. www.wipo.int/wipolex/en/about.html (accessed March 27, 2015).

Conclusion to Part I

In her book *Power & Ideas* (1998), Susan Sell emphasized the importance of the role that ideas, beliefs, and learning play in determining the outcome of North–South anti-trust and intellectual property negotiations. While economic and political power have undeniable roles in determining the outcomes of these negotiations, ideas, beliefs, and learning, as well as the availability and dissemination of models, also play two additional important roles: first, in forming the basis for conceptualizations of negotiators' goals, identities, and visions of development; and second, in implementing the outcomes of the negotiations.[1]

In this part, I have focused on the rise and fall of particular visions of development, and of particular ideas and beliefs surrounding principles of access within international copyright negotiations. In the history of copyright negotiations under the Berne Union, particular agendas of development, particular ideas about access and how it should or could be achieved, and the perceived national interests in supporting or challenging principles of access, changed dramatically over time.

Ideas surrounding the principle of access to scientific knowledge changed with the exit of Louis-Joseph Janvier, a Haitian medical doctor, and the rise of proprietary market visions of scientific development came to dominate in international copyright discourse. Copyright in scientific works saw scientific development conform to a proprietary model. However, this model is currently subject to challenge from the open access movement and, at the international level, by the A2K movement and proponents of minimum standards of limitations and exceptions pertaining to research and science.

[1] Susan Sell, *Power & Ideas: The North–South Politics of Intellectual Property and Anti-Trust* (New York: State University of New York Press, 1998), 1–39.

Ideas surrounding access to educational materials, and the types of materials viewed as educational have changed. As with principles of access to scientific knowledge, principles of access to educational materials were narrowed over the history of the current system of international copyright. However, the A2K movement has sought to restore principles of access to educational materials to the international copyright system.

In the case of the principle of access to news, ideas about the need for free copying of news items among newspapers changed to reflect prevailing market models. However, the market model continues to be challenged by open source journalism, participatory journalism, and open data, associated loosely with the A2K movement.

Ideas on the importance of access to copyright works in translation have also shifted dramatically over time, with free translation originally being viewed as crucial to domestic education and publishing industries, and later being viewed as of continuing importance in the field of education. The development of increased access to translation in new crowdsourced and machine translation business models may challenge the existing regime of translation rights.

Ideas about *who* should benefit from principles of access have also shifted over time. People in developing countries, as opposed to people in all countries, came to be seen as the proper beneficiaries of special principles of access to copyright works following postwar decolonization. The principles that were established were narrow and buried in red tape. The idea that principles of access should be directed at developing countries alone has, however, recently been challenged, as the A2K movement moves to promote minimum standards of exceptions and limitations that would apply worldwide. This shift arises from the combining of developing country representatives and NGO representatives under the umbrella of the A2K movement, and perhaps from the realization that "development" takes a variety of forms and is not confined to developing countries alone.

More recently, in the development of the *Marrakesh Treaty to Facilitate Access to Published Works for Persons Who Are Blind, Visually Impaired, or Otherwise Print Disabled*, we have seen the rise of the idea that limitations and exceptions could serve the goal of "accessibility." Here, we see the rise of the idea that the copyright limitations and exceptions could solve the "book famine" that affects the blind and visually impaired (see Chapter 8 below).[2]

[2] Francis Gurry, "Opening Speech by Francis Gurry, Director General, World Intellectual Property Organization, to the Marrakesh Diplomatic Conference," June 17–28,

Changes in the core ideas surrounding principles of access occurred, at times, because of new learning at the domestic level in key negotiating parties that shifted conceptualizations of their national interest. At other times, negotiating-party interests changed as a result of changes in the perceived bargain that was before them at the international level. In the first case, domestic-level learning was not necessarily scientific or neutral but was often the result of industry lobbying. The Swedish emphasis on free translation shifted, as noted in Chapter 6, as a result of lobbying by Swedish authors and publishers, who argued that stronger translation rights were, in fact, in their interests. This led to changes in Swedish legislation and changes to the Swedish position in relation to the *Berne Convention.*

Negotiating-party interests also sometimes changed as a result of changes in the perceived bargain that was before negotiating parties at the international level. For example, the (false) promise of American adherence to the convention was, in part, what brought British negotiators to the table in the 1880s.[3] The (largely false) promise of protection for traditional knowledge was, in part, what brought African countries to the table in the 1960s.[4]

Ideas' strengths, as will be discussed in Part II of this book, are not determined so much by an assessment of their real power to provide the forms of access they promise; ideas' strengths are determined in part by the strength of the states and interest groups that brought them to the table, and in part by the ability of those groups to point to, demonstrate, and promote particular models as embodying their ideas.[5] Such abilities are constrained by the loss of those actors who promote alternative models and principles of access, and also by the constraints on alternatives placed by the norm-setting nature of the international copyright system itself. The exit of Louis-Joseph Janvier from the negotiations was important in the decline in emphasis on access to news and scientific and medical knowledge, whereas the entry of other developing countries to the negotiations in the 1960s was important in the rise in emphasis of access to educational materials and translation. At the same time, path dependency has meant that decisions taken earlier in time have had greater effect than those taken later. Today, the increasing presence of developing country

2013, www.wipo.int/about-wipo/en/dgo/speeches/dg_dc2013.html (accessed March 27, 2015).

[3] Lionel Bently and Brad Sherman, "Great Britain and the Signing of the Berne Convention in 1886," *Journal of the Copyright Society of the USA* 48, 3 (2001), 311–340.

[4] See Chapter 4. [5] Braithwaite and Drahos, *Global Business Regulation*, Chapter 25.

and NGO representatives has been important in driving the establishment of the WIPO Development Agenda and the A2K movement. While it may be unable to undo past policy directions entirely, the A2K movement has brought important alternative models of copyright and open access, alternative visions of development, and alternative visions of the future of access to knowledge to the table, recognizing development, in various forms, as something in which all people have a stake.

PART II

Interests

Introduction to Part II

Many histories tend to focus on powerful actors, and there are good reasons to do so. The most powerful players often, after all, exert the most influence, and their visions of the future often dominate because they have the resources and power to put them in place. However, the histories of the *less* powerful states and interest groups in the international copyright system are also interesting and important for a number of reasons.

First, it is obvious that the major state powers such as France, Germany, Italy, the United Kingdom, and the United States have been the most powerful players in the international copyright system; that these states operate, much of the time, in service of economic and corporate interests and copyright holders; and that the international copyright system largely serves the interests of powerful states and corporations. These fundamental facts are well documented.[1]

Even so, the most influential players are not the only players, and the influence of core states must be seen against the shifting relative power of others. The international system is often seen as hierarchical, characterized by power groupings of great, medium, and small powers; economic groupings of "developed," developing, and least developed countries; or in terms of cores, semi-peripheries, and peripheries.[2] Within these

[1] Ronald V. Bettig, *Copyrighting Culture: The Political Economy of Intellectual Property* (Westview Press, 1996); Chang, Kicking Away the Ladder; Drahos, Peter, and John Braithwaite. *Information Feudalism: Who Owns the Knowledge Economy?* (London: Earthscan Publications, 2002); Susan K. Sell, *Private Power, Public Law: The Globalization of Intellectual Property Rights* (Cambridge: Cambridge University Press, 2003); May, The World Intellectual Property Organization; Christopher May and Susan K. Sell. *Intellectual Property Rights: A Critical History* (Boulder and London: Lynne Reinner, 2006); Christopher May, "The World Intellectual Property Organization." *New Political Economy* 11, 3 (2006), 435–445; Christopher May, "Direct and Indirect Influence at the World Intellectual Property Organization," in *Business and Global Governance*, eds. Mortgen Ougaard and Anna Leander (London and New York: Routledge, 2010), 39–56; Peter Drahos, "'IP World'", 197–216.

[2] Ian Clark, *The Hierarchy of States* (Cambridge: Cambridge University Press, 1989), 2.

categorizations, shifts take place. The decline of the British Empire in the early twentieth century led to the emergence of former British dominions as independent countries within the world system. The end of formal imperialism after World War II led to the emergence of an additional set of states operating as formally independent actors on the world stage. More recently, a number of countries have been classed as "emerging" economies. The rise of transnational NGOs and civil society actors have also transformed, to some extent, international affairs. Such shifts may have significant effects on international institutions and on the visions and strategies that they adopt.

Second, the trajectory that saw WIPO gain almost universal domination, its strategies and tactics for so doing, and its openness (or not) to new or peripheral voices, reveals a great deal about WIPO. It speaks about the institution's legitimacy, its relationship to its peripheries, and its relationship to modern forms of empire.

Third, institutions shape actors in important ways. Whereas critical political economists often assume that actors have fairly fixed interests and motivations based on their position in domestic or international class hierarchies, others have observed that institutions play a role in the socialization of actors, the opportunities available to them, and their interaction with other groups.[3] This is especially true of WIPO; it has shaped many countries' trajectories in international copyright relations by providing model laws and norms, by posing as a "gold standard" to be striven for, by providing recognition and rewards to diplomats, and by giving states a platform from which to speak and to be recognized as players on the international stage.

Finally, it is a premise of postcolonial theory and of this work that less powerful actors must be viewed as active, even if less influential, players in history. One of the key questions that this work asks is what role less powerful players played in establishing principles of access. In this part I examine more fully the relationship of developing countries, NGOs, and indigenous peoples with the *Berne Convention*, and with WIPO and its predecessors, focusing on their roles in shaping international copyright norms and institutions.

Related to this final point, it must be noted that it is not always the case that the most powerful actors are the most influential. Drahos and

[3] Thelen, Kathleen and Sven Steinmo. "Historical Institutionalism in Comparative Politics," in *Structuring Politics: Historical Institutionalism in Comparative Analysis*, eds. Sven Steinmo, Kathleen Thelen, and Frank Longstreth (Cambridge: Cambridge University Press, 1992), 1–32.

Braithwaite show that patterns of modeling, influenced by inequities of power, have a great deal to offer in explaining the outcomes of battles of principles. They argue that although "economically powerful actors have a greater capacity to make models work for them," battles of models can be won by economically weaker actors who find and point to cracks in dominant systems, offering concrete models as solutions to those problems.[4] Modeling processes are therefore "crucial resources for emancipation" because of their potential to be used to exploit cracks in dominant systems and introduce new and favorable models.[5] Access to international forums, where alternative models can be presented, transposed, translated, and disseminated internationally, presents important opportunities to less powerful groups.

This final point is also related to the second form of access to knowledge outlined in Chapter One: the ability to be recognized as a source of knowledge, to influence the direction and shape of the discourse that defines what knowledge is, what knowledge is valued, and what knowledge is recognized as being knowledge. Part II of this book focuses on this second form of access to knowledge.

"Developing" countries and least developed countries have long had a majority in the Berne system of international copyright. Nevertheless, copyright has expanded, and rarely has it been reduced, whereas access provisions have been, in many cases, whittled down. Given the important opportunities for influence that international institutions offer, why is this the case?

While the entry of the former British commonwealth countries that gained independence in the early twentieth century had little impact on the construction or revision of the *Berne Convention*, the entry of the countries that gained independence in the mid-twentieth century have had, and continue to have, a greater impact on both the norms of the international copyright system and on its power structure. The rise of transnational NGOs, especially those advocating principles of access, and the increasing involvement of indigenous peoples at WIPO, have also been significant. At the same time, none of these shifts has, as of yet, changed the overall trajectory of the international copyright system toward increasing protection and declining principles of access, nor will they necessarily ever. Rights-holders continue to reap the rewards of a system formed on the basis of colonialism.

[4] Braithwaite and Drahos, *Global Business Regulation*, 579, 581, and 594–595.
[5] Ibid., 579.

Nonetheless, the A2K movement has had a significant impact at WIPO, and many of its proposals could change the picture of access to knowledge around the world, if adopted not only by the relatively peripheral developing countries and NGOs that promote them but also by WIPO's core member states.

We might expect to see a relationship between increasing developing country participation in international copyright negotiations and increasing access provisions. However, as noted in Part I of this book, this has not, historically, been the case. Instead, we see, alongside a general downward trend, instances of limited jumps in the grant of access rights sparked by coordinated spurts of activity by developing countries, first at the time when they joined the UCC and then became active, around 1967 and 1971, in negotiating for special provisions in the *Berne Convention* and, second, following the negotiation of the *TRIPs Agreement* and the WIPO Internet Treaties in the establishment of a Development Agenda for WIPO. The *Marrakesh Treaty to Facilitate Access to Published Works for Persons Who Are Blind, Visually Impaired, or Otherwise Print Disabled* of 2013 (see Chapter 8), and the new proposals for minimum limitations and exceptions to copyright for educational, teaching, and research institutions and persons with other disabilities may also be seen as related to the burst of activity surrounding the WIPO Development Agenda starting in 2004. Overall, rising (though still limited) levels of participation by developing country representatives, NGOs, and indigenous peoples have not transformed the overall shape and direction of international copyright as of yet. It remains to be seen whether the A2K movement will have a greater impact than have prior campaigns in transforming, globally, access to knowledge in the second sense, as well as the visions of development promoted by international institutions and the global conditions of access to knowledge more broadly.

7

The role and inclusion of developing countries in international copyright

Developing and emerging countries are often left out of the histories of international copyright, or portrayed as marginal players. In this chapter, I review the history of international copyright negotiations, asking what role developing country representatives have played, synthesizing and elaborating the discussions in the first part of this book. Second, I evaluate the impact of the establishment in 2007 of a Development Agenda for WIPO. The Development Agenda has, I will argue, seen partial success in giving developing country delegates greater influence at WIPO, but it has also deepened, entrenched, and expanded WIPO's view of intellectual property as a "power tool" for development. In the third part of this chapter, I note the ways that developing countries' identities and interests in international copyright have been in part shaped by their participation in international copyright institutions.

Developing countries and international copyright: a history

The 1880s

The founding of the *Berne Convention* took place "during the heyday of colonialism" and, as mentioned in Chapter 1, only European, North and South American, and Caribbean states were invited.[1] The continents of Africa and Asia, seemingly deemed "uncivilized," fell outside the realm of the negotiation of international law.[2] This imagined geography would play a fundamental role in the construction of the international copyright system by establishing a privileged role for European powers as modelers of copyright provisions.

Even a number of those countries considered at the time to be "civilized" did not join the Union when it was founded, including

[1] Actes 1884, 9; Alan H. Lazar, "Developing Countries and Authors' Rights," *Copyright Law Symposium* 19 (1971), 6.

[2] Anghie "Finding the Peripheries."

Austria-Hungary, Portugal, the Netherlands, the Scandinavian countries, the Russian Empire, the United States, and the American republics.[3] Among states of the Western Hemisphere, only Costa Rica, El Salvador, Haiti, and Paraguay sent representatives to the first meeting at which the draft convention was discussed.[4] The United States attended the second session at which the convention was negotiated, as did representatives from several Caribbean, South and Central American countries: Argentina, Costa Rica, Haiti, Honduras, and Paraguay. However, of those, only the Haitian government sent a delegate to the final conference in 1886 and signed the *Berne Convention*.[5] The United States, which could be viewed at the time as a developing country, attended but did not sign.

The non-participation of many states in the establishment of the Berne system of international copyright highlighted enormously differing conceptualizations of the relationship between international copyright and development. It also highlighted the differing development agendas, public policy goals, and national conditions of the countries concerned.

The United States' refusal to join the *Berne Convention* was an exception to the general trend of American participation in international organizations that took off in the 1880s.[6] The United States had joined the Universal Postal Union (1874), the International Bureau of Weights and Measures (1878), the International Union for the Protection of Industrial Property (1884), and the International Center for the Exchange of Publications (1889 and 1968).[7] However, citing the need to take into account a range of interest groups, including the paper manufacturers, typesetters, printers, bookbinders, and others who then enjoyed the ability to reproduce European works for the American market (American law did not grant copyright in foreign works), it did not join the negotiations, later sending a representative in observer capacity only.[8]

Other states of the Western Hemisphere, as well as from Europe, rejected the invitation to join the negotiations. Governments of the

[3] Ricketson and Ginsburg, *International Copyright*, 82–83.

[4] Actes de la première conférénce internationalle pour la protection des œuvres littéraires et artistiques du 8 septembre 1884 à Berne, 9; Ricketson and Ginsburg, *International Copyright*, 52–59; Kampelman, "The United States and International Copyright," 411.

[5] Francis Adams and J.H.G. Bergne to the Earl of Iddelsleigh. Report on the Third International Copyright Conference at Berne, September 10, 1886, in Library and Archives Canada, RG6 A3, Vol. 214, file: "Copyright Conference at Berne, 1886."

[6] Elmer Plischke, *U.S. Department of State: A Reference History* (Westport, Conn.: Greenwood, 1999), 139.

[7] Ibid., 138–139.

[8] Ricketson and Ginsburg, *International Copyright*, 59; Actes 1884, 9.

Dominican Republic, Nicaragua, Mexico, as well as Greece and Denmark, were invited but declined to attend in consideration of the state of their domestic copyright legislation and their literary "underdevelopment."[9]

Although various Latin American countries did participate in the meetings leading up to the formation of the Berne Union, none joined.[10] In 1889 Latin American countries, instead, formed a copyright Union of their own. The *Montevideo Convention*, also referred to as the first *Pan American Convention*, was ratified by Argentina, Bolivia, Paraguay, Peru, and Uruguay in the 1880s and 1890s, building on the separate and different intellectual property histories of Latin American and Caribbean countries.[11]

Canada, though not represented at the negotiations – it not being yet the norm for British dominion representatives to attend international negotiations – would be brought in to the *Berne Convention* by the British Imperial government. The dominion government would soon embark on a decade-long attempt to denounce the treaty, though such denunciation would never receive approval from Great Britain.[12]

The *Berne Convention* was viewed by North Americans as a European treaty ill-suited to the requirements of society in the Americas. Canadian Prime Minister John Thompson saw the *Berne Convention* as a model of copyright inappropriate to North American settler society:

> The Berne Convention had in view considerations of society which are widely different from those prevailing in Canada. In Europe the reading population in the various countries is comparatively dense; – in Canada, a population considerably less than that of London is dispersed over an area nearly as large as that of Europe. In the cities of Europe, especially in Great Britain, the reading public is largely supplied from the libraries, while, in Canada, as a general rule, he who reads must buy. In European countries the reading class forms but a fraction of the whole population, while in Canada it comprises nearly the whole population.[13]

[9] Actes 1884, 9, referring to the Dominican Republic as "Saint-Domingue."

[10] Ricketson, "The Birth of the Berne Union," 30.

[11] Caroline Deere, *The Implementation Game, 34–35: The TRIPS Agreement and the Global Politics of Intellectual Property Reform in Developing Countries* (Oxford: Oxford University Press), 34–37.

[12] Bannerman, *The Struggle for Canadian Copyright.*

[13] John Thompson to Governor General in Council, 1892, 7, in Library and Archives Canada, RG13 A-2 Vol. 85 File 892–217.

The colonies and dominions of the British Empire, though not present, shaped the British approach to negotiations. The dominions, for example, confined the British delegation's position, since some of the provisions under discussion during the negotiations of the 1880s might have disturbed British colonies' and dominions' settlements or ambitions with regard to the importation of American reprints of British books, the ability to translate copyright works into local languages (a key strategy of Anglicization and colonialism, especially in India) and the ability of British dominions to adopt increasingly independent copyright laws to address local concerns.[14] Only once it was determined that the treaty would adopt fairly general principles, allowing certain flexibilities to innovate in local regimes, and once the British negotiators had affirmed that specific colonies and possessions could be exempted from the convention, was the British government able to sign.[15]

While many governments, of both core and peripheral countries, opted not to take part in the Berne negotiations, a number of less powerful states did send representatives. Of those representatives, only one spoke. As has been described in Part I of this book, Louis-Joseph Janvier, the Haitian delegate to the conferences of the 1880s, played a role in establishing principles of access to scientific information, educational materials, and news in the founding of the *Berne Convention.*

With the representative of Haiti standing out as the one possible exception, the presence of many of the less powerful states at the foundation of the *Berne Convention* was substantively different from that of the major powers. Many had only recently achieved independence, and their diplomatic resources were generally quite limited.[16] Some were represented by accredited diplomats, others by academics, and some by representatives serving dual functions, being both diplomats and writers or businessmen, or being the delegate for multiple countries. Others, while intending to send delegates, had difficulty in actually doing so.

Argentina, whose independence from Spain had been established earlier in the nineteenth century, was represented by an Argentinean government representative based in Berne.[17] However, as an observer, Argentina was not an active participant in the negotiations.

Similarly, both Costa Rica and Honduras, also Latin American countries that gained independence in the early nineteenth century, sent

[14] Bently and Sherman, "Great Britain and the Signing of the Berne Convention in 1886."

[15] Ibid., 311–340. [16] Ricketson and Ginsburg, *International Copyright*, 61.

[17] Actes 1885, 7.

representatives to the early negotiations, although neither spoke on record.[18] El Salvador, a country in a similar position, chose as a delegate Torres Caicedo, a diplomat in Europe and former author, although he seems not to have participated.[19] Finally, the government of Paraguay also registered observers to the 1884 and 1885 meetings, but did not ultimately sign the agreement,[20] demonstrating the same interest in the convention as the other Latin American countries mentioned, along with the same decision not to become a signatory.

A Liberian representative was also in attendance. William Koentzer, Imperial Advisor and Consul General of the Republic of Liberia, represented Liberia in 1886 and signed the *Berne Convention* on Liberia's behalf.[21]

Liberia had declared independence in 1847, but indigenous Africans were excluded from citizenship until 1908, and often-corrupt and incompetent Americo-Liberian governors and managers took part in what was effectively a form of colonial rule.[22] Liberia had no specific copyright organizations or legislation; copyright was granted through customary or common law, without formalities.[23] Most of Liberia's population had not been in contact with or very much influenced by the Liberian administration, who held a strong sense of cultural superiority and did not view the African people as possessing any tangible or distinctive culture of their own.[24] It is therefore not surprising that the cultures and cultural works of the indigenous peoples of Liberia, nor their modes of governance, were little represented by Koentzer. He is on record as speaking only to indicate that he did not have specific instructions on a particular matter pertaining to the administration of the Union.[25]

Despite signing, Liberia was the only one of the original signatories not to ratify the *Berne Convention* in 1887. Twenty years later in 1908, though formally independent, Liberia acceded to the convention under signature

[18] Actes 1885; Actes 1886; Adams and Bergne, *Report on the Third International Copyright Conference*, September 10, 1886, in Library and Archives Canada, RG6 A3, Vol. 214, file: "Copyright Conference at Berne, 1886."

[19] "Jose Maria Torres Caicedo," Famous Americans, http://famousamericans.net/josemaria torrescaicedo/ (accessed March 27, 2015); Actes 1884.

[20] Actes 1885, 69. [21] Ibid.

[22] M.B. Akpan, "Black Imperialism: Americo-Liberian Rule over the African Peoples of Liberia 1841–1964," *Canadian Journal of African Studies* 7, 2 (1973), 217–236.

[23] Bowker, *Copyright: Its History and Its Law*, 62, 124, 419.

[24] Akpan, "Black Imperialism." [25] Actes 1886, 44.

of the German delegation to the 1908 diplomatic conference to revise the *Berne Convention.*[26]

Tunisia, which had been invaded by France in 1881 and made a French protectorate, was represented at the negotiations in 1885 and 1886 by Louis Renault, a prominent French international lawyer who was also a member of the French delegation.[27] He was the only representative of a small country to participate actively in the deliberations of the conferences, aside from Janvier of Haiti.[28] Since the Tunisian delegation always voted with the French delegation (the two being represented by a common delegate) France effectively had an extra vote in the deliberations. On at least one occasion, this vote was a deciding one in favor of France.[29]

In sum, less powerful countries were represented at the founding of the *Berne Convention* by an irregular mix of representatives, many who acted only as observers, some who were unable to attend, and some who were represented by foreign or imperial representatives. With the exception of Haiti, whose representative spoke almost strictly on a single issue, the voices of less powerful states at the founding of the *Berne Convention*, though present, were markedly silent.

Due to the exclusion of, and inadequate representation from, countries who were generally net importers of copyright works, those with the greatest interest in access to copyright works were structurally underrepresented. In the face of the general inadequacy of representation from many less powerful countries, Haiti's participation in the conferences of the 1880s was highly significant. Louis-Joseph Janvier might be seen, somewhat anachronistically, as the first voice of the A2K movement in the multilateral copyright system.

As noted in Part I, a number of principles of access were embedded in the original Berne regime. This was due, in a large part, not to the efforts of Janvier alone, but to a convergence of interests held between Janvier and those expressed by other state delegates. Janvier was able to leverage a

[26] Ricketson and Ginsburg, *International Copyright*, 82; Serge L. Levitsky, "The Union of Berne at 100: What Keeps the Superpowers at Bay? Thoughts and Apprehensions," in *Law and the Gorbachev Era: essays in honor of Dietrich André Loeber* (Dordecht: Martinus Nijhoff, 1988), 367.

[27] Kenneith Perkins, *The History of Modern Tunisia* (Cambridge: Cambridge University Press, 2004), 37–40.

[28] Actes 1885; Actes 1886.

[29] In rejecting the 1884 draft of the article on translation rights; Actes 1885, 44; see also Chapters 6 and 10.

weakness in the British imperial copyright system (its lack of cohesiveness due to divergences of imperial and colonial interests) in arguing for less detailed, and thus broader, principles of access to serial publications.[30]

The American government, though not participating in the negotiations directly, exerted significant influence; delegates were conscious of and hopeful regarding the potential that, in the near future, the United States might join the Union. This consciousness played a role in preventing the adoption of provisions that might make more difficult or prevent future American adhesion.

Other principles of access – such as access to knowledge through translation – were not supported by the delegates of Haiti and Tunisia (the latter, as mentioned, being controlled by France). Rather, it was the Scandinavian countries, supported in part by the British, who pressed for more open access to translation.[31]

Middle powers had a particularly important role in establishing principles of access and mediating differences at the founding of the *Berne Convention.* From the beginning, middle powers began to take on some characteristically middle-power roles. Numa Droz, a Swiss legal figure and bureaucrat who had advocated for an international copyright union, acted as president of the meetings as a result of the Swiss government's role as host, and he often played the role of mediating between state interests.[32] Austria-Hungary, along with Sweden, resisted strong translation rights, as their domestic laws included formalities and a shorter term associated with the translation right.[33]

Major powers, at times, also played important roles in promoting principles of access. Great Britain, as mentioned, was weighed down by copyright conflicts within the British Empire, and therefore emerged as a proponent of access as it attempted to avoid copyright commitments that might complicate its relations with its colonies and dominions. Germany was an important advocate of the principle of access to educational materials.[34]

Beginnings are extremely important. Inertia, stickiness, and enduring consequences characterize political development, reinforcing inequalities of power and causing inequalities to become deeply embedded in organizations and dominant modes of understanding. Histories that celebrate the birth of the Berne Union as a triumph of civilization and progress and

[30] See Part I. [31] See Chapter 6.
[32] Ricketson and Ginsburg, *International Copyright*, 52.
[33] Actes 1884, 48–49. [34] Actes 1885, 29.

as the orderly carrying out of the internationalization of international institutions ignore these dynamics, which have had a permanent effect on what has become the international copyright system we know today.

History matters because key causes are located in the past, as are possible alternatives that have been "lost" due to the self-reinforcing nature of paths taken.[35] "It is hard," Braithwaite and Drahos note, "for interest groups to break free of the frameworks imposed by received models."[36] For less powerful states, market actors, and civil society NGOs who sought greater access to foreign works in line with their specific visions of development, many of whom saw the convention as irrelevant and inappropriate, the founding of the *Berne Convention* can largely be seen as the beginning of a losing battle with forces beyond their control.

1908

The next full revision of the *Berne Convention* took place in 1908, a crucial year for access principles, and – despite the presence of several additional developing country representatives advocating for such principles – a year of significant losses. The *Berne Convention*'s provisions on serial publications were, as noted in Part I, adjusted to reduce the scope of permitted reproduction, and the translation right was assimilated to the full term of copyright, as noted in Chapter 6, although reservations to previous versions of the *Berne Convention* would still be permitted. At the same time, further incursions on permitted uses were prevented.

The absence of the Haitian delegate, Louis-Joseph Janvier, as well as the Scandinavian countries' concessions on the right of translation, can be viewed as contributing to the decline of the principles of access to news and scientific works. The Haitian government did not send a delegation but rather committed itself in advance to whatever the outcome of the conference might be.[37] In Janvier's absence, copyright, rather than free reproduction, for the first time became the default for scientific articles and other articles not falling into the category of literary or artistic works articles under the *Berne Convention.*

The loss of former advocates of access through translation was also strongly felt. The Norwegian government, having previously been a leader on this issue, bowed out of the battle for limitations on the translation

35 Paul Pierson, *Politics in Time: History, Institutions, and Social Analysis* (Princeton and Oxford: Princeton University Press, 2004), 11.

36 Braithwaite and Drahos, *Global Business Regulation*, 582.

37 Actes 1908, 153.

right. Norwegian delegate Klaus Hoel explained that the Norwegian government's thinking had evolved on the question, having found that both Norwegian publishers and authors felt they benefited from the translation right; publishers of translations were protected against concurrent translations, and authors' royalty claims were not extreme.[38] The Swedish delegation did not engage on the question, having recently joined the *Berne Convention* in 1904, and the Danish delegation, while present as a member of the Union since 1903, did not go on record with any position on any issue. What had been an alternative Scandinavian model of copyright in relation to translation would disappear.

Even as old stalwarts were lost, three countries joined the battle for more limited translation right. However, the Japanese, Dutch, and Russian delegates, who argued for the retention or recognition of a principle of access to works in translation, did not prevail.

At the same time, some further incursions on permitted uses were prevented – and absent territories were, despite their absence, influential in this. Canada's position of wishing to denounce the *Berne Convention* had the effect, in 1908, as it had in 1896, of causing the British to refuse imposition of additional international obligations in the *Berne Convention*.[39] It also led to the creation in 1914 of a special protocol to the *Berne Convention* allowing Canada to put in place a form of reciprocity *vis-à-vis* the United States via compulsory licensing provisions.[40] In this, Canada's resistance to the Berne model of international copyright resulted from Canada's emulation of the American model of copyright at a time when the United States still refused to join the *Berne Convention*.[41] Thus, alternative models had power, and Canada, despite the absence of any Canadian representative at the Berne negotiations (Canada was represented by the British) had a form of influence on the negotiations and the position of the British negotiators.

Thus, advocates of principles of access lost a key player in Janvier's absence, and the thinking of several previous players on the question of translation had evolved such that their previous role in that debate was abandoned. Despite the interventions of the Japanese, Russian, and Dutch delegates, the battle over access via translation – or what had previously been considered to be a method of encouraging access to works through translation by limiting translation rights – had been lost. Canada, though absent, held back the extension of further principles of protection.

[38] Actes 1908, 246–247.

[39] Bannerman, *The Struggle for Canadian Copyright*, 64–68. [40] Ibid. [41] Ibid.

1928

Leading up to the 1928 diplomatic conference to revise the *Berne Convention*, a number of increasingly independent British dominions had joined the agreement in their own right, having been previously party to the convention only as colonies. These new players included Australia, New Zealand, Canada, South Africa, and the Irish Free State. The political settlement after the First World War also meant that the emerging states of Austria, Czechoslovakia, Danzig, Estonia, Finland, Hungary, and Poland would join the Union.[42] Brazil acceded in 1922, the only country from South America to do so.[43] A number of countries sent observers, including Bolivia, Chile, Columbia, Cuba, Ecuador, Guatemala, Latvia, Mexico, Nicaragua, Peru, Salvador, Uruguay, and Venezuela.[44]

The participation of delegates from Brazil, the British dominions, and the emerging European states did little to shift the balance in struggles over principles of protection and access, especially given the loss of past key proponents of access principles. No Haitian delegate attended the meeting in 1928.[45] Japan and the Scandinavian countries had lost their key battles over translation in 1908 and their role, by 1928, was also less active.[46]

Access principles gained little ground in 1928, but two gains are worthy of mention. First, delegates of Australia, Japan, Norway, Brazil, and the UK called for a new article allowing domestic legislation to permit the reproduction of oral works and speeches by the press, leading to the establishment of a new Article 2*bis* under the convention.[47]

Second, governments in the process of establishing national public radio systems had goals of regulating copyright in such a way as to facilitate this, such as by creating licensing regimes for broadcasting, which was becoming an important new mode of access. The delegates from Australia and New Zealand, "reflecting the emerging public service ethos of broadcasting in countries with vast distances between small communities," defended the view that the matter of radio broadcasting rights was open to the intervention of public authorities to protect cultural and social interests linked to this new format – especially for the popular dissemination of musical works.[48] Here, they faced off against the British and French delegates, who took the view that the right of radio broadcasting

[42] Ricketson and Ginsburg, *International Copyright*, 104. [43] Ibid. [44] Ibid., 106.
[45] Actes 1928, 134. [46] Actes 1928. [47] Ibid., 195–196.
[48] Actes 1928, 310; May, *The World Intellectual Property Organization: Resurgence and the Development Agenda*, 21.

should be assimilated with other rights. The result was a compromise that granted the right of radio broadcasting, requiring governments to grant to copyright owners a right of equitable remuneration for the broadcast of their works, while also allowing governments to regulate the conditions under which this right could be exercised.[49]

Other access principles advocated by countries new to the Union failed to take hold. Though efforts were made by the delegations of Siam and the Irish Free State to obtain compulsory licensing of translations, as detailed in Chapter 6, they were not successful. This battle over translation rights had been lost before those countries had become part of the discussion.

The Irish Free State's position on translation is especially interesting because it represents an instance where the international copyright system was viewed as an instrument that could be used to circumvent the British imperial copyright system, and as allowing greater scope of access than did the imperial system. The Irish Free State wished its copyright relations with Great Britain and the other parts of the British Empire to be regulated by the *Berne Convention* rather than by the imperial copyright system because the *Berne Convention* gave greater freedom to legislate on copyright than did British imperial law. The Irish Free State wished, in particular, to retain its shorter term of translation, which was consistent with the 1896 revision of the *Berne Convention* and with later revisions, which allowed reservations to the 1896 level, but not with imperial copyright law. When this failed – the format of signature of the *Berne Convention* ultimately meant that copyright relations between the parts of the British Empire would be governed by imperial rather than international law – the Irish Free State refused to sign the *Berne Convention.*[50]

[49] *Berne Convention,* 1928, Article 11bis.

[50] H. M. Whitton, Memo dated May 3, 1928 and approved May 9, 1928. National Archives of Ireland, DFA LN 6/5. Letter, The Secretary, Department of External Affairs, Dublin, May 2, 1928, National Archives of Ireland, DFA LN 6/5. Declaration made by Mr. MacWhite, delegate of the Irish Free State, at the closing session of the conference for the protection of copyright, Rome (translation), in Library and Archives Canada, RG25, Vol. 1490, file 1827–278, pt. 2. See also Roy and Désy, *Confidential Memo for the Prime Minister (Secretary of State) on Certain Inter-Imperial Aspects of the Rome Conference on Copyright,* July 17, 1928, in Library and Archives Canada, RG25 G-1, Vol. 1491, file 278, pt. 3, 3–4; *Alternative Proposals: C.D.A. 34 and C.D.A. 38,* in Library and Archives Canada, RG25 G-1, Vol. 1491, file 278, pt. B.7. For background on the Irish Free State's relationship to the *Berne Convention* leading up to the Rome conference, see Ricketson and Ginsburg, *International Copyright,* 1104. Actes de la conférence réunie à Rome du 7 mai au 2 juin 1928, 308.

While the Siamese and Irish efforts failed, the entry of a number of emerging countries was influential in ensuring that existing principles of access to scientific publications, educational materials, and works in translation were retained, as detailed in Part I. In some instances, such as in the case of discussions of copyright in news, the delegates of core states, including Italy and the UK, as well as emerging countries and middle powers, defended the existing balance, or pressed for stronger principles of access.[51]

1948

Up to and including the conference to revise the *Berne Convention* in 1948, the influence of developing countries at Berne Union negotiations was, overall, still fairly minimal. This remained the case in 1948. None of the Berne Union's African territories were yet responsible for their own foreign affairs; India and Pakistan were in the process of becoming independent; and, of the seven remaining developing countries, the Philippines and Turkey had not yet joined the convention.[52] Only Siam was an independent sovereign developing-country member of the Union at the time of the negotiations of 1948.[53]

Whereas the principle of access to translation remained at the status quo – indeed, no delegation to the 1948 conference proposed its expansion, other principles saw more mixed results. As countries continued to join the Union, the strength of countries' resistance to what had become Berne norms was reduced. Countries that objected to the full assimilation of translation rights joined on the basis of reservations to the 1896 level of translation rights, on the knowledge that, to move to more recent revisions of the *Berne Convention*, these reservations would have to be abandoned.

By 1948, Siam had joined the 1908 revision of the *Berne Convention*, declining to adhere to the 1928 revision at which it had argued, without success, for the freedom of expansive reservations, and opting instead to adhere to the previous 1908 revision, which had permitted a wider range of reservations.[54] On adhering, it had made six reservations, including to the 1896 level of translation rights and to the 1896 level of rights pertaining to periodicals.[55]

[51] Actes 1928, 248. [52] Lazar, "Developing Countries," 15. [53] Ibid.
[54] Actes 1948, 22. [55] Ibid., 17; see also Lazar, "Developing Countries," 16.

Iceland had also gained membership, joining the 1928 revision as the sole new member to join at that level, making use of the ability to reserve the right of translation. Iceland declared, upon joining, that it would reserve to the 1896 level as regards translations into Icelandic.[56] A number of other countries had declared that they would maintain some or all of their prior reservations on ratifying or adhering to the Rome revision.[57] Greece, Ireland, Japan, and Yugoslavia declared that they would maintain their reservations pertaining to the right of translation.[58] The Nordic countries, as promised in 1928, had abandoned their reservations to the translation right.[59] Overall, while many reservations had been eliminated, some were still in active use, particularly on the question of translation.

With the assimilation of the Nordic countries to full translation rights, the controversies over freedom of translation had passed, for the moment, from discussion. Despite the fact that a number of other countries were not in accord with the full assimilation of the translation right, they sufficed with retaining the reservations to the 1896 level and, indeed, as no change had been suggested on this aspect of the convention, they were able to retain said reservations under the 1948 revision.[60] Former advocates of greater freedom of translation, Siam and Japan, were not present at the 1948 diplomatic conference.[61]

Other principles of access saw mixed results. France, as noted in Chapters 3 and 4, was forced to moderate its position on the excerpts and borrowings in light of the positions of the host Belgian administration, the UK, Austria, Hungary, Czechoslovakia, and Denmark.[62] The UK, Czechoslovakia, and Switzerland were the biggest opponents of the narrowing of these provisions proposed by France.[63] The convention's provisions relating to news were, in fact, slightly expanded as a result

56 Ibid., 20. 57 Ibid., 20–21. 58 Ibid., 21. 59 Ibid., 20.

60 Austria proposed a redrafting of the relevant Article 25 but withdrew its proposal: Actes 1948, 393–395; discussion related to the question of which authors were eligible to claim the right of translation under the convention. A Hungarian proposal to require that the original title of works be displayed on translated copies was rejected in light of objections from British and French delegates: Actes 1948, 227.

61 Actes 1948, 54.

62 "In so far as this inclusion was justified by its purpose" was a new phrase, added to the convention and slightly narrowing the application of Article 10; *Berne Convention*, 1948, Article 10.

63 Including Australia, Belgium, Canada, Denmark, Finland, Great Britain, Hungary, India, Ireland, Lichenstein, Norway, New Zealand, Pakistan, Netherlands, Poland, Portugal, Sweden, Switzerland, Czechoslovakia, and South Africa. Austria, Bulgaria, Luxembourg, Monaco, and Vatican City abstained; Actes 1948, 163.

of proposals by Belgium, speaking for Luxembourg, Netherlands, and Nordic countries, and by Monaco, to leave the regulation of excerpts and reproduction of works in the reporting of current events in photography, film, and broadcast to national legislation.[64]

Overall 1948, in general, saw most principles of access in a holding pattern. Principles of access were promoted or defended by a mix of established and emerging states. Translation rights remained the most contentious issue of those principles of access discussed here, leaving the door open to the formulation of a more accommodating model under the new UCC.

1952

The formation of the *Universal Copyright Convention* (UCC) in 1952 acted as a critical juncture in international copyright relations, creating an alternative model of international copyright with lower levels of protection. The United States, which still viewed itself as a "user country" in international copyright relations, and which was invested in protectionist copyright policies that granted international copyright on condition of domestic manufacture in order to encourage domestic industry, had been unwilling to join the Berne system of international copyright relations. It therefore initiated a new system of international copyright that would be welcoming of lower standards of copyright protection and that would allow it to keep its domestic manufacturing clause. The new system attracted many developing countries, setting up an alternative model of international copyright and a competitor with the Berne system.

This new system went a distance to address developing countries' difficulties with the Berne model of international copyright. The UCC did not guarantee royalties to copyright owners from the reproduction of their works in other countries; rather, it guaranteed a "right of equitable remuneration" that could take forms other than royalties.[65] Exporting royalties was a particular problem for developing countries facing crises in foreign exchange.[66]

[64] Actes 1948, 234–235. [65] Lazar, "Developing Countries," 33–34.

[66] Some have questioned the guarantee of royalties to foreign rights-holders who are granted such royalties whether or not they undertake any investment in foreign markets – that is, unlike traditional foreign investors, intellectual property holders often assume no risk in terms of additional investment, creativity, or foreign printing or publishing operations in exchange for the foreign copyright ownership that they claim; Lazar, "Developing Countries," 33–34.

At this critical juncture, international copyright policies could be reimagined. As discussed in Chapter 6, this allowed the question of freedom of translation to come once again to the forefront of debate and, as a result of the efforts of six of the seven reservatory countries under the Berne system (Japan, Turkey, Greece, Ireland, Thailand, and Yugoslavia), with the former three leading this charge, greater scope of access through translation was achieved.[67] As noted in Chapter 3, while it appeared that an opening might have appeared allowing special provisions for access to scientific works, a broad right of access to scientific works was not adopted.

The UCC created a competing copyright regime that, as noted in Chapter 2, provided a forum for new visions of the relationship between copyright and development. This led, ultimately, to the reformulation of both the *Berne Convention* and the UCC in 1971 as both institutions became embroiled in a copyright crisis.

1960s and 1970s

Following the wave of postwar decolonization, the diplomatic conference at Stockholm to revise the *Berne Convention* in 1967, as well as the conference at Paris to attempt a new revision of the *Berne Convention* simultaneously with a revision of the UCC in 1971, brought a large number of new players to the table of the Berne Union. This included, most prominently, the Indian subcontinent and a number of African countries.

The Indian government had, since the 1952 negotiation of the UCC, become an important leader in international copyright negotiations. India had first emerged "as a prominent advocate of special concessions in favour of developing countries" at a 1960 UNESCO conference at which resolutions were made regarding developing countries.[68] The Indian Patent Enquiry Committee and the Ayyangar Committee in the 1940s and 1950s had sparked domestic reform of intellectual property laws.[69]

The emergence of the African countries into international copyright negotiations and the Berne negotiations in particular was also hugely

[67] See Chapter 6. Thailand: UCC 1952 records, 172, item 415; Ireland: 236, item 1064; UCC 1952 Actes, 43; Yugoslavia: UCC 1952 records, 172 item 413; Turkey: UCC 1952 Records, 268, item 1470. Iceland, also a reservatory country, was not in attendance.

[68] Ricketson and Ginsburg, *International Copyright*, 887; see also Deere, *The Implementation Game*, 42.

[69] Deere, *The Implementation Game*, 39–40.

important. The views of the African representatives have been summarized as follows:

> Their opinion of the world copyright situation as of 1963 was that it was essentially European in orientation and therefore opposed to their interests. They expressed the view that the major conventions needed to be re-examined in light of the specific needs of the African continent. In this connection, they recommended that African experts be included in all international copyright meetings, especially the committees which were then preparing for the revision of the Berne Convention.[70]

Among African countries, Tunisia – which had been nominally represented at the early negotiation of the *Berne Convention* by French delegates – now became active it its own right. Tunisia, which had gained independence from France in 1965, was a member of the Monrovia Group in the lead-up to the formation of the Organization of African Unity (OAU). The Monrovia Group favored a gradualist policy on African unity and closer ties with France and the West.[71] Of the Monrovia Group, Tunisia was one of the most active representatives at the 1967 conference to revise the *Berne Convention.*

Other African countries, including Algeria, Egypt, Ghana, Guinea, Libya, Mali, and Morocco of the Casablanca Group, adopted a vision of development that entailed a stronger move toward Pan African Unity and greater distancing from the West. Of this group, Algeria participated actively in the 1967 copyright negotiations, as did Morocco and (less actively) Kenya, but the other members of the Casablanca Group either did not attend or were present only as observers, and by the time of the 1971 revision were less engaged.[72]

In some ways, greater dependence on colonial structures may have fostered greater independence in copyright. Ghana is especially illustrative of this. A process of gradual independence tended to leave in place a fuller

[70] Johnson, "The Origins of the Stockholm Protocol," 107.

[71] Norman J. Padelford, "The Organization of African Unity." *International Organization* 18, 3 (1964), 521–542.

[72] See generally Records 1967 Vol. 1. Algeria joined the UCC in 1973 but delayed joining the *Berne Convention* until 1998. Ghana joined the UCC in 1962 but delayed joining the *Berne Convention* until 1991. Guinea joined Berne in 1980 and the UCC in 1981. Libya joined Berne in 1988 and did not join the UCC. Egypt joined the *Berne Convention* in 1977, but did not join the UCC. Mali declared continued adhesion to the *Berne Convention* in 1962 and did not join the UCC. Morocco had been bound to the *Berne Convention* since 1917 under France and remained a member through successive revisions; it also acceded to the UCC in 1972.

administrative structure in former colonies. Following independence, the Ghanaian government, for example, passed copyright legislation inconsistent with Berne standards, thereby signifying nonmembership.[73] This stance was informed by Ghanaian President Kwame Nkrumah's strong sense of nationhood. Ghana did not join the Berne Union until 1991, although it had joined the UCC in 1962.

On the other hand, many former French colonies received little help in preparing for independence, creating a structural dependence on the metropole for legal and bureaucratic functions. In a sense, this tended to lead to continuing Berne membership.[74] The ability to create, adopt, or promote alternative models of copyright was dependent on the availability of the necessary administrative structures to do so. That notwithstanding, many of those countries became active participants in conference negotiations, including especially Congo-Brazzaville and Côte d'Ivoire.[75]

Despite their more active participation post-independence, developing countries were disadvantaged by the difficulty of joining forces, given their differing membership statuses within international copyright institutions. Some had joined the Berne Union, others the *Universal Copyright Convention*, and some had uncertain status as Berne members, having been signed on by their colonial masters and, upon independence, their status as members of the Berne Union was left uncertain.[76]

Nevertheless, some groups of developing countries forged common approaches to intellectual property at the time. The Andean countries adopted common rules on intellectual property in 1970 and asserted a distinct developing country voice in international intellectual property negotiations; and Argentina, Brazil, Columbia, Mexico, and Peru adopted reforms of the rights of (often foreign) patent holders.[77] Yet, while Argentina, Brazil, Mexico, and Uruguay joined the *Berne Convention* by 1970, most Latin American countries did not. As Deere Birkbeck notes, "like some of the newly independent states no longer bound by the Berne Convention, they were reluctant to join what they perceived as a 'developed' country grouping, that demanded standards they considered too high."[78]

On copyright, moreover, not all of the developing countries took the same position. While African and Asian countries took similar stances to

[73] Lazar, "Developing Countries," 28. [74] Ibid., 14.
[75] Thanks to Nicholas Must for these observations.
[76] Lazar, "Developing Countries," 17.
[77] Deere *The Implementation Game*, 39–42. [78] Ibid., 41.

India in favoring concessions to developing countries, some Latin American countries, such as Mexico, Argentina, and Uruguay, who already had a long tradition of copyright law and who often identified culturally with Europe, took the position that advancement and progress were impossible if copyright was weakened.[79]

Several delegations attempted to take a middle ground in the interests of achieving consensus between the different camps. Israel, in particular, took a middle position. Along with Israel, some countries who could have been seen as "emerging" at some of the earlier revision conferences were, by the time of the diplomatic conference to revise the *Berne Convention* of 1967, in the odd position of being, like developing countries, net copyright importers, but also considered by most to be "developed." In the time leading up to the conference of 1971, Canada made efforts to create a coalition of "intermediate countries" who, as net copyright importers, would also benefit from provisions similar to those planned for the benefit of developing countries.[80] Australia took a similar position: that "representation on different international bodies concerned with copyright had tended to include only two groups of countries, namely the developing countries and the large developed countries; and that developed countries with comparatively small populations had not been adequately represented."[81]

Though the Canadian delegation noted there was "growing dissatisfaction" among "intermediate countries" with the state of international copyright, efforts to create a coalition of intermediate countries never came to fruition.[82] The Canadian delegation reported that "the concept of intermediate countries and their place in international copyright has yet to be fully explored."[83]

The biggest gains won by developing countries in 1967 and 1971 were embedded in the *Berne Appendix*. They primarily related to, as discussed

[79] Actes 1967, 949–950, as cited in Ricketson and Ginsburg, *International Copyright*, 899.

[80] Bannerman, *The Struggle for Canadian Copyright*, Chapter 11.

[81] *Paris Revision Conference of the Universal Copyright Convention and the Berne Copyright Convention*, Paris, July 5–24, 1971: *Report of the Canadian Delegation*, 19. RG25 Vol. 10904 File 55–19–4-BERNE pt. 6–2; *Records of the Conference for Revision of the Universal Copyright Convention*, UNESCO House, Paris, July 5–24, 1971, 179. See also related remarks by Australia, *Records of the Diplomatic Conference for the Revision of the Berne Convention* (Paris, July 5 to 24, 1971), 49.

[82] *Paris Revision Conference of the Universal Copyright Convention and the Berne Copyright Convention*, Paris, July 5–24, 1971: *Report of the Canadian Delegation*, 20. RG25 Vol. 10904 File 55–19–4-BERNE pt. 6–2.

[83] *Paris Revision Conference*, 20.

in Part I, access to educational materials and works in translation. At the same time, what initially appeared to be tremendous wins for developing countries proved narrow and has rarely been put into effect.[84]

Other countries continued to play a non-speaking role, their absence from the negotiations a symbol of their disagreement with the Berne system of international copyright and their commitment to alternative models of knowledge governance and visions of the course of history and development. Although a 1946 trade agreement between China and the United States had included copyright provisions, the Communist Party, in coming to power in 1949, repealed all the laws and treaties of its predecessor, and put all property under state control. During the Cultural Revolution from 1966 to 1969, foreign book imports were stopped, universities were closed, and scholars and writers were sent to be farm laborers.[85] Copyright was ideologically opposed under the communist ideology of the time.

This would change in 1979 when the United States and China established a trade pact under which China agreed to "take appropriate measures" to protect the copyright of each other's nationals "equivalent to the copyright protection correspondingly accorded by the other party."[86] China, at the time, had no copyright law. Rather, authors were generally paid a salary. Following the agreement, China embarked on a process of study and planning, forming numerous study groups to examine the copyright legislation of various countries and international copyright agreements, and planning the necessary infrastructure. They received training and assistance in this process from the American Copyright Office, and the Chinese government abandoned its alternative model in favor of a more market-oriented vision of trade and development.[87] China would join the *Berne Convention* in 1992.

A second country today known as one of the "BRICS" also remained outside of the Berne Union for some time, opting for a communist vision

[84] Ricketson and Ginsburg, *International Copyright*, 957; Armstrong et al., eds. *Access to Knowledge in Africa*, 326–327; and see generally *Berne Convention Notifications*, www.wipo.int/treaties/en/ip/berne/.

[85] Natasha Roit, "Comment: Soviet and Chinese Copyright: Ideology Gives Way to Economic Necessity," *Loyala Entertainment Law Journal* 6 (1986), 53–70, 64–65.

[86] David Ladd, "Address: Copyright and the Re-Emergence of the Middle Kingdom," *American Bar Association, Section of Patent Trademark and Copyright Law Proceedings* 94 (1984), 94–97.

[87] Ibid., 94–97.

of development and progress. Emerging from isolationist international copyright relations, in 1973 the USSR joined the *Universal Copyright Convention*, in a *quid-pro-quo* agreement with the United States for tax concessions on Soviet imports to the US.[88] Shortly thereafter, the USSR established the VAAP (All-Union Copyright Agency), through which all foreign licensing of Soviet copyright, as well as all Soviet licensing of foreign copyright, was negotiated. The VAAP established foreign offices in other countries for these purposes. Soviet compliance with international copyright agreements was, in practice, minimal, since they were somewhat unwilling to pay high levels of foreign royalties. Russian law permitted the reproduction of works without consent or royalties for non-profit scientific, educational, enlightenment purposes.[89] The Russian Federation would not join the Berne Union until 1995, though it joined the UCC in 1973.[90]

The 1960s and early 1970s thus saw the emergence of a number of significant shifts in international copyright negotiations. First, and most significantly, some developing countries emerged as agenda-setters in international copyright negotiations, having in previous revision conferences played only peripheral roles on specific issues. At the same time, not all developing countries adopted the same "agenda of development"; views and approaches differed to some degree. Second, awareness emerged of a middle ground in international copyright, though this did not result in a coalition of "intermediate" countries or have a significant impact on the negotiations, which remained highly polarized. Third, whereas previously developing countries had been active on only one or two issues of concern to them at international copyright negotiations, in the 1960s and 1970s a few developing country delegations emerged, for the first time, as active on a full range of issues in the negotiations.[91]

While the United States was able to successfully initiate an alternative model of international copyright through forum-shifting to UNESCO, things changed when the American government announced its exit from UNESCO in 1984, resulting from the fact that UNESCO had become a

88 Roit, "Comment: Soviet and Chinese Copyright," 53–70, 59–60.
89 Ibid., 53–70, 60–63.
90 WIPO, Berne Notification No. 92 Accession by the Russian Federation Geneva: WIPO, December 9, 1994, www.wipo.int/treaties/en/notifications/berne/treaty_berne_162.html (accessed March 27, 2015); Ricketson and Ginsburg, *International Copyright*, 1202.
91 These included India, Monaco, Japan, and Tunisia. See *Records 1967* and *Records 1971* generally.

forum for developing countries to oppose American media hegemony. As well, UNESCO "tended to consider the issue of copyright from the perspective of users."[92] The American withdrawal from UNESCO would leave the American government without influence in international copyright. It thus paved the road for American entry into the Berne system and the decline of the UCC as an alternative model of international copyright. In consequence, when the *TRIPs Agreement* was established in 1994, it was the Berne system of international copyright, rather than the UNESCO system in which developing countries had historically had greater influence, that would provide the foundation stone. Following the establishment of *TRIPs*, developing country membership in the Berne system grew dramatically, and the UCC, along with the visions of development that it had embodied, faded in significance.

The TRIPs Agreement

Whereas developing country negotiators, in a large part, set the agenda of the international copyright negotiations of 1967 and 1971, the United Sates and other "developed" country negotiators took the lead in the negotiation of the 1994 *TRIPs Agreement* and the 1996 WIPO Internet Treaties. The establishment of the 1994 *TRIPs Agreement* put developing countries again on the sidelines of international intellectual property negotiations, and the 1996 WIPO Internet Treaties also reflected, in a large part, an agenda that was led by the United States, the European Union, and Japan.

Beginning at the Tokyo round of the General Agreement on Tariffs and Trade (GATT) talks in 1979, American negotiators, under pressure to alleviate the US trade deficit, began to advocate for a trade-based approach to intellectual property, pushing for the inclusion of intellectual property provisions in other trade agreements. In 1986 countries agreed to the inclusion of intellectual property in the GATT talks.[93] GATT became the main forum for norm-setting efforts in international intellectual property. When the WTO was established in 1994, Annex 1C of the *Marrakesh Agreement Establishing the World Trade Organization* (the *Agreement on Trade-Related Aspects of Intellectual Property Rights* or *TRIPs Agreement*)

92 Braithwaite and Drahos, *Global Business Regulation*, 568–569.

93 Sunny Handa, "A Review of Canada's International Copyright Obligations," *McGill Law Journal* 42, 4 (1997), 972–976.

required compliance with Articles 1 through 21 of the 1971 revision of the *Berne Convention* and the appendix thereto, with the exception of Article 6*bis* regarding moral rights.[94] These provisions led to a dramatic expansion in the membership of the Berne Union.

By the time of the Uruguay Round of international trade negotiations, intellectual property laws in developing countries varied widely. Some did not have any intellectual property laws at all, others had remained unchanged since the colonial era, and still others – especially in Latin America – had tailored intellectual property laws to local priorities.[95]

These events left developing countries further on the periphery. Whereas at WIPO and UNESCO, developing countries had developed stronger activist positions, Deere Birkbeck notes that "only a small and loosely coordinated grouping of ten developing countries engaged in IP discussions at the GATT in the early days of the Round."[96] As Deere Birkbeck explains, "no more than twenty developing countries had the resources and expertise to follow the IP negotiations and their implications closely."[97] Brazil and India were, at this point, the most vocal.[98] Argentina, Brazil, Cuba, Egypt, India, Nicaragua, Nigeria, Peru, Tanzania, and Yugoslavia pressed to exclude comprehensive intellectual property negotiations from the GATT,[99] and ultimately fourteen developing countries (Argentina, Brazil, Chile, Colombia, Cuba, Egypt, India, Nigeria, Peru, Tanzania, and Uruguay, joined later by Pakistan and Zimbabwe) became active participants in GATT negotiations, together submitting a proposal aimed at minimizing substantive intellectual property provisions in the new agreement.[100] Only India, Argentina, and Brazil were tenacious in the complex negotiations.[101] As Deere Birkbeck notes, "less than 20 of the 106 developing country WTO members that are now bound by the Agreement were involved in the negotiations. Most of these countries had limited input into the technical aspects of the discussion."[102]

The *TRIPs Agreement*, Vandana Shiva notes, "is not the result of democratic negotiations between the larger public and the commercial interests, or between industrialized countries and the Third World. It is the imposition of values and interests of Northern multinational corporations on

[94] *Final Act Embodying the Results of the Uruguay Round of Multilateral Trade Negotiations*, Annex IC: *Agreement on Trade-Related Aspects of Intellectual Property Rights*, Article 9.
[95] Deere, *The Implementation Game*, 8. [96] Ibid., 52. [97] Ibid., 8. [98] Ibid.
[99] Ibid., 52. [100] Ibid., 54. [101] Ibid. [102] Ibid., 56.

the diverse societies and cultures of the world."[103] The regime shift to the WTO had weakened developing countries' influence further.

WIPO Internet Treaties

While the GATT and TRIPs negotiations took place, processes were also underway at WIPO, beginning around 1989, to revise the *Berne Convention* or create an additional protocol to it, covering a wide range of topics including new technologies such as copyright in databases, artificial intelligence and computer-produced works, and computer software.[104] What emerged from the negotiations, which ultimately focused on digital issues, was not a revision or an additional protocol to the *Berne Convention* but a set of two new treaties: the WIPO Internet Treaties.

While the WIPO Internet Treaties largely, based on an agenda set by American players, focused on digital issues, there were several victories for developing countries in the negotiations. First, developing countries and some industrialized countries together were successful in curtailing many of the more controversial American proposals to extend copyright. Second, developing countries pressed for, and won, some limited protections for performers of folklore.

The United States has been widely acknowledged to have set the agenda of the negotiations of the WIPO Internet Treaties, through which they set out to establish a treaty that would grant new intellectual property rights in every possible digital use of works, including in ephemeral copies. However, member states of WIPO rejected this approach, instead affirming rights that existed previously under the *Berne Convention* and extending more modest new provisions covering technological protection measures, rights management information, and ISP liability.[105]

The negotiations of the WIPO Internet treaties were marked by a greater diversity of voices than had been the case in prior revisions of the *Berne Convention*. The influence of countries such as Singapore, South Africa, Canada, and Denmark loosened some of the terms that were ultimately

[103] Vandana Shiva, "TRIPs, Human Rights, and the Public Domain," *The Journal of World Intellectual Property* 7, 5 (2004), 665. Bannerman, *The Struggle for Canadian Copyright*, 195–196.

[104] Bannerman, *The Struggle for Canadian Copyright*, 195–196.

[105] Samuelson, "The U.S. Digital Agenda."

set under the treaties.[106] Many countries objected to some of the most controversial proposals put forward by the American negotiators.[107] Japan also played a role in softening the terms of the treaty, arguing against rights in ephemeral copying.[108]

Many developing countries pressed for a focus on the protection of folklore in the negotiation of the WIPO Internet Treaties, and they were somewhat successful.[109] Performers of folklore were granted protection under the terms of the WIPO Performances and Phonograms Treaty (WPPT).[110]

Despite these successes, the WIPO Internet Treaties reflected the continuing dominance of "developed" country agendas in international copyright negotiations at WIPO. While the entry of large numbers of developing countries into the organization has somewhat moderated the ability of "developed" countries to dictate the terms of international copyright to developing countries, and while WIPO has provided opportunities for minor concessions to developing countries, such as the WPPT provisions on folklore, "developed" country agendas, or those of the market actors they represent, have continued to dominate.

The development agenda

The rising agenda of intellectual property maximalism that led to the formation of the *TRIPs Agreement* and the WIPO Internet Treaties provoked both criticism and the formation of a group of countries at WIPO calling themselves the "Friends of Development," and later the formation of the "Development Agenda group" of countries.[111] The establishment of the "Friends of Development" group of countries, which is not recognized by WIPO as a formal group, represented, to some degree, a departure from WIPO's reliance on regional groupings, to be discussed further below in Chapter 10.

The rise of these new coalitions of developing countries has strengthened developing country influence at WIPO, perhaps even sparking a shift

106 Samuelson, "The U.S. Digital Agenda," 388 and 414; Blayne Haggart, *Copyfight: The Global Politics of Digital Copyright Reform*, (Toronto: University of Toronto Press, 2014), 120–122.

107 See generally Samuelson, "The U.S. Digital Agenda."

108 Ibid., 382–392.

109 See generally CRNR/DC/101.

110 WPPT Art. 2; Von Lewinski, *Indigenous Heritage and Intellectual Property*, 354–356.

111 See Chapter 2.

away from WIPO by "developed" countries to form plurilateral arrangements unhindered by such coalition interests.[112] At the same time, these coalitions suffer from very significant weaknesses in sustaining engagement within the coalition, in their capacity to monitor the projects and actions resulting from the WIPO Development Agenda, and in their capacity to monitor and engage with the actions of what has become an enormous bureaucracy in the WIPO Secretariat, whose power in agenda setting and technical assistance is tremendous.[113]

It should be noted that the establishment of forty-five recommendations as the Development Agenda for WIPO in 2007 represented a compromise between the original proposals of the Friends of Development for a developing agenda for WIPO in 2004, and those of countries initially staunchly opposed to it. Although many of the main elements of the Friends' proposal were retained, others were not. Proposals calling for major institutional changes at WIPO were replaced by proposals to undertake work under existing bodies. Proposals that involved new treaties, such as a treaty on access to knowledge, were also dropped in the wake of proposals simply to encourage discussions on access to knowledge.[114]

The implementation of the Development Agenda, which is, as of this writing, still in progress, has taken two forms. The first is concerned with mainstreaming the Development Agenda throughout WIPO as an organization, while the second has taken the form of a set of projects, each associated with one or more of the forty-five recommendations of the Development Agenda.

The WIPO General Assembly, in 2010, agreed to a "coordination mechanism" that would see "the relevant WIPO bodies" report annually on their contribution to the implementation of the Development Agenda.[115] However, some WIPO bodies, including the Program and Budget Committee and the WIPO Standards Committee, have been resistant to this, not viewing themselves as "relevant bodies" that are required to implement the Development Agenda.

A number of Development Agenda projects have been put in place, and resourced, as of this writing, with 26,536,000 Swiss francs (about 28

112 Bannerman, "WIPO and the ACTA Threat."
113 As discussed in Chapter 10.
114 Bannnerman, "The Development Agenda at WIPO: Where is Canada?"
115 WIPO, Coordination Mechanisms and Monitoring, Assessing and Reporting Modalities, 2010. www.wipo.int/ip-development/en/agenda/coordination_mechanisms.html (accessed March 1, 2014).

million US dollars) total.[116] While this is significant, it makes up only a small percentage of WIPO's annual budget of 673,993,000 CHF, or 672 million USD.[117]

Evaluation of the Development Agenda for WIPO

The Development Agenda can be judged against various criteria: whether it has caused WIPO to engage, to a greater extent, with concerns of development; whether it has interrupted the dominant narrative that saw, simplistically or ideologically, intellectual property as a "power tool" for (economic) development; and whether it has encouraged greater developing country and NGO engagement with WIPO and greater influence of developing countries in WIPO norm-setting and other activities.

As regards the first criterion, it is clear that the Development Agenda has caused WIPO to engage more fully with questions of development. At the same time, WIPO's history is not that of a UN or a development organization, and this lack of experience with development work has come out in several of WIPO's Development Agenda projects. As well, it may be that the type of development with which WIPO has engaged remains narrow and focused on the "power tool" vision of IP's role in development, rather than a fuller and more nuanced view. As further outlined in Chapter 10, institutional factors that make it difficult for developing countries and civil society groups to engage at WIPO mean that developing country and civil society visions of development, while driving the original proposal for a development agenda for WIPO, have been less influential in guiding the implementation of the Development Agenda.

Judged against the second criterion (whether the implementation of the Development Agenda has interrupted an overly simplistic or ideological narrative that saw stronger intellectual property as a "power tool" for development), the success of the Development Agenda is less clear. Abdel Latif notes that, while some of the rhetoric of the Development Agenda has been widely adopted at WIPO, much of the rhetoric of the Friends of Development's IP-skepticism has been co-opted. The term "flexibility," for example, used by the Friends to mean the flexibility

[116] WIPO, Committee on Development and Intellectual Property, Thirteenth Session, *Draft Report* CDIP/13/13 Prov. (Geneva: WIPO, 2014), 4.

[117] WIPO, WIPO Program and Budget for the 2014/15 Biennium (Geneva: WIPO, 2013), 14.

to *reduce* intellectual property rights, has now been used to mean the flexibility to *increase* intellectual property rights. Similarly, the importance of "balance," emphasized by the Friends of Development, has been adopted in ways that suggest that the *current* intellectual property system is "balanced" – the very position that the Friends had originally set out to challenge.[118] Knutsson notes that mainstream development thinking often co-opts alternative visions of development, sometimes evolving or broadening the mainstream version.[119] While broadening may occur, co-optation might alternatively involve adoption of ideas that, while in tension with mainstream visions, nevertheless, neither shatter nor significantly disrupt the mainstream, possibly even lending legitimacy to the dominant conceptualization.

The material outputs of the Development Agenda also evidence a lack of success in interrupting the "power tool" view. Of the thirty-two Development Agenda projects, several have, as a central element, a component that interrupts WIPO's unitary focus on the promotion of intellectual property as a "power tool" of development, while a far greater number continue to focus on the promotion of mainstream IP norms, training, systems, and institutions.[120] Projects aimed at transforming WIPO and making WIPO more transparent have mainly produced smaller-scale outputs such as studies and databases.[121] Some of these have not been fully

[118] Abdel Latif, "Change and Continuity," 45–47.

[119] Knutsson, "The Intellectual History of Development," 5.

[120] In the former category, two of the 32 Development Agenda projects stand out. First, the project "IP and the Public Domain" commissioned several studies relating to the public domain and "resulted in an increased interest among a cross-section of WIPO stakeholders on the issue of IP and the public domain." WIPO, *Evaluation Report*, CDIP/9/7, Annex, p. 3. A second, titled "IP and Competition Policy," commissioned studies and surveys pertaining to the possible role of intellectual property as a barrier to market entry, and to the anti-competitive use of intellectual property. Many of the projects connected to WIPO's traditional activities have channeled WIPO resources into the creation of significant growth in WIPO's bureaucratic footprint and service offerings. For example, WIPO has put in place five projects to implement Recommendation 10, which calls on WIPO to "assist Member States to develop and improve national IP institutional capacity through further development of infrastructure and other facilities." WIPO, Projects for Implementation.

[121] For example, from WIPO's Projects for Implementation of Development Agenda Recommendations, the projects "IP and the Public Domain," "IP and Competition Policy," "IP, Information and Communication Technologies (ICTs), the Digital Divide and Access to Knowledge," "Developing Tools for Access to Patent information," "Project on IP and Socio-Economic Development," "IP and Technology Transfer: Common Challenges – Building Solutions," "Open Collaborative Projects and IP-Based Models," and "Patents and the Public Domain" have mainly resulted in studies.

successful, suffering from lack of use and lack of integration with WIPO's other activities.[122]

Judged against the third criterion, the success of the Development Agenda is clearer. Developing countries and NGOs have become more engaged in WIPO as a result of the Development Agenda processes and, arguably, have achieved greater influence at WIPO.[123] However, the Development Agenda has not reached all of its goals in this regard; recommendation 2 of the Development Agenda had called on WIPO to "provide additional assistance to WIPO through donor funding, and establish Trust-Funds or other voluntary funds within WIPO specifically for LDCs," but WIPO has been unsuccessful in creating a fund for the participation of LDCs at WIPO.[124]

As well, despite increased engagement, some groups' priorities are less reflected in the agenda's implementation – as is true of the A2K movement more broadly. Some LDCs' priorities in particular have resulted in only relatively minor projects within the overall budget and outcomes of the Development Agenda. This is seen in the work aimed at studying and reversing the brain drain out of Africa, an LDC priority, which was budgeted at 339,000 Swiss francs (about $337,437 USD) compared with the over 3 million Swiss francs (about $2.9 million USD) budgeted for a "Improvement of National, Sub-Regional and Regional IP Institutional and User Capacity" project, which was dedicated to assisting the development of national IP strategies and sets the technical basis for the creation of a Caribbean Regional Patent Administration System.[125]

A disconnect from developing or LDC priorities can be seen in the A2K movement more broadly as well. The movement's preoccupation with access to digital materials through the Internet has been criticized "when, in fact, many parts of the South, especially in the poorest countries, lack even rudimentary Internet access for a variety of reasons."[126]

[122] WIPO, *Project Evaluation: Intellectual Property Technical Assistance Database* CDIP/9/4 (Geneva: WIPO, 2012).

[123] Some have argued that this greater influence of developing countries at WIPO has sparked norm-setting to go elsewhere to plurilateral forums. Susan K. Sell, "Cat and Mouse: Forum-Shifting in the Battle over Intellectual Property Enforcement," Paper presented at the *American Political Association Meeting*, Toronto, September 3–6, 2009.

[124] WIPO, *Project Evaluation has this greater influence of developing countries at WIPO has sparked normative 6 and Chapter* CDIP/9/3 (Geneva: WIPO, 2012).

[125] WIPO, *Evaluation Report of the Project on Intellectual Property and the Brain Drain CDIP/13/6* (Geneva: WIPO, 2014); WIPO, *Progress Reports CDIP/8/2* (Geneva: WIPO, 2011), Annex VIII.

[126] Story, Darch, and Halbert, *The Copy/South Dossier*, 162.

The movement tends, as well, not to focus on concerns surrounding traditional knowledge, also an LDC priority.[127] Vying priorities and visions of development – cultural, economic, and technological – thus compete within the movement.

WIPO's institutional biases, including its historical expertise and specializations, as well as its pro-IP ideology, have been resistant to the kind of wholesale change envisioned by those who initially advanced the idea of a development agenda for WIPO. There continues to be conflict over who directs WIPO: the funders (intellectual property owners who pay application fees, from which a large part of WIPO's budget is generated – see Chapter 10 below[128]) or the member states. Whereas some "developed" countries have underlined that WIPO is "financed by users of the global IP system, and whose main goal is the promotion of the protection of intellectual property," developing countries emphasize WIPO's status as a UN agency "with development at its core."[129]

Abdel Latif asks whether the international intellectual property system can be "reformed in any significant way beyond the minimalist concessions and adjustments that its most powerful backers – that is, industrialized countries and their intellectual property-based industries" are willing to make.[130] Given the possible limits of the Development Agenda there is concern that the incremental approach taken under it might "detract, or even undermine, more far-reaching proposals that could better serve the goals of access to medicines and knowledge and the public interest."[131]

Although the Friends of Development and the A2K movement have seen the establishment of the WIPO Development Agenda as evidence of the increasing influence of developing countries at WIPO, and as a tool for the spread of more development- and access-friendly copyright norms, and although the movement has achieved notable success, there is nevertheless a danger that such optimism is misplaced.[132] It is

[127] Ibid.

[128] Center for International Environmental Law, *A Citizen's Guide to WIPO* (Washington, DC, and Geneva: Center for International Environmental Law, 2007), 13; WIPO, Results, Budget and Performance, www.wipo.int/about-wipo/en/budget/ "Developed" countries, in recognition of WIPO's role in the implementation of the TRIPs Agreement, increased their budget contributions "to facilitate the capacity building and legislative advice functions of the organization"; May, *The World Intellectual Property Organization*, 53.

[129] Catherine Saez, "Crisis at WIPO over Development Agenda; Overall Objectives In Question," IP-Watch, May 25, 2014.

[130] Abdel Latif, "Change and Continuity," 51. [131] Ibid., 53.

[132] Peter Drahos and John Braithwaite suggest that actors can be enrolled on behalf of weaker powers, but developing countries' efforts to enroll WIPO have been less than successful, in Information Feudalism; and Braithwaite and Drahos, *Global Business Regulation*. See

possible that WIPO, historically, institutionally, and financially, is simply too entrenched in an ideological view that intellectual property serves development in all cases, that sees development flow from the North to the South, and that institutionally is unable to incorporate substantive change to its organizational culture or vision. Further, it is possible that, as WIPO's bureaucratic footprint expands (see Chapter 10), it may become more difficult to undertake transformation. If it is the case that WIPO's capacity for change is not as great as advocates of access require, it is also possible that future projects brought to WIPO by either the A2K movement or the Friends of Development will ultimately be co-opted by more powerful states seeking to serve intellectual property owners, bolstering the existing system's legitimacy, expanding its bureaucratic footprint, and furthering WIPO's traditional mission of protecting and expanding intellectual property rights in the interests of intellectual property owners. The danger is that such developments could ultimately sideline alternatives, such as many of those proposed by the originators of the development agenda, that could better serve the goal of greater access to knowledge. On the other hand, there would also be danger in abandoning the WIPO system without first establishing an alternative, as WIPO may, at the moment, be the best of available options among international IP norm-setting institutions.

Developing countries have been shaped by Berne Union

Institutions have an important role in shaping actors and their interests. They play a role in socializing, educating, and building processes that can shift or alter the possibilities available to state actors, shifting the interests that may come to the forefront of state assessments of national interests and priorities.[133] WIPO has, in assisting, educating, and socializing officials, diplomats, and bureaucrats, played a role in shaping the construction and calculation of national interests. Its growing role in this regard, extended under the 2007 Development Agenda, may even outpace its role as a forum for setting international intellectual property norms.[134]

First, WIPO provides extensive "technical assistance" – assistance in drafting legislation and in the establishment and operation of intellectual property institutions – to developing countries. This assistance can be

also May and Sell's pessimistic outlook on the potential for WIPO to be transformed as a result of the Development Agenda in Intellectual Property Rights, 214–215.

[133] Thelen and Steinmo, "Historical Institutionalism in Comparative Politics," 1–32.

[134] See May, *The World Intellectual Property Organization*, 35.

traced back to the 1963 African Study Meeting on Copyright in Brazzaville aimed at assisting "the African Member States and Associate Members of Unesco in defining the general principles applicable in their respective territories to the protection of authors, notably writers, composers, and artists, with regard to their literary, musical and dramatic works."[135]

WIPO technical assistance has been a central focus of criticism issued by the Friends of Development. First, the Friends argued, technical assistance tended to "be provided as a means for enhancing enforcement measures in receiving countries," and was "too often planned and delivered in isolation from development goals of developing countries."[136] Little attention, the Friends noted, was "given to different levels of development and cultural differences."[137] Second, the Friends also raised concerns that assistance might be provided by staff and consultants with conflicts of interest in the matter. For example, assistance might be provided by staff or contractors working for rights-holder groups who might therefore "assist" governments in establishing stronger rights-holder protection than strictly required. Third, the Friends implied that WIPO technical assistance might, at times, be "perceived as being a reward system for supporting certain positions in WIPO negotiations."[138]

The WIPO Development agenda, following negotiations, called on WIPO to ensure that "technical assistance shall be, inter alia, development-oriented, demand-driven and transparent, taking into account the priorities and the special needs of developing countries, especially LDCs, as well as the different levels of development of Member States."[139] The Development Agenda called for increased WIPO resources to be dedicated to technical assistance, that WIPO assist in "making national intellectual property institutions more efficient and promote fair balance between intellectual property protection and the public interest," and emphasized that conflicts of interest in the provision of technical assistance should continue to be avoided.[140]

In 2009, two years following the beginning of the Development Agenda's implementation, WIPO commissioned a study to review WIPO technical assistance activities, aimed at measuring the extent to which

[135] *G.H.C. Bodenhausen and René Maheu*, circular, undated, received May 1960, in Library and Archives Canada, RG25, Vol. 5169, file 5582-U-2–40.

[136] Friends of Development, *Proposal to Establish a Development Agenda for Wipo: An Elaboration of Issues Raised in Document WO/GA/31/11 IIM/1/4*, para. 19 and 56.

[137] Ibid., para. 59. [138] Ibid., para. 65–67.

[139] WIPO, The 45 Adopted Recommendations under the WIPO Development Agenda.

[140] Ibid.

WIPO's technical assistance contributed "towards the reduction of the knowledge gap and the greater participation of the developing and least-developed countries (LDCs) in deriving benefits from the knowledge economy."[141] The review found that "a relatively small proportion of expected results related to these two objectives."[142] A dominant view among WIPO staff that WIPO's primary role was "the guardian of the international IP system" may have contributed to a bias in technical assistance toward promoting accession to WIPO treaties and focused on "promoting the use and usefulness of the system to existing and potential IP right-holders in developing countries."[143] The review found that work towards "assisting developing countries to derive broader benefits from the global IP system" was stronger than it was in the "flip-side" of the Development agenda in contributing to goals such as:

> a) the use of TRIPs flexibilities; b) promoting access to medicines and education; c) enlarging the public domain; d) ensuring efforts to address counterfeiting and piracy are aligned with national needs and conditions; e) the alignment of IP laws with efforts to protect natural resources, cultural expressions or TK and genetic resources from unfair use; and/or f) the promotion of competition in the area of IP.[144]

Technical assistance, while strong on developing traditional intellectual property institutions, was relatively weak in addressing geographical indications and traditional knowledge, two areas of special import to many developing countries.[145] Instead, WIPO's web site reveals that support is offered on a philosophy of standardization that views "all IP offices" as having "similar business processes" and facing "similar challenges in processing applications for IP rights."[146] WIPO provides "generic and customizable solutions" for IP office business processes.[147] By strengthening intellectual property legislation and institutions in developing countries in ways that conform to standardized conceptualizations of how intellectual property works, and by focusing especially on strengthening institutions that serve rights-holder interests, WIPO helps to change the

141 This review was called for under recommendation 41 of the Development Agenda. WIPO, The 45 Adopted Recommendations under the WIPO Development Agenda; Carolyn Deere Birkbeck and Santiago Roca, *An External Review of WIPO Technical Assistance in the Area of Cooperation for Development CDIP/8/INF/1/ANNEX1* (Geneva: WIPO, 2011), iv.

142 Ibid. 143 Ibid., v. and vii. 144 Ibid., v. 145 Ibid.

146 WIPO, Technical Assistance (Geneva: WIPO, n.d.), www.wipo.int/global_ip/en/activities/technicalassistance/ (accessed March 27, 2015).

147 Ibid.

construction and calculation of developing country national interests and priorities.[148]

Moreover, WIPO has developed an extensive educational apparatus in all areas of traditional intellectual property. This apparatus is aimed at shaping the knowledge and views of diplomats and government officials, including most particularly developing country diplomats and government officials.[149] It is also aimed at altering or "modernizing" the intellectual property institutions of developing countries. WIPO conducts formal intellectual property training through the WIPO Academy that, established in 1998, provides professional development for diplomats and government officials, master's degrees, distance learning on intellectual property in seven languages, and a summer school on intellectual property.[150] According to WIPO, the WIPO Academy "plays a central role in WIPO's activities to enhance the capacity of countries to use the intellectual property (IP) system."[151] Its courses, according to the Academy web site, "are taught by people versed in IP and how it works to stimulate innovation, creativity and development."[152] Under the Development Agenda, a pilot project was launched to establish start-up academies, or National IP Academies, under which WIPO is, as of this writing, in the process of establishing IP training centers in Colombia, the Dominican Republic, Egypt, Ethiopia, Peru, and Tunisia.[153]

The Development Agenda, despite originating in developing countries' insistence that "IP protection is a policy instrument the operation of which may, in actual practice, produce benefits as well as costs," now used to forward projects based on the intellectual property-as-a-power-tool-for-development ideology and WIPO's work in expanding intellectual property training and institutions.[154] The *WIPO Academy Education and Training Portfolio* for 2015 introduced its programs as responding to "increasing needs" and as "endeavoring to upgrade knowledge and skills in various areas of IP with a view to promoting the use of IP as a tool for economic, social, cultural and technological development."[155]

148 On this see also May, *The World Intellectual Property Organization*, 61–68.

149 May, "Direct and Indirect Influence," 39–56.

150 WIPO, WIPO Academy (Geneva: WIPO, n.d.), www.wipo.int/academy/en/ (accessed March 27, 2015).

151 Ibid. 152 Ibid.

153 WIPO, Start-Up Academies (Geneva: WIPO, n.d.), www.wipo.int/academy/en/about/startup_academies/ (accessed March 31, 2015).

154 Argentina and Brazil, *Proposal by Argentina and Brazil*, Item II.

155 WIPO, *WIPO Academy Education and Training Portfolio* (Geneva: WIPO, 2015).

Finally, WIPO plays a role in socializing both diplomats and government officials and local elite who participate in WIPO events and WIPO-supported institutions into a transnational intellectual property community. Jean-Frédéric Morin found that ideas about intellectual property among international intellectual property professionals are shaped within a transnational network, rather than along national lines or North–South divides.[156] Transnational systems can thus come to dominate over locally produced alternative models of IP. Peukert argues that this transnational socialization can create local copyright elite "having a strong individual interest to push a pro-IP agenda irrespective of the general effects of this policy for a developing country."[157] WIPO and other transnational intellectual property institutions have constructed an international network that not only provides formal technical assistance and education, but that also diffuses legal, social, and cognitive norms, making competing norms less likely to be viewed as alternatives. Morin and Gold observe that socialization is an important mechanism of the diffusion of legal transplants.[158] They point to a process called "norm cascade":

> [u]nder this process, once a critical mass of countries adopts a given norm, the norm reaches a tipping point after which it begins to diffuse independently, without the need for the material incentive initially required to reach that point. As an increasing number of countries transplant a set of rules, those rules become normalized and create social and cognitive pressure for conformity.[159]

It is clear that, in entering WIPO, member states' government officials and diplomats also enter a social environment in which pressure exists to adopt, support, and even disseminate WIPO norms, and an environment in which alternative models and institutions, which have historically been so important in driving change and instituting principles of access in copyright, disappear.

[156] Jean-Frédéric Morin, "Paradigm Shift in the Global IP Regime: The Agency of Academics." *Review of International Political Economy* 21, 2 (2014), 275–309; Jean-Frédéric Morin, *Mapping Prevailing Ideas on Intellectual Property: Preliminary Findings from a Survey* (Geneva: ICTSD, 2013).

[157] Peukert "Intellectual Property," 12.

[158] Jean-Frédéric Morin and Edward Richard Gold, "An Integrated Model of Legal Transplantation: The Diffusion of Intellectual Property Law in Developing Countries," *International Studies Quarterly* 58 (2014), 783.

[159] Morin and Gold, "An Integrated Model of Legal Transplantation," 784.

Conclusions

Several overall observations can be made about the role of developing country representatives in the history of the international copyright system. First, developing countries have rarely been successful in establishing or expanding principles of access and, where they have, they have had the support of at least one powerful state. Second, and perhaps more importantly, we observe that the growing numbers and strength of developing country participation at WIPO and its predecessors has led to few substantial shifts or victories for access principles in the overall international copyright regime.

There may be several reasons for this. One may be that the proponents of copyright principles intended to promote access to translation, news, education, and scientific and medical information have been a historically changing cast of characters. Whereas those states advocating strong international copyright protection have remained a fairly stable group, the state-advocates of access principles have shifted over time. First Haiti, then the Scandinavian countries, then Japan, then (to a very limited extent) Australia, New Zealand, and Canada in the 1920s, then Tunisia, India, and other newly independent countries in the 1960s, and most recently, Brazil, India, Egypt, Chile, and Argentina have taken the lead. There is a reduced ability, therefore, to carry forward institutional knowledge and expertise on particular issues. Some have noted that, as emerging countries grow economically, gaining greater interest in intellectual property exports, their positions on principles of access may change, and they may become proponents of principles of protection more so than principles of access.[160] While this does not explain all instances of countries' discontinuance of access advocacy, it may partially explain some cases, such as those of Japan and Korea.[161] On the other hand, there is no guarantee that rising intellectual property powers will not, alternatively, advocate for different systems of intellectual property based more closely on their historical traditions and cultural backgrounds.[162]

Second, we can note that when developing countries did take an active role in Berne negotiations, they usually did so on specific issues only.

[160] Peter K. Yu, "Intellectual Property and Asian Values," *Marquette Intellectual Property Law Review* 16, 2 (2012), 374.

[161] Jean-Frédéric Morin and Sara Bannerman, "Tigers and Dragons at the World Intellectual Property Organization (WIPO)," in *Rising Powers in Multilateral Institutions*, eds. Dries Lesage and Thijs Van de Graaf (Basingstoke: Palgrave Macmillan, 2015).

[162] Yu, "The Rise and Decline," 563. Burke, *A Social History of Knowledge*, 2.

Whereas core countries like the UK, France, or Germany tended to speak on almost every element under negotiation, developing country representatives often stayed silent except on select issues such as serial publications or translation rights. There could be a number of reasons for this, including lack of negotiation capacity, the smaller number of delegates that peripheral countries tended to send, or the ability of delegates to network and prepare for the negotiations. Whatever the reason, it meant that developing country interests, and, insofar as they coincided, the interests of users, were far more sparingly and far less consistently represented.

Third, we can observe that, often, delegations from countries that were not members of the *Berne Convention* were among the strongest proponents of principles of access. Indeed, their countries' nonmembership gave these delegates leverage in the negotiations; they could argue that particular provisions, if adopted, would either allow or prevent their country from joining the convention. At the same time, because it was often the case that the provisions adopted were not satisfactory and the country did not join the convention, these peripheral actors, as nonmember states, did not consistently attend the negotiations. This meant that proponents of access principles were both peripheral and, often, disappearing actors.

Fourth, we observe that, as more countries have joined the international copyright system, the power of not joining has been reduced. As more countries join, only the most marginal players are left on the outside. While WIPO continues to expend some effort in assisting countries to join the international copyright system, the influence of non-joiners on international copyright negotiations, either as outsiders who are not present, or as nonmembers present as observers or negotiators, is minimal. Nonmembership, and the ability to negotiate the terms on which a state was willing to join the Union, once a powerful source of negotiation power, is no longer a viable strategy.

Fifth, *WIPO*'s fundamental characteristic as a norm-setting institution, intended to encourage consistency and conformity among member states, means that by its very nature it eliminates peripheral and nonnormative models of knowledge governance and visions of development. Its technical assistance, educational programs, and socialization processes contribute to this norm-setting power, which may now have overtaken its role in providing a forum and voice-opportunities for developing country participation in setting international intellectual property norms.

Finally, it must be observed that, throughout the history of the international copyright system, developing countries have been successful, in some cases, in preventing or delaying the elimination of access norms over time. They have been less successful in proposing, establishing, or extending models and principles of access, and where they have done so, they have been backed by a more powerful country. Developing countries are influential, we might conclude, when they want something that a powerful entity also wants.

What can we conclude about developing country involvement today, and about the international copyright system in general? Rather than being a forum where developing countries gain some degree of influence, the results of this study indicate that the Berne-based international copyright system is a forum where developing country alternative norms and models disappear, and where developing countries can (occasionally) enroll, or (far more often) be enrolled by, more powerful states toward a particular copyright norm. It is not clear that developing countries' ability to enroll more influential states is stronger under postcolonial multilateralism than it was under colonial multilateralism. This means that the visions of development and of access to knowledge held by less powerful states tend to be overridden by those of the more powerful states and those whose interests more powerful states most represent – often intellectual property owners.

Overall, we might also observe that the structures and effects of colonialism are stickier and more difficult to shift than may be expected by those who look to WIPO as a site of possible transformation of the international copyright regime. This raises questions about the current strategy whereby NGOs or other entities concerned with establishing principles of access have aligned with developing country governments to work toward establishing norms of access. It may be the case that such a strategy is overly optimistic about the ability of developing countries to transform international copyright norms and about the capacity for transformation at WIPO in general. At the same time, the A2K movement has made important inroads, at times enrolling more powerful states in some of its projects and its visions of access to knowledge, as shall be discussed in the next chapter.[163]

[163] For example, UK Prime Minister David Cameron called British copyright laws too restrictive in 2010 and commissioned the Hargreaves Report, which in turn called for increased flexibility and openness in copyright law. Ian Hargreaves, *Digital Opportunity: Review of Intellectual Property and Growth* (London: Department for Business, Innovation, and Skills, 2011); Halbert, *The State of Copyright*, 77–78.

8

The role and inclusion of NGOs in international copyright

The nature of NGO participation in international communication policy debates has changed dramatically since the rise of international institutions dealing with communication policy in the 1880s.[1] These shifts are reflected in the visions of access and development embedded in the international copyright system. In tracing the history of NGO participation in the development of the *Berne Convention,* a complex picture emerges of the role and impact of NGOs. The breadth and depth of NGO participation has changed over time, as have the prescribed avenues of participation. Although significant contributions have been made by NGOs to the Berne Union and WIPO, NGOs have historically represented just a limited range of interests in these fora. This has begun to change with the rise of the A2K movement.

Pippa Norris has noted the growth, since the 1960s, of international nongovernmental organizations and social movements. Such movements, she argues, constitute a new form of political participation that contrasts with previous forms. While participation in traditional politics and civic organizations, when measured by voting activity and political party membership, has declined since the 1960s, Norris observes that participation in new social movements has grown dramatically, on national and international scales.[2]

These changes in the type of political action that we observe, especially in the international sphere, have been accompanied by changes in the targets of political action. Just as privatization and deregulation have seen decision making flow from public bodies to nonprofit and private agencies, the avenues and targets of political participation have widened beyond the nation state.[3] Further, as the targets of political action have

[1] Stefania Milan, *Social Movements and their Technologies: Wiring Social Change* (New York: Palgrave Macmillan, 2013) 19–20.

[2] Pippa Norris, *Democratic Phoenix: Reinventing Political Activism* (Cambridge: Cambridge University Press, 2002), 188–214.

[3] Ibid., 193–194.

broadened, so have the repertoires of political action, which now include not only the rise of social movements but also everything from volunteering, fundraising, internet networking, to street protests, consumer boycotts, and direct action.[4]

These trends are reflected in the realm of international copyright policy making. On one hand, international NGOs have always been at the heart of the Berne system of international copyright, given the integral role that the *Association littéraire et artistique international* (ALAI) played in its founding. On the other hand, NGOs' participation in the Berne regime of international copyright has varied greatly over the course of its history. While they have recently been incorporated in greater numbers and breadth into the international copyright policy-making regime, reflecting the broader rise of international NGOs that Norris remarks upon, their participation has also shifted, in some ways, further to the margins of the international norm-setting processes. Even so, the A2K movement has had a significant impact in articulating alternative visions of the development of international copyright to those already in place.

For many international organizations, the term "NGO" applies to non-profit organizations that seek to advance the public interest. However, at WIPO, the term "NGO" applies to any organization that is independent from government, including private sector organizations. There is no requirement that the NGO be non-profit or that it be associated with public interest. This differs from other international institutions such as the World Bank, which defines NGOs as "private organizations that pursue activities to relieve suffering, promote the interests of the poor, protect the environment, provide basic social services, or undertake community development."[5] This means that at WIPO, unlike at other international institutions, business groups and private sector organizations are considered to be NGOs. This failure to distinguish between NGOs representing rights-holders and those representing the public interest has recently been challenged by developing countries.[6]

NGOs and international copyright: a history

We can group the history of NGO participation in Berne negotiations into four periods. During the first period, in the years leading up to

[4] Ibid., 190–193.

[5] World Bank, *Nongovernmental Organizations in World Bank-Supported Projects* (Washington, DC: World Bank, 1999), ix. As cited in CIEL, *A Citizen's Guide to WIPO*, 5.

[6] CIEL, *A Citizen's Guide to WIPO*, 5.

1886, a single NGO – the *Association littéraire et artistique international* (ALAI) – exerted enormous influence on the negotiations, setting the agenda and acting as a primary source of expertise on international copyright. Second, from 1886 to 1908, only very few NGOs participated in the negotiations, either as representatives embedded in country delegations or in the views documented by the international office of the Berne Union and presented with the program of the conference. Third, from 1928 to 1948, an expanding range of NGOs participated in the negotiations, both as delegates embedded in country delegations and in documented comments presented along with the program of the conference. As well during this period, some intergovernmental organizations (IGOs) came to participate in the revision conferences. Fourth, the period from 1967 to 1971 marked the beginning of independent NGO delegations and the practice of calling on NGO representatives to speak at the end of discussions and meetings. This period also marked the rise of participation of IGOs in the negotiations. Finally, recent trends have seen NGOs reach levels of influence that have helped to spark the negotiation of new treaties, such as the *Marrakesh Treaty to Facilitate Access to Published Works for Persons Who Are Blind, Visually Impaired, or Otherwise Print Disabled* of 2013, which resulted from the efforts of advocates for the visually impaired as well as the A2K movement. Even so, NGO participation at WIPO remains highly unbalanced.

Up to 1886

The movement for international copyright was one of the earliest transnational social movements active in the realm of communication policy. The ALAI, originally established as the *Société des gens de lettres* in 1878, chaired by Victor Hugo, provided a draft convention that sparked the negotiation of the *Berne Convention.* ALAI enrolled the Swiss government to take forward this draft and to invite governments around the world to convene in creating an international copyright convention and international copyright union. The draft convention created by ALAI was the basis for a second draft, drawn up by the Swiss Federal Council, which was used as the basis for negotiations beginning in 1884.[7]

Perhaps reflecting the primacy of copyright owners in the new Berne Union, and also the relatively advanced stage of the international copyright movement as compared with other international groups representing users and publics, the primary NGOs present at the diplomatic

[7] Ricketson and Ginsburg, *International Copyright*, 52–60.

conferences that founded the *Berne Union* in the 1880s were authors' groups, with ALAI first among them. These groups did not have seats at the negotiations as independent delegates; instead, reflecting the character of the Berne Union as an intergovernmental organization, their representatives were embedded in national delegations alongside state representatives. Louis Ulbach, author and President of ALAI, was one of France's several delegates throughout the negotiations in the 1880s, and Fredrik Baetzmann, author, journalist, translator, and the vice president of ALAI, stood as Norway's sole delegate. One of Italy's delegates, the lawyer Enrico Rosmini, was the vice president of the Italian Authors' Society. User groups were more sparsely represented but not entirely absent at the founding conferences of the *Berne Convention.* One of Spain's two representatives in 1885, Manuel Tamayo y Baus, was the director of the National Library of Spain.[8]

Along with delegates sent in person, interest groups, including those that were not represented in person, also sent correspondence and proposals to be taken on board during the negotiations.[9] Organizations that expressed their interest in the early negotiations underway included groups of French authors in Italy, the *Association internationale des juristes* in Vienna, and the *Bureau international de correspondances pour la press* in Frankfurt, which requested that it be kept apprised of developments.[10]

In some cases, these groups wished simply to express their appreciation and approval of the efforts of the conference, but in other cases, groups were critical of the direction being taken.[11] In 1885, Numa Droz, the Swiss delegate voted president of the conference, noted that some wished the Union to establish a form of international legislation on copyright, setting out a law that would apply universally in all countries, rather than simply general principles or minimum standards. Nevertheless, Droz declared that, overall, support of the project of the Union was overwhelming, and that the establishment of the Union, even one that did not go so far as to establish a universal copyright law, was the "necessity of our epoch."[12]

1886–1908

NGO in-person presence was sparse at the conferences to revise the *Berne Convention* in the years to follow. In the early years of *Berne Convention*

[8] Actes 1884. [9] Ibid., 27; Actes 1885, 13. [10] Actes 1884, 27. See Chapter 5.

[11] The *Association internationale des juristes* in Vienna, for example, sent such a note to the 1884 conference. Actes 1884, 40.

[12] Actes 1885, 13.

revision, the only delegations represented were state delegations and the International Office of the Berne Union; no NGOs or IGOs had stand-alone delegations.[13] In 1896, the first revision conference took place, and perhaps more than any other conference, it was an affair of diplomats, with a few academics also in attendance.[14]

While few NGOs attended in person, the views of NGOs were front-and-center of the early negotiations of the *Berne Convention*; by the time of the 1896 conference such views had begun to be systematically documented and compiled in the program of the conference, presented alongside the French organizers' proposals for revision.[15] Many of the views represented had been selected from the published minutes of the meetings of select international associations and published in the monthly newsletter of BIRPI, *Le Droit d'Auteur*.[16]

From 1886 to 1908, only a few NGOs participated in the negotiations, either by being present in country delegations or in the views documented in the program of the conference. The hundreds of views presented in 1896 were primarily those of three associations: the *Congrès artistique international*, the various national chapters of ALAI, and the *Assemblée des écrivains allemandes*. These three groups' views and proposals were far more numerous than those of the French organizers. Included in the compilation of NGO views were comments pertaining to each of the articles of the convention. These, proposed new provisions in the convention, calls to extend the Union to new countries, comments on the internal legislation of specific countries, and calls for the extension of the functions of the international office of the Union.[17] A few peripheral comments not pertaining to the Union directly were also made by a small number of other groups.[18] In sum, three NGOs representing writers and artists were given significant agenda-setting capacity in 1896.

[13] Actes 1896, 85–88.

[14] Only Belgium and France sent NGO delegates; Belgium sending a member of the Royal Academy of Belgium, Edouard Descamps, along with two other regular delegates, and France sent a member of the *Acadamie française* and senator, Charles de Saulce de Freycinet, as its lead delegate. Actes 1896, 85–88.

[15] Actes 1896, 53–82. [16] Actes 1908, 79–80.

[17] Suggested functions included the creation of a universal deposit library for, or a list of, all works published in countries of the Union; the collection of international copyright statistics; the establishment of a library on copyright at the international office; and the establishment of an international copyright tribunal.

[18] These included *Congrés des littérateurs et journalistes allemandes*'s observations about the state of German–American copyright relations, the *Congrès ibéro-américain*'s declaration that "until uniform legislation is achieved, each country will grant, in its own regime, the same rights for foreigners as it does to its own nationals," and the *Conférence du livre*,

By 1908, NGOs were represented not only by their written views tabulated as part of the program for the conference, but also, in greater numbers, in person. Several were embedded in country delegations. Germany sent the secretary general of the *Association pour la protection de la propriété industrielle* as one of eight delegates, France sent the presidents of the *Société des auteurs et compositeurs dramatiques*and the *Société des gens des lettres* as two of its of seven delegates, Italy sent the vice president of the Italian Society of Authors as one of its five delegates, and the Netherlands sent a member of the Association of Writers of Amsterdam as one of its four delegates.[19]

Not only did NGOs have a more substantial presence in 1908 country delegations, but so also did government officials. Whereas in the initial years, the diplomatic conferences of the Berne Union had been attended primarily by diplomats, lawyers, and academics, along with a number of representatives of writers and artists, in 1908 these were joined by a greater number of government officials working in the departments concerned with intellectual property. In most cases the departments of justice and commerce were the primary departments concerned, but occasionally so were departments of culture and education.[20]

Also by 1908, the International Office of the union had begun to document a broader but still limited range of associations' views in its preparation for the revision conference. Alongside the voluminous views on every aspect of the revision provided by the previously noted NGOs, the office also included the views issued by additional European societies and congresses of artists, writers, theatrical artists, printers, photographers, architects, journalists, music sellers, and printers – each of whom wished to see copyright extended in their particular domain. Almost none of the associations included were groups that met outside of Europe.

Few, if any, associations or congresses requesting limitations or extensions on copyright were documented, while numerous calls for the elimination or narrowing of exceptions or limitations were included in the tabulated views. ALAI and the *Association des auteurs allemands* called for the harmonization of translation rights. Calls from press and editors' associations, along with writers' societies, for greater copyright protection of scientific and medical articles were noted in the views tabulated

Anvers' hope that duties would not be imposed on books, and that governments should purchase a copy of all books published in their countries. See Actes 1896, 72–75. Also noted were the *Bourse des libraries*' request to the German government that no duties be imposed on books. Actes 1896, 69.

19 Actes 1908, 139–144. 20 Ibid., 85–88.

for the 1908 conference, which saw serial works removed from the public domain.[21] No views to the contrary were included in the conference documents. Several writers' groups, along with ALAI, called for the elimination of the educational exceptions that allowed the production of educational anthologies, but these were retained in 1908.[22] Overall, it was almost solely the interests of those groups that wished to expand copyright whose views were presented.

1928–1948

By 1928, a greater number of countries embedded NGO representatives in their delegations.[23] The NGOs included continued to be those representing authors, composers, playwrights, and other rights-holders. The presence of these embedded representatives was palpable and was remarked upon by Sir Harrison Moore, the Australian delegate, as he described a warm and cohesive atmosphere completely committed to extending copyright protection.[24]

While NGOs' in-person presence had risen, fewer NGOs' views were documented in writing in the preparation for the 1928 conference. This may be explained by the state of war, which had prevented international organizations from conducting normal operations in the time leading up to the conference.[25] Those NGOs that did manage to make statements at their meetings and congresses about the revision of the *Berne Convention* included the same groups that had dominated the documented views at previous conferences, and most prominently ALAI.[26]

In 1948 the number of NGOs embedded within country delegations continued to balloon. These embedded delegates continued to represent, with a few exceptions, rights-holder groups, including, as before, representatives of societies of authors, editors, and composers.[27] The President of ALAI was, as usual, among the delegates.[28] A number of countries also included representatives from radio broadcasting organizations on

[21] Including the *Congrès international de la presse*, the *Congrès international de la presse médical*, the *Congrès international des délégués d'Association de presse médicale, the Association allemande des éditeurs de journaux*, the *Congrès international des éditeurs*, and the *Association général des écrivains, Berlin.*

[22] Actes 1908, 79–128. [23] Actes 1928.

[24] W. Harrison Moore, *Report of the Australian Delegate*, 4 July 1928, 3–4, in Library and Archives Canada, RG25 G-1, Vol. 1491, file 278, pt. 3.

[25] Actes 1928, 29. [26] Ibid., 29–40. [27] Actes 1948, 54–61.

[28] Marcel Boutet was a delegate on the French delegation. Actes 1948, 55.

their delegations.[29] Several other non-rights-holder delegates were also embedded in the country delegations. France sent a member of *l'Institut* and a former legal counselor for the *Institut de cooperation intellectuelle*, and Italy sent the president of the *International Institute for the Unification of Private Law*.

A similar set of groups dominated the written proposals compiled for 1948, and many proposed narrowing some of the principles of access that had formed a part of the *Berne Convention*. Various chapters of ALAI, for example, proposed narrowing the exceptions for educational and scientific publications, so that payment would be required for taking short excerpts from works to include in educational and/or scientific publications.[30]

Whereas previously there had been few documented proposals by NGOs promoting provisions of access, there were several of note documented in advance of the 1948 conference. First, the *Cercle des libraires allemands*' short proposal that the term of copyright should not be extended to fifty years after the death of the author, but rather should be retained at thirty years, was included.[31] Second, although several NGOs, including various chapters of ALAI, proposed the further narrowing of exceptions for the press, including the possible protection of facts and breaking news, there were also proposals that would allow the republication of journal articles following their initial publication.[32] Some NGOs, including the *Congrès international de droit comparé* and the *Congrès de la presse médicale latine*, suggested that journalists should retain the right to publish their works, insofar as this did not conflict with the interests of the journal in which the article was originally published.[33]

The origins of NGO and IGO delegations

1928 was the first year that outside organizations sent their own delegations. While most NGO representatives were embedded in country delegations, two international organizations sent independent delegations: the League of Nations and the *Institut international de coopération*

[29] Belgium, Denmark, France, Luxembourg, Monaco, the Netherlands, Norway, Poland, and Sweden sent such representatives.

[30] Actes 1948, 447. [31] Ibid., 441.

[32] The *Congrès international de droit comparé* resolved that the question of how facts and news published for the first time in a daily newspaper could be protected and should be studied. Actes 1948, 446.

[33] Actes 1948, 446–447.

intellectuelle. Their presence reflected, perhaps, the growing role of international institutions after World War One, led by the creation of the League of Nations.[34]

The *Institut international de coopération intellectuelle*, headquartered in Paris, had been founded in 1926 by the French government in response to the League of Nations' call for member states to support the *Commission International de coopération intellectuelle*'s work.[35] The latter, founded in 1922 by the League of Nations, was tasked with completing the disarmament policy of the League by encouraging close cooperation between member states in cultural and social policy.[36] The *Institut*, which became a working arm of the *Commission*, would be charged, by the end of the conference in 1928, with the project of unifying the Berne Convention with the Pan American conventions.[37] Through such an initiative, driven by NGO participation, the Berne Union had come to be seen as more than a tool for securing political and economic control of foreign markets; it was now seen as a vehicle for promoting peace: a vision connected to the second and third "development agendas" of the Berne Union identified in Chapter 2, those of developing a sense of international society, and of developing arts and culture.

Representatives of both the League of Nations and the *Institut* made general statements during the first meeting of the conference.[38] Whereas the practice of allowing outside organizations to speak *after* state delegations would one day be established, in 1928 these two organizations made their statements between those of country delegations, making a number of specific proposals relating to the revision of the treaty.[39] This marked the first time that outside organizations not embedded in country delegations made proposals concerning the revision of the convention from the floor of the formal negotiations.

[34] Antony Anghie, "Colonialism and the Birth of International Institutions: Sovereignty, Economy, and the Mandate System of the League of Nations," *New York Journal of International Law* 34, 3 (2002), 514.

[35] Isabella Löhr, "Selling Books: The League of Nations and the Globalization of Intellectual Property Rights in the 1930s." Paper presented at the *11th Annual Conference of the European Business History Association*, September 13–15, 2007.

[36] Löhr, "Selling Books." [37] Ibid. [38] Actes 1928, 169.

[39] They promoted four specific proposals: (1) the extension of the minimum term of copyright for 50 years following the death of the author; (2) the elimination of reservations to the 1908 revision of the *Berne Convention*, (3) the inclusion of works of applied art to the convention, and (4) the concepts of *droit du suite* and the paying public domain, while also promoting the inclusion of moral rights in the convention, Actes 1928, 199.

In 1948, UNESCO sent a delegation of two. In the period between 1928 and 1948, the idea of unifying the *Berne Convention* and the Pan American system had matured, after having been raised at the conference in 1928. Preparations for this project were begun, but World War II intervened and it was never carried out. Instead, UNESCO took over the project, which led to the creation of the *UCC* in 1952.[40] This is the reason for UNESCO's participation at the 1948 revision conference of the *Berne Convention*, and the reason for the presence, in the French and Italian country delegations, of the delegates from the former two institutes that had contributed to those preparations.

Thus, the initial inclusion of NGO and IGO delegations was a special case. The possibility of other organizations sending delegates was, at the time, rejected. In 1948 a controversy arose over a French proposal that the president of the *Confédération internationale des Sociétés d'Auteurs* be admitted as an observer.[41] While this proposal was supported by a number of delegations, including the Italian, Portuguese, Polish, Hungarian, Czech, Canadian, and Norwegian delegations, the president of the conference, supported by the British delegation, spoke against it on the grounds that the conference was of an intergovernmental nature, and if one group representing private interests were admitted, many other groups might also wish to participate.[42]

1967–1971

In the years of the crisis in international copyright during the 1967 and 1971 revision conferences over proposals of principles of access intended to developing countries, the tradition of embedding NGO representatives in country delegations continued. However, along with an expanding range of rights-holder organizations representing artists, authors, publishers, composers, film producers, film directors, and playwrights, a smaller number of representatives was also embedded from private broadcasting organizations as well as government broadcasting, film, and arts organizations. Even a few library representatives were included.[43]

[40] See Ricketson and Ginsburg, *International Copyright*, 111–112 and Löhr, "Selling Books."

[41] Actes 1948, 69. [42] Ibid.

[43] *Records 1967*, 583–599. For a general view of the role of librarians in international copyright, see Marietta Daniels Shepard, "International Dimension of US Librarianship," *ALA Bulletin* 62, 6 (June 1968), 699–710; and Chin Kim, "Librarians and Copyright Legislation: The Historical Background," *American Libraries* 2, 6 (June 1971), 615–622.

A broader transformation occurred as well: 1967 represented the first year that NGOs representing industry groups were specifically invited to send delegations to the conference. Groups representing broadcasters, telegraphy, mechanical reproduction, authors, composers, actors, film exhibitors, film distributors, film producers, journalists, musicians, newspaper publishers, the phonographic industry, publishers, radio and television organizations, film theaters, and others were invited. This represented a far broader range of NGOs than had been involved in past revision conferences but also a set dominated by industry groups rather than, as in the past, by authors' and professional organizations. While industry groups dominated, no consumer groups were invited. However, some, including those representing broadcasters, film exhibitors, the phonographic industry, and the International League against Unfair Competition, might be thought of as representing certain user interests. As well, a wider range of IGOs were invited.[44]

The treatment of these new delegations was not equal to that of state delegations. Whereas state delegations were guaranteed three seats in the rooms, observers and NGOs were guaranteed only a single seat each.[45] NGO delegations were classed as observers and were not empowered to make formal proposals to the conference.[46] Occasionally, at the invitation of the meeting chair, they were empowered to speak, and at other times were invited to take part in general discussion. For example, the delegate from the International Confederation of Societies of Authors and Composers spoke during the general discussion at the opening of the conference to denounce the proposed changes that would reduce the requirements of the convention for developing countries.[47] At other points, NGO delegations and other observer delegations were invited to speak at the end of meetings.[48] On one such occasion, the delegate from the European Broadcasting Union spoke in favor of the proposed provisions.[49]

This new form of in-person participation by NGOs, including industry groups, came with a loss; NGO delegations' proposals were not, as they had been in the past, tabulated and presented alongside the formal proposed revisions to the convention. The ability to make occasional speeches at the conferences and to interact with delegates, therefore, replaced the written accounting of their views as a part of the program and

[44] *Records 1967*, 577–582. [45] Ibid., 575–581. [46] Ibid., 594.
[47] Ibid., 838, item 479. [48] For example, see Ibid., 952, item 2011.
[49] Ibid., 955, item 2016.

agenda-setting of the conference. This severely restricted the agenda-setting power that NGOs had previously had in revision conferences. NGOs were now restricted to the role of responding to events already taking place, rather than helping to construct the vision and objectives of international copyright.

Despite the restricted nature of their participation, some NGOs' proposals did have influence. For example, the International Federation of Journalists' proposal to eliminate the provisions allowing the reproduction of articles in the press became a suggested reform that formed part of the program of the conference.[50]

It must be noted that, overall, the *Berne Convention* was not negotiated over the course of its history among a "balanced" set of interest groups. Rather, the *Berne Convention* was negotiated in an environment that nearly excluded consumer, user, and public interest groups. By the time consumer, user, and public interest groups were included in the negotiating conferences, NGO voices had been moved from an agenda-setting to a peripheral position in the institution.

Since 1971

The tradition that began in 1967 of accepting independent NGO delegations, including industry groups, rather than requiring that these be embedded in country delegations, has continued since the most recent Berne revision was conducted. NGO observer delegations have attended all of the major diplomatic conferences for the formulation of new WIPO copyright treaties since that time. The tradition of allowing NGO delegates to make statements following the statements of country delegations has also continued, often under strict time constraints – another way in which NGOs have been included, although in peripheral or informal ways. Finally, IGOs and NGOs can circulate papers but must do so outside of the meeting room, whereas member states may circulate proposals and papers inside, including as formally recognized documents.[51]

Despite the broadening, in some ways, of NGO participation, civil society NGOs' power at WIPO has been reduced from what it was at the founding of the *Berne Convention* and in the years up to 1967. On the other hand, the role of rights-holder industry groups was strengthened

[50] Ibid., 114.

[51] Geoffrey Yu, "The Structure and Process of Negotiations at the World Intellectual Property Organization," *Chicago-Kent Law Review* 82, 3 (2007), 1448.

by the strong support of the American delegation's maximalist agenda in the negotiation of the *WIPO Internet Treaties* in 1996. In some ways this reflected the early role of rights-holders' groups in founding the *Berne Convention.* At the same time, while a lengthy list of NGOs was invited to attend the diplomatic conference, and while a great number of NGOs were present, there were no recorded interventions by NGOs at the conference.[52] Delegates from IGOs also participated, but only two are recorded as having spoken: the delegates of UNESCO and the International Labour Organization.[53] Civil society NGOs did have, nevertheless, some significant influence at the negotiation of the WIPO Internet treaties in, as noted in Chapter 3, helping to prevent the adoption of a treaty to protect databases, which was viewed by many in the scientific community as having the potential to stand in the way of access to scientific knowledge.[54]

Despite the noted shortcomings, WIPO is more inclusive of NGO participation than are other forums of international copyright norm-setting. The negotiation of the *Anti-Counterfeiting Trade Agreement* (ACTA), for example, invited no participation from NGOs, and some other UN agencies do not provide for NGO participation. A number of WIPO's practices contribute to NGOs' abilities to participate in deliberations. Along with WIPO's practice of accrediting NGOs and IGOs to attend its deliberations, WIPO publishes extensive documentation and minutes of its formal meetings online. NGOs and other state and civil society representatives can examine and comment on developments taking place at WIPO and can follow them in detail via this documentation. WIPO also publishes translations of these documents in a variety of languages. As well, WIPO webcasts many of its meetings, enabling remote and live viewing of the discussions underway. Finally, NGOs often also host side events, to which WIPO delegates are invited. This is an important venue for the expression or exploration of questions related to WIPO negotiations and to agenda-setting.

While NGO and IGO formal in-person participation in the negotiation of the *WIPO Internet Treaties* was minimal, trends such as those just noted may have increased the influence that NGOs have been able to have at WIPO since the 1996 negotiation of those treaties. Groups representing user and public interests, as opposed to rights-holder interests,

52 *Records 1996*, CRNR/DC/INF.4, 4–7; Records 1996, CRNR/DC/INF.2, 55–66.
53 *Records 1996*, CRNR/DC/101, 60–62.
54 Samuelson, "The U.S. Digital Agenda," 418–427.

have increasingly engaged at WIPO, although they are still by far in the minority. Some have wielded notable influence.

The Marrakesh Treaty

The World Blind Union (WBU) and the International Federation of Library Associations and Institutions (IFLA) were significant instigators of the *Marrakesh Treaty*, which created a minimum set of limitations and exceptions to benefit the blind, visually impaired, and otherwise print-disabled that permit the reproduction, distribution, and making available of published works in accessible formats. The treaty also requires member states to put in place provisions permitting the exchange of accessible-format works across borders by organizations that serve visually impaired people. It is the first international copyright treaty put in place primarily to create principles of access rather than principles of protection, and its founding in 2013 was, for that reason, historic.

The work toward the *Marrakesh Treaty* was sparked by advocates for the visually impaired, beginning in the new millennium. While WIPO, since the 1980s, had done previous work on copyright provisions for the visually impaired, it was only following advocacy by the WBU, IFLA, and others that work towards a treaty began.[55]

David Mann of the WBU led a delegation to initiate contact with WIPO by attending the December 2000 Diplomatic Conference on the protection of audiovisual performances. The delegation's purpose was "to make initial contact with WIPO and put our concerns on its agenda."[56] The delegation met with WIPO officials and began discussions of how WIPO might facilitate the WBU's aims. Mann, in a 2001 proposal circulated at the WBU and at the International Federation of Library Associations and Institutions (IFLA), proposed for international treaties to "allow the creation of non-commercial alternative, accessible versions and their free flow across international boundaries," that would empower member states to facilitate access to works that would be otherwise inaccessible.[57]

The following year, WBU and IFLA officials asked WIPO's Standing Committee on Copyright and Related Rights (SCCR) to study the

[55] See Manon Ress, *Timeline: Addressing Copyright Related Barriers to Overcoming Reading Disabilities* (Washington, DC: Knowledge Ecology International, 2009).

[56] David Mann, "WIPO – Advancing Access to Information for Print Disabled People," Paper presented at the *67th Council and General Conference of the International Federation of Library Associations and Institutions (IFLA)*, August 16–25, 2001, 6.

[57] Ibid., 8.

copyright problems facing the visually impaired.[58] Following this, in 2004, the WBU and other groups continued to lobby for the international establishment of such an agreement, and this was further reinforced when the delegate of Chile presented a proposal to the SCCR calling for "access to the most vulnerable or socially prioritized sectors" to be ensured in national legislation.[59] Then, in 2008, the WBU and Knowledge Ecology International (KEI) convened a meeting of experts to consider a possible WIPO treaty for the visually impaired. This draft treaty was presented to WIPO in October of that year.[60] The governments of Brazil, Ecuador, and Paraguay, in May 2009, presented the draft WBU treaty to the SCCR, and work from there culminated in the 2013 diplomatic conference at which the *Marrakesh Treaty* was founded.[61]

Not only was the *Marrakesh Treaty* a watershed because it marked the first time that an international treaty focused on establishing minimum standards of rights for copyright users rather than owners, it also marked the first time that an international intellectual property treaty enshrined human rights in its preamble. The first statement in the preamble to the *Marrakesh Treaty* recalls "the principles of non-discrimination, equal opportunity, accessibility and full and effective participation and inclusion in society, proclaimed in the Universal Declaration of Human Rights and the United Nations Convention on the Rights of Persons with Disabilities."[62] No other WIPO intellectual property treaty to date contains a reference to human rights.

Some called the establishment of the *Marrakesh Treaty* the "miracle at Marrakesh": the end of a troubled period in which the very idea of international copyright was questioned – a period of doubt as to whether international copyright institutions could take on board and "balance"

[58] *Report SCCR 7*, May 13–17, 2002.

[59] World Blind Union, *Policy Position Agreed by the World Blind Union (WBU), the Daisy Consortium and IFLA Libraries for the Blind Section (LBS)*. www.worldblindunion.org/English/our-work/Position%20Statements/wbu%20ifla%20lbs%20and%20daisy%20Joint%20Policy%20Position.doc (accessed March 27, 2015); Chile, Proposal by Chile on the Analysis of Exceptions and Limitations *SCCR/13/5* (Geneva: WIPO, 2005).

[60] See Ress, *Timeline*.

[61] See Ibid., Brazil, Ecuador and Paraguay. Proposal by Brazil, Ecuador and Paraguay, Relating to Limitations and Exceptions: Treaty Proposed by the World Blind Union (WBU) *SCCR/18/5* (Geneva: WIPO, 2009).

[62] *Marrakesh Treaty to Facilitate Access to Published Works for Persons Who Are Blind, Visually Impaired, or Otherwise Print Disabled adopted by the Diplomatic Conference to Conclude a Treaty to Facilitate Access to Published Works by Visually Impaired Persons and Persons with Print Disabilities in Marrakesh, on June 27, 2013* (Geneva: WIPO, 2013): Preamble.

various interests.[63] It remains to be seen whether the *Marrakesh Treaty* offers any such proof, but its establishment was indeed historic.

The Pirate Party

While some NGOs have become influential at WIPO, others' participation has been disallowed. In September 2013 the General Assembly of WIPO rejected the application for observer status of the Pirate Parties International (PPI). Given various objections to PPI's admittance from the floor of the Assembly, the chair closed debate and declared that the PPI's application was not accepted.[64]

The PPI, headquartered in Brussels, is the umbrella organization for national Pirate Parties around the world. Working through the established political system, their goal is to promote "consumer and authors [sic] rights-oriented reform of copyright and related rights, support for information privacy, transparency and free access to information."[65] Pirate Parties exist in more than forty countries around the world, and its members have been elected nationally in Sweden, the Czech Republic, Iceland, as well as to regional and local offices in Germany and elsewhere.[66]

WIPO requires that organizations granted observer status "be essentially concerned with intellectual property matters,"[67] be "able to offer constructive, substantive contributions," and that their aims and purposes be "in conformity with the spirit, purposes and principles of WIPO and the United Nations," among other criteria.[68] The PPI's application

63 Mihály J. Ficsor, "Commentary to the Marrakesh Treaty on Accessible Format Copies for the Visually Impaired." *Copyright See-Saw.net* (2013), www.copyrightseesaw.net/archive/?sw_10_item=50 (accessed March 20, 2015).

64 William New, "WIPO Approves 15 New Observers, Including DNDi, COHRED; Pirate Parties Rejected," *IP-Watch*, September 25, 2013, www.ip-watch.org/2013/09/25/wipo-approves-15-new-observers-including-dndi-cohred-pirate-party-rejected/ (accessed March 27, 2015); WIPO, General Report of the Assemblies of the Member States of WIPO *A/51/20* (Geneva: WIPO, 2013), 101 item 161.

65 Pirate Parties International, *About the PPI* (Brussels: PPI, 2015). www.pp-international.net/about (accessed March 31, 2015).

66 Pirate Parties International, *Elected Pirates* (Brussels: PPI, 2015). http://wiki.pp-international.net/Elected_Pirates (accessed March 31, 2015).

67 Interestingly, the International Air Transport Association, the International Organization of Hotel and Restaurant Associations and the International Poetry for Peace Association are among WIPO's accredited observers. WIPO, *Accredited* Observers (Geneva: WIPO, n.d.), www.wipo.int/members/en/organizations.jsp?type=NGO_INT (accessed March 27, 2015).

68 WIPO, *Observers*, www.wipo.int/members/en/admission/observers.html (accessed March 27, 2015).

was rejected by member states of WIPO based on a number of delegates' arguments – namely, that PPI is an umbrella organization of political parties, and that the PPI's objectives run contrary to those of WIPO.[69] In rejecting participation by a group promoting copyright reform and access to information, WIPO closed itself off from alternative visions and models of national and international copyright.

Other NGOs have also experienced difficulty in achieving observer status at WIPO. Several civil society NGOs that wished to participate in the discussion of the proposed WIPO development agenda were not given accreditation until a *WIPO Manifesto on Transparency, Participation, Balance and Access* gathered more than 1,200 signatures.[70] Direct participation has since made it "possible for members to exchange ideas with other international institutions, personally meet their representatives, get to know country delegates, and better engage in relevant discussions."[71] Such participation is extremely important in promoting alternative visions and models of access and development.

Overall trends

The history of the negotiation of the *Berne Convention* exhibits a number of trends. First, the number and types of NGO participation has broadened, from the substantive participation of a single NGO, ALAI, to the participation of many, representing a (somewhat) broader range of interest groups.[72] Second, industry groups have, since 1967, come to take up a dominant presence among NGOs represented at WIPO, outnumbering the civil society and professional groups that were once central. Third, the history of *Berne Convention* negotiations witnessed the rise and fall

[69] The representative of Knowledge Ecology International observed that Socialists International is an observer at the UN International Labour Organization. www.ip-watch.org/2013/09/25/wipo-approves-15-new-observers-including-dndi-cohred-pirate-party-rejected/ (accessed March 27, 2015).

[70] Pedro Paranaguá, "Strategies to Implement WIPO's Development Agenda: A Brazilian Perspective and Beyond," Chapter 11 in *Implementing the World Intellectual Property Organization's Development Agenda*, ed. Jeremy de Beer (Waterloo, ON: Wilfrid Laurier University Press, CIGI, IDRC; 2009), 147–148.

[71] Ibid., 148.

[72] 245 international nongovernmental organizations, as well as 73 national nongovernmental organizations, have currently been accredited with observer status at WIPO. Accredited groups include various rights-holder groups, user groups, and general business groups. WIPO, *Accredited* Observers (Geneva: WIPO, n.d.), www.wipo.int/members/en/organizations.jsp?type=NGO_INT (accessed March 27, 2015).

of the ability of NGOs to have written proposals taken into account with the official program of the conference. Fourth, the reduced ability to have written proposals taken into account has been accompanied by a new ability to attend negotiations, first within country delegations and then as independent delegations. The participation of independent delegations entails, however, a loss of influence and ability to speak and make written proposals compared with participation within country delegations.

As a result of these patterns, fundamental decisions made early on took place in an environment of extremely unbalanced and circumscribed NGO presence. Those that were party to negotiations, or whose views were collected by the international office of the Berne Union, were able to make detailed written proposals that were prominently presented in the preparatory documents for the conference. These were predominantly rights-holder groups. The increased interest in both economic and technological development in the 1950s and 1960s coincided with the declining prominence of NGO written proposals, and the sidelining of many NGOs into independent delegations that could not make proposals and rarely, or only secondarily, spoke. These patterns have contributed to the continuous strengthening of the rights accorded to copyright owners under the convention, and the continuous weakening of principles of access.

Recent trends have been toward greater influence on the part of NGOs seeking to enshrine principles of access in international law. It remains to be seen whether the *Marrakesh Treaty* will be successful in establishing or improving access to works by the blind and visually impaired. However, the *Marrakesh Treaty* represents the first time an international copyright treaty has been established with a primary purpose of establishing an international principle of access to knowledge. In that sense, it might be seen as a watershed moment in the history of international copyright and a true victory for advocates of the visually impaired and the A2K movement.

Looking ahead

Two possibilities have been discussed that might extend NGO influence in international organizations in general, and in WIPO in particular. First, multistakeholderism has arisen as a new model of international governance. Second, some have focused on the potential and necessity of forming coalitions – especially between groups advocating for principles of access and middle or emerging powers.

Whereas some areas of international communication governance have shifted to a multistakeholder model, WIPO remains an intergovernmental organization.[73] The World Summit on the Information Society (WSIS) and the Internet Governance Forum (IGF), for example, represent a new model of international governance – one that allows government, corporate, and advocacy groups to contribute to debates under a single umbrella.[74] Under the multistakeholder model, NGOs and corporations participate, to an extent, alongside state delegations and take a much more active role in discussions on matters of communication policy. However, multistakeholder forums remain limited as forums of discussion; they are not, as of yet, empowered to take binding decisions.

Some scholars have also examined the potential of coalitions between NGOs and middle or emerging powers. Some have speculated that progressive NGOs may (or should) attempt to enroll middle or emerging powers in their efforts.[75] As Neufeld notes, dissident groups use the language of middlepowermanship "to signify the influence enjoyed by a country like Canada, and the potential such influence offers to effect radical progressive change in terms of disarmament, economic development and wealth re-distribution, environmental policy and democratization of the foreign policy-making process."[76]

However, the idealized view of middle powers as particularly able to advocate for progressive change may not necessarily reflect the reality of the Berne system of international copyright, at least historically. While in some cases Canada and the Scandinavian countries have either advocated progressive principles of access or proposed middle ground, neither they nor any of the other emerging countries of the early twentieth century that are now viewed as middle powers were stalwart proponents of principles of access in the way that some developing countries and NGOs are able to be today.

From the opposite side of the coin, some have asked whether NGOs are taking up the traditional role formerly played – theoretically at least – by middle powers: that of finding common ground.[77] Jordaan argues that:

[73] Milan, *Social Movements.* [74] Ibid., Chapter 1.

[75] Braithwaite and Drahos, *Global Business Regulation*; Peter Drahos, "When the Weak Bargain with the Strong: Negotiations in the World Trade Organization," *International Negotiation* 8 (2003), 79–109.

[76] Mark Neufeld, "Hegemony and Foreign Policy Analysis: The Case of Canada as Middle Power," In *Readings in Canadian Foreign Policy: Classic Debates and New Ideas*, eds. Duane Bratt and Christopher J. Kukucha (New York: Oxford University Press, 2006), 94–107.

[77] Eduard Jordaan, "The Concept of a Middle Power in International Relations: Distinguishing between Emerging and Traditional Middle Powers," *Politikon* 30, 2 (2003), 165–181.

> The increasing influence of transnational issue networks have in many instances usurped many of the roles traditionally performed by middle powers, acting as the conscience of a global civil society that sees foreign policy elites as being too closely knitted into the web of conformity with hegemonic rules and the benefits derived from such conformity.[78]

Jordaan argues that "closer cooperation between middle powers and transnational issue networks are important in effecting more bottom-up change that does not concur with the hegemon's wishes."[79] Such cooperation may now be taking place, but less with the traditional middle powers that emerged to independence in the early twentieth century than with the new BRICS group of countries. Some NGOs advocating on behalf of principles of access now turn to these emerging powers to form alliances; Brazil, Egypt, and India, and, to a lesser extent, South Africa, have been important NGO allies in the A2K movement and in pushing forward the development agenda for WIPO.

While international NGOs may look to middle and emerging powers for support in taking their views forward, in turn, domestic civil society advocates of principles of access may look to international NGOs rather than to their own state representatives to have views promoted. This may be for many of the reasons outlined here: those groups located in developing countries may find that their state representatives have little capacity to take issues forward, or have been enrolled by larger states and proponents of principles of protection.

While the turn to NGOs may be a practical choice, it has two important consequences. First, if proponents of principles of access turn to NGOs rather than to their state representatives to promote their cause, state representatives may in turn be left in the hands of rights-holder groups, rather than being enrolled as agents for progressive change. Lack of opportunity for NGO engagement with many Group B state representatives may exacerbate this trend.[80] Second, NGOs are less powerful in actual negotiations than are state delegations; they can assist and inform state delegations, but they have little direct influence on the negotiations themselves. Thus, enrolling state delegations in access to knowledge work remains of great importance.

[78] Ibid., 170. [79] Ibid.

[80] Claire Cassedy, "KEI Comments regarding USTR Public Interest Trade Advisory Committee," *Knowledge Ecology International*, March 25, 2014, http://keionline.org/node/1983 (accessed March 27, 2015).

It may be that proponents of principles of access in international copyright are seeking, in NGOs and middle or emerging countries, moral heroes to advocate for the underdog or the oppressed. Neither NGOs nor middle powers, however, truly or consistently fit this ideal; NGOs have little power in international copyright negotiations, and middle powers today are very often embedded in the Group B coalition of industrialized countries, the significance of which is outlined further below in Chapter 10. At the same time, there have been instances and cases where NGOs and today's emerging BRICS state representatives have played this role. Their ability to do so depends on, first, their position as being peripheral to the hegemon and their ability, therefore, to form different and independent views and expertise from core actors. Second, it depends, similarly, on their ability to act independently outside of the core of most powerful rights-holder groups.

While the rising number and breadth of NGOs engaged at WIPO, and the rise of information and communication technologies that facilitate that engagement, have altered WIPO's relationships with civil society, WIPO continues to fall far short of the ideal of an international organization that is responsive to its public. NGOs now have an extensive ability to monitor and comment on WIPO negotiations informally, in informal statements distributed at WIPO and online, and in formal interventions at WIPO, but their participation remains peripheral; unlike in the early days of WIPO, they rarely have agenda-setting ability at formal negotiations, and they have no ability to make formal proposals directly during negotiations. As well, NGO participation continues to be highly unbalanced; while industry groups take on active roles, some groups promoting alternative models of knowledge governance are entirely excluded from WIPO meetings by WIPO's refusal to accredit them.

The A2K movement's successes at WIPO, represented most prominently by the establishment of the *Marrakesh Treaty*, comes following a legacy of international copyright in which NGOs advocating principles of access have played only the most peripheral of roles. The visions of development and of access to knowledge already embedded in the Berne system of international copyright are therefore primarily those of states and copyright holders. Against this history, the accomplishments, and the challenges, faced by the A2K movement seem all the more significant.

9

The role and inclusion of indigenous peoples in international copyright

While WIPO's record on welcoming NGO voices in its activities may be better than that of many other international organizations, its record on the inclusion of indigenous peoples in intellectual property norm-setting falls short of a number of articulated ideals. Representatives of indigenous peoples have been entirely excluded from Berne negotiations. In the 1960s, when decolonization brought a number of African countries' representatives to the table, the question of folklore began, as a result, was discussed (see Chapters 4 and 7 above). Since then, WIPO discussions have expanded to encompass the possibilities of protecting not only folklore but also other forms of traditional cultural expressions and knowledge. This, in turn, has opened the door, to a greater extent, to the concerns and voices of indigenous peoples and to promoting a greater understanding within the international intellectual property community of the perspectives, expectations, and needs of traditional knowledge holders.[1] However, indigenous peoples' participation has been perhaps the most inadequate of all the groups examined in this book.

As noted in Chapter 4, the desire to maintain institutional relevance and preeminence in an international environment filled with a growing number of institutions (such as UNESCO) dealing with intellectual property in the 1960s and 1970s drove BIRPI to seek to bring developing countries into its ambit. Similarly WIPO sought to maintain and extend its role following the establishment of the *TRIPs Agreement* under the WTO and the *CBD* in 1992 and 1994, respectively. The establishment of the IGC in 2001 has led to increased norm-setting work in the area of traditional knowledge that is, as of this writing, still underway.

While undertaking substantial efforts to establish traditional knowledge as a realm of expertise, WIPO has taken incremental steps to include, to some extent, voices of indigenous and local communities and other holders of traditional knowledge in some WIPO processes.[2] For example,

[1] Von Lewinski, *Indigenous Heritage and Intellectual Property*, 65. [2] Ibid., 68.

at meetings of the IGC, indigenous delegations were, like NGOs, originally allowed to speak only after all country delegations had spoken. These procedures were adjusted to allow indigenous delegations to intervene at any relevant time.[3] However, indigenous peoples still do not have the ability to submit written proposals to the IGC directly; they must do so through a state delegation.

The long absence of indigenous peoples' voices from international norm-setting reflects, in some ways, the historical absence of recognition of indigenous peoples' as creators of literary and artistic works. As Brad Sherman points out, indigenous peoples were long viewed, under Western traditions of copyright law, as anonymous craftspeople whose work lacked the requisite originality to confer copyright, or as conduits of tradition whose individual identity collapsed into the broader group, tribe, or community.[4] Intellectual property institutions are but one of the institutions that have framed indigenous creators as anonymous craftspeople rather than as creators in the tradition of romantic authorship upon which copyright is premised; museums and art galleries similarly, until the 1960s, treated aboriginal works as ethnographic or scientific, rather than aesthetic, objects.[5] Increasing recognition of the commercial value of indigenous peoples' knowledge, both in the realms of science, where biopiracy has become a concern, and in the realm of the arts, has led to a focus on intellectual property mechanisms to ensure attribution for and equitable sharing of the benefits in such knowledge.[6] At the same time, existing intellectual property systems may not recognize indigenous ownership systems because most national intellectual property law systems do not recognize ancestors, for example, as legal persons.[7]

The invisibility of indigenous authors as authors of literary and artistic works has also been reflected in the absence of recognition of indigenous peoples' as authors of law. The exclusion of indigenous people's voices and concerns in the *Berne Convention* reflects the absence of provisions dealing with indigenous peoples' rights in multilateral treaties more generally, prior to 1957. Hurst Hannum notes that:

[3] Foundation for Aboriginal and Islander Research Action, *Submission to the WIPO Secretariat on Indigenous Peoples' Effective Participation in WIPO on GRTKF*, (WIPO, 2011), 4.

[4] Sherman, "From the Non-Original to the Ab-Original," 111–130. [5] Ibid., 112.

[6] Peter Drahos and Susy Frankel, "Indigenous Peoples' Innovation and Intellectual Property: The Issues," in *Indigenous Peoples' Innovation: Intellectual Property Pathways to Development*, eds. Peter Drahos and Susy Frankel (Canberra: Australian National University E Press, 2012), 8–9; Shiva, "TRIPS, human rights and the public domain," 665–673.

[7] Drahos and Frankel, "Indigenous Peoples' Innovation," 9.

> [i]ndigenous rights, unlike the rights of other minorities, were never recognized as separate issues of international concern. In fact, apart from treaties to which Indian nations themselves were parties and the agreement which established the Inter-American Indian Institute in 1940, no multilateral treaty or agreement addressed the issue of indigenous rights per se prior to the adoption of International Labour Organisation (ILO) Convention No. 107 in 1957.[8]

Whereas national independence movements ultimately saw developing countries gain representation at international institutions, the same has not usually been an option for indigenous peoples. "The prevailing discourse of the nation-state," Halbert notes, "could not conceive of returning sovereignty to indigenous groups, meaning that often the decolonizing efforts associated with a transfer of sovereignty to postcolonial administrators is not available to indigenous peoples who remain trapped within settler-state political systems."[9]

WIPO's history of excluding indigenous people's voices from international forums also reflects indigenous peoples' history with the UN more broadly. However, it seems that, over time, indigenous peoples have gained stronger representation in other UN agencies than they have at WIPO. The UN has permitted narrow cracks that "allow the political space and authority for nongovernmental organizations (NGOs) and individual spokesmen to penetrate the boundaries of national sovereignty to speak directly, in spite of their governments' wishes, to an international audience."[10] However narrow, such affordances were crucial, for example, in the campaign against South African annexation of South West Africa and South African apartheid when Reverend Michael Scott, supported by the American National Association for the Advancement of Colored People (NAACP) and representatives of the indigenous peoples of South West Africa, were invited to speak to the UN against the wishes of the ruling South African government. These events were "the beginning of the transformation of the [Union of South Africa] into a pariah nation" and a major step towards Namibian independence.[11] Further strides were

[8] Hurst Hannum, "New Developments in Indigenous Rights," *Vanderbilt Journal of International Law* 28 (1988), 652, as quoted in Elsa Stamatopoulou, "Indigenous Peoples and the United Nations: Human Rights as a Developing Dynamic," *Human Rights Quarterly* 16, 1 (1994), 58–81.

[9] Halbert, *The State of Copyright*, 148.

[10] Carol Anderson, "International Conscience, the Cold War, and Apartheid: The NAACP's Alliance with the Reverend Michael Scott for South West Africa's Liberation, 1946–1951," *Journal of World History* 19, 3 (2008), 297–298.

[11] Ibid.

made for indigenous peoples' representation at the UN when, in the 1980s, the United Nations opened its doors to large numbers of indigenous peoples' representatives; in 1992, when indigenous leaders addressed the UN General Assembly for the first time, and in 2002 when the UN Permanent Forum on Indigenous Issues was established.[12] Such events are linked to the growth and strengthening of both indigenous identity and indigenous organizations operating in relation to the UN since the 1970s, when the indigenous movement had only recently started in North America.[13]

As Halbert notes, efforts to circumvent the nation state and speak directly to the international community are also important in efforts to disrupt the illusion that "the state spoke for all the people within its boundaries, when all too often it only spoke for specific settler groups":[14]

> As indigenous people in myriad communities across the globe have sought to establish their autonomy, to resist the colonial powers of the settler state, and to articulate authentic positions from which to ground their daily lives, they have turned to international governance systems to forge relations with each other that bypass the nation-state. Gaining international visibility has been instrumental in disrupting the idea of the unitary state that speaks for all its citizens.[15]

The efforts of indigenous peoples to gain supranational recognition goes back at least as far as the 1880s, when delegations of Māori traveled to England in attempts to meet with British kings and queens, and to 1923 when Deskaheh spoke for the Six Nations at the League of Nations.[16] While early efforts failed, indigenous peoples persisted in their efforts to "globalize their fight for justice."[17] With the creation of the UN system arose new opportunities for such struggles.[18]

The right of indigenous peoples to participate in UN decision-making has, in recent years, gained greater recognition. In 2007, the same year that the Development Agenda for WIPO was established, a new *Declaration on the Rights of Indigenous Peoples* (UNDRIP) was adopted by the UN General Assembly.[19] Article 18 of that declaration provides that "Indigenous

[12] Stamatopoulou, "Indigenous Peoples and the United Nations," 59–61, 68; United Nations, Permanent Forum: Origin and Development, http://undesadspd.org/IndigenousPeoples/AboutUsMembers.aspx (accessed March 27, 2015).

[13] Stamatopoulou, "Indigenous Peoples and the United Nations," 67–69.

[14] Halbert, *The State of Copyright*, 147. [15] Ibid., 144.

[16] Drahos and Frankel, "Indigenous Peoples' Innovation," 6. [17] Ibid. [18] Ibid.

[19] UNPFII, *Declaration on the Rights of Indigenous Peoples*. http://undesadspd.org/IndigenousPeoples/DeclarationontheRightsofIndigenousPeoples.aspx (accessed March 27, 2015).

peoples have the right to participate in decision-making in matters which would affect their rights, through representatives chosen by themselves in accordance with their own procedures, as well as to maintain and develop their own indigenous decision-making institutions."[20] While WIPO notes that "[t]he Declaration is frequently referred to in WIPO's work on these issues, including in the IGC's negotiations," WIPO's efforts to implement Article 18 have been deemed inadequate by some indigenous peoples, and WIPO has been called on by the United Nations Permanent Forum on Indigenous Issues to improve its implementation of the declaration (see this chapter, below).[21]

WIPO has taken certain limited steps to include representatives of indigenous peoples in WIPO discussions about traditional knowledge. WIPO's work in this regard must be seen in light of Article 31 of the *Declaration on the Rights of Indigenous Peoples*, which provides that Indigenous peoples "have the right to maintain, control, protect and develop their Intellectual Property over such cultural heritage, traditional knowledge and traditional cultural expressions."[22]

One of the hurdles to indigenous peoples' participation at WIPO is financial. Some WIPO member states have therefore contributed to a voluntary fund used to bring indigenous representatives to meetings of the IGC.[23] The *Voluntary Fund for Accredited Indigenous and Local Communities* was established in 2005. In further efforts to involve indigenous peoples in WIPO negotiations, the IGC in 2005 decided to hold half-day panel presentations chaired by representatives from local or indigenous communities prior to each session of the committee. Such panels have been held for each session of the IGC since 2005.[24]

The steps that WIPO has taken in the field of traditional knowledge, and to include indigenous peoples in its proceedings, however, have proved

[20] Ibid.

[21] WIPO, "Traditional Knowledge, Genetic Resources and Traditional Cultural Expressions/ Folklore: Frequently Asked Questions," www.wipo.int/tk/en/resources/faqs.html (accessed March 27, 2015).

[22] United Nations, *United Nations Declaration on the Rights of Indigenous Peoples* (United Nations, 2007).

[23] William New, "Experts Debate Access to Knowledge," IP-Watch, February 15, 2005, www.ip-watch.org/2005/02/15/experts-debate-access-to-knowledge/ (accessed March 27, 2015), (n. 65).

[24] WIPO, Information Note for the Panel of Indigenous and Local Communities WIPO/GRTKF/IC/23/INF/6 (WIPO, 2012), 1.

unsatisfactory. The inability to make proposals directly remains a problem. WIPO negotiations have traditionally taken place between states, and indigenous delegates have urged that indigenous peoples be given a place at the table as well, to "ensure the full, equal and direct participation of Indigenous Peoples" and the "creation of a new category of participation for Indigenous Peoples that includes the right to submit proposals, amendments, motions, and the right to vote."[25] "It is not acceptable," said the International Committee for the Indigenous Peoples of the Americas (Incomindios) in a statement, "to reduce our rights to the lowest common denominator for Indigenous Peoples while promoting broader "state rights" standards that allow States and other parties to take our property without our free, prior and informed consent."[26]

In February 2012 most indigenous observer delegates to the IGC stood and walked out of IGC negotiations in protest of "the continuing reduction in the quantity and level of their participation."[27] The Foundation for Aboriginal and Islander Research Action (FAIRA) had noted, in an earlier submission to a WIPO consultation related to a *Study on Observer Participation in the Work of the Intergovernmental Committee on Intellectual Property and Genetic Resources, Traditional Knowledge and Folklore*, that:

> in the more recent sessions of the IGC when important drafting was being conducted, States mostly ignored, and in some cases were openly hostile towards, the Indigenous Peoples' comments. This loss of effective engagement is problematic for Indigenous Peoples, and ultimately weakens the credibility of WIPO and the IGC and their outcome documents.[28]

Indigenous delegates announced that they would withdraw "until the States changed the Rules of Procedure so as to allow their full and fair

[25] Incomindios, "Statement presented by Ambassador Ronald Barnes to the 50th General Assembly of WIPO on behalf of Incomindios," IP-Watch, October 4, 2012. www.ip-watch.org/weblog/wp-content/uploads/2012/10/WIPO-GA-50-Incomindios-statement.pdf (accessed March 27, 2015).

[26] Ibid.

[27] WIPO, *Report of the Twentieth Session of the Intergovernmental Committee on Intellectual Property and Genetic Resources*, Traditional Knowledge and Folklore February 14–22, 2012 (Geneva: WIPO, 2012), 94.

[28] Foundation for Aboriginal and Islander Research Action, *Submission to the WIPO Secretariat on Indigenous Peoples' Effective Participation in WIPO on GRTKF*, (Geneva: WIPO, 2011), 4.

participation in the elaboration of the IGC's work," and sought particularly the ability to submit textual proposals independently, rather than through state representatives.[29]

In some ways, indigenous peoples' focus on recognition within international institutions is similar to the that of emerging countries as they first entered international copyright negotiations, whether in 1928 or in the 1950s and 1960s. In other ways the emphasis on recognition is even more complex in the case of indigenous peoples.

The need for recognition and inclusion is possibly more fundamental than any emphasis on particular norms or provisions dealing with traditional knowledge in international norm-setting. This was true, for example, of the British dominions who first sent delegates to the 1928 diplomatic conference to revise the *Berne Convention* and whose primary focus was on the status conveyed by the order of signature on the convention (see Chapter 7).[30] When the recognition of a country or a people's legitimate right to standing, recognition, and negotiating status is either in doubt or in the process of being established, the focus of their representatives can tend to rest on the fundamental matter of the achievement of recognition and status, and, depending on the administrative resources available, may not extend as fully to the substantive matters under negotiation. As Coombe observes, "Any new alienable right, however, is only as valuable as the position its holder occupies in a market; for this reason many indigenous peoples NGOs view commitments to local capacity-building and self-governance as more important than the creation of new intellectual property rights."[31]

The struggle for recognition of indigenous peoples in international institutions, however, is more complex than was the recognition of newly independent states, in that the participation of indigenous peoples in WIPO negotiations further troubles the notions of "representativeness" upon which the multilateral system is based, given that representation falls outside the container of the state. Such participation challenges positivistic notions of international law that construed indigenous peoples as falling outside the realm of international law and as failing to meet the

[29] WIPO, *Report of the Twentieth Session of the Intergovernmental Committee on Intellectual Property and Genetic Resources, Traditional Knowledge and Folklore*, Geneva: WIPO, February 14–22, 2012, 94 and 102.

[30] See Rosemary Coombe, "The Recognition of Indigenous Peoples' and Community Traditional Knowledge in International Law," *St. Thomas Law Review* 14 (2001), 277.

[31] Ibid., 281.

requisite standards of sovereignty.[32] Who can speak for indigenous peoples, and who can be spoken to as a representative of an indigenous group remains, at times, in question.[33] In one instance, following, ironically, on the withdrawal of indigenous delegates from IGC work, the representativeness of indigenous peoples participating at WIPO was called into question when the North American Indigenous Peoples' Caucus expressed disapproval about "a small number of Indigenous organizations, some state-funded, that appear willing to participate in the WIPO process."[34] As Bowrey and Anderson point out, the problem of representativeness goes all the way to the classification of aboriginality itself, which "as with circumscribing any cultural or ethnic identity, is inherently unstable" and difficult to define.[35]

Following the February 2012 withdrawal, and following a consultation with WIPO in May 2012, the United Nations Permanent Forum on Indigenous Issues issued a number of recommendations to WIPO aimed at addressing some of the problems that had been identified.[36] The Forum called on WIPO, among other things, to recognize and respect the *UN Declaration on the Rights of Indigenous Peoples* as an instrument that must be incorporated into WIPO work, to "explore and establish modalities to ensure the equal, full and direct participation of indigenous peoples in all negotiations of the Intergovernmental Committee," and to incorporate an indigenous person as a co-chair of the IGC.[37]

The Permanent Forum also called upon states "to organize regional and national consultations to enable indigenous peoples to prepare for and participate effectively in sessions of the Intergovernmental Committee."[38] In July 2012 some of the recommendations of the Permanent Forum were discussed at one of the IGC's half-day panel presentations chaired by representatives from local or indigenous communities, although, as of

32 Anghie "Finding the Peripheries."
33 Bowrey and Anderson, "The Politics of Global Information Sharing," 492–494 (n. 45).
34 *Recommendations of the North American Indigenous Peoples' Caucus* (n. 81), 9.
35 Ibid., 493.
36 United Nations Economic and Social Council, Information Received from Entities of the United Nations System and other Intergovernmental Organizations: World Intellectual Property Organization E/C.19/2012/5 23 February 2012 (United Nations Economic and Social Council, 2012).
37 United Nations Permanent Forum on Indigenous Issues, *Report on the Eleventh Session* 7–18 May 2012 E/C.19/2012/13 (Economic and Social Council, 2012), 9.
38 Ibid.

March 2015, these recommendations had not yet been formally addressed at the IGC.[39]

The recognition of customary law

Some have called not for the codification of new forms of legal protection of traditional knowledge, but instead for the recognition of the local context and customary law of indigenous communities as the legal basis of protection.[40] This approach, unlike approaches based in transnational law that position the Western world as a paternalistic protector and may impose external models and visions of development, would put indigenous peoples at the center of decision making about protection and access.[41]

Doyle and Gilbert argue that:

> For indigenous peoples the next and long overdue phase in the history of development has to be one where development models are not imposed on, or designed for, them by external actors, be they international institutions, governments or multinational corporations. Instead it must be one that sees indigenous peoples themselves as having the determining say in the process to be followed and the ends to be aimed for in their own development path.[42]

The North American Indigenous Peoples' Caucus has recommended that "Indigenous Nations and Peoples . . . set their own legal standards for the protection of our traditional knowledge, traditional cultural expressions, and genetic resources," and has called on the UN to "inform WIPO that it must respect Indigenous Peoples laws on these issues."[43] It argued

[39] WIPO, *Report of the Twenty-Second Session of the Intergovernmental Committee on Intellectual Property and Genetic Resources*, Traditional Knowledge and Folklore July 9–13, 2012 (Geneva: WIPO, 2012), 9–10.

[40] Von Lewinski, *Indigenous Heritage and Intellectual Property*, 66.

[41] Andreas Rahmatian, "Neo-Colonial Aspects of Global Intellectual Property Protection," *The Journal of World Intellectual Property*, 12, 1 (2009), 62. See also Antony Taubman, "Preface: Indigenous Innovation: New Dialogues, New Pathways," in *Indigenous Peoples' Innovation: Intellectual Property Pathways to Development*, eds. Peter Drahos and Susy Frankel (Canberra: Australian National University E Press, 2012), xxiii.

[42] Cathal Doyle and Jérémie Gilbert, "Indigenous Peoples and Globalization: From 'Development Aggression' to 'Self-Determined Development,'" *European Yearbook of Minority Issues* 7 (2008/9), 236.

[43] *Recommendations of the North American Indigenous Peoples' Caucus to the Eleventh Session of the United Nations Permanent Forum on Indigenous Issues*, United Nations Permanent Forum on Indigenous Issues, 2012, 10.

that WIPO "cannot regulate indigenous traditional knowledge and access to such and associated genetic resources, and that those remain under the control of Indigenous Peoples."[44] Such calls have been consistently articulated by indigenous and local communities.

Recognition of customary law could take a range of formats, from taking it as a fundamental source of law for communities' legal rights over traditional knowledge, to using customary law in guiding the definition of traditional knowledge, or by establishing its relationship to a community, determining rights and exceptions, and determining appropriate remedies, sanctions, and restitution after a breach of rights in traditional knowledge.[45] Rosemary Coombe calls for such recognition to be full:

> it is important that WIPO and the CBD have recognized that indigenous customary law has to be respected when considering the use of traditional knowledge and that indigenous customary law principles provide legitimate juridical resources for a consideration of alternative forms and norms of property. The promise of a cross-cultural conversation in the international intellectual property arena that is thereby posed cannot be indefinitely postponed.[46]

Debora Halbert notes that a great diversity of possible ownership models are available within indigenous knowledge systems. While the Berne model of copyright, among other Western regimes of intellectual property, has become predominant, it is far from the only model available. The problem of how to address traditional knowledge within Western-based intellectual property institutions is less a problem of lack-of-fit, she argues, than it is "a problem of refusing to recognize alternative systems of property rights."[47] Antony Taubman asks whether there is a need "for a more pluralistic system or at least a system that is more representative of or practically responsive to the diverse needs, interests and values of peoples across the globe, in particular indigenous peoples and local communities" and suggests that international dialogue might lead to "more positive and culturally appropriate forms of IP protection that transcend the constraints, limitations and embedded values" of the current

[44] Ibid. [45] Von Lewinski, *Indigenous Heritage and Intellectual Property*, 89–90.

[46] Coombe, "The Recognition of Indigenous Peoples' and Community Traditional Knowledge," 275.

[47] Debora J. Halbert, *Resisting Intellectual Property* (London and New York: Routledge, 2005), 41.

intellectual property system.[48] In fact, Taubman suggests that such a recalibration has already begun:

> Ideas, concepts and concerns that were perhaps considered tangential or barely relevant to the IP system a little more than a decade ago are now central to work being done by two of the main international institutions – WIPO itself and the WTO . . . This recognition is surely a remarkable sign of a more pluralistic understanding of what IP is and whose interests should be recognized within an IP system – an indication of a broader and more inclusive framework than was conceived of some two decades ago when the main elements of the TRIPS Agreement were concluded.[49]

Conclusion

WIPO may provide one forum for the sort of cross-cultural conversation that Coombe calls for, and that Taubman suggests has begun, but it is far from an ideal or an egalitarian one. While NGOs have had long-standing voices within country delegations, have been influential in making many of the foundational proposals on which the *Berne Convention* was constructed, and have long had places as stand-alone delegates, indigenous peoples struggle to gain recognition, to make proposals to WIPO forums, and to have their views recognized in WIPO meetings.

The discussions that have taken place at WIPO on traditional knowledge have provided an international forum for the articulation of alternative visions of development. While some indigenous peoples' voices have been included, these voices are marginal to the voices of state representatives. While the international intellectual property system is certainly more inclusive than it has been in the past, it is clear that it falls far short of even UN standards.

While the participation of indigenous peoples in WIPO has been circumscribed, WIPO has actively created for itself a central place defining the legal contours of traditional knowledge. There is reason to be critical about the implications of the knowledge/power regime thus constructed within WIPO, and to be skeptical of the effects of this regime as recognizing global institutions at the expense of local or transnational indigenous peoples. That is, by bringing traditional knowledge into the realm of international copyright largely according to its own terms and those of

48 Taubman, "Preface: Indigenous Innovation: New Dialogues, New Pathways," xvi.
49 Ibid., xxii.

member states, WIPO may undermine as much as protect such forms of knowledge and their traditional rights-holders. Despite WIPO's relative openness (when compared against some other international institutions) to outside observer organizations, and its limited openness to participation by indigenous peoples and individuals, its work in this area falls far short of the articulated ideals of global polity.

PART III

Institutions

10

Institutional aspects of international copyright at WIPO

WIPO is seen, by some, as a positive example of a multilateral institution whose relative transparency, and whose work to include NGOs and indigenous peoples as observers in its meetings, stands out among other multilateral institutions.[1] According to this view, WIPO is working well: it is a site for the legitimate expansion of international legal norms in general and of the rights of copyright holders in particular, as well as a fruitful forum for work toward the internationalization of principles of access to knowledge. The proponents of the WIPO Development Agenda, the *Marrakesh Treaty*, and ongoing work at WIPO toward new international instruments that would codify principles of access, have seen these events, and the influence that developing country representatives and NGOs have had in sparking them, as a turning point – or a potential turning point – for WIPO as an institution and for the A2K movement. Not all agree.

Some assess the situation more harshly, viewing the WIPO/Berne system as one among an array of neoliberal or neo-imperialist institutions that serve to extend the power of a transnational capitalist class of intellectual property owners and the power of North over South, West over East, and neocolonial over indigenous.[2] In part, these analyses are based on a framing of the question in a broader structural context: one that includes questions of international structural and cultural inequalities as part of the frame.

WIPO, as an international institution, it has been noted, falls far short of a number of ideals. This is due not only to the inadequacies of developing country, NGO, and indigenous peoples' participation, but also, in part – as

[1] Toby McIntosh, "WIPO Transparency Wins Praise, Gaps Remain," *Freedominfo.org* January 7, 2014, www.freedominfo.org/2014/01/wipo-transparency-wins-praise-gaps-remain/ (accessed March 27, 2015).

[2] Story, "Burn Berne"; May, *The World Intellectual Property Organization*; May and Sell, *Intellectual Property Rights*.

shall be discussed in this chapter – to the resiliency of structures and norms that were established in the days of formal colonialism, and to procedures, provisions, and institutional features that prevent the development of alternatives.

May and Sell argue, and this book further illustrates that, while the current era may be a time of contestation, offering opportunities to balance private interests "with some nascent notion of a (global) *public interest*,"[3] the mechanisms of such balancing, "remain difficult to enact at the global level," despite existing at the national level in some countries.[4] This is because:

> any mechanisms for the realization of a global polity or community interest within [global governance of IPRs], are currently severely underdeveloped . . . the world is far too insufficiently globalized for the imposition of a global legal settlement that does not allow for the divergent social developmental interests of all countries to be recognized (and acted upon).[5]

As a result, May and Sell argue, "further harmonization of intellectual property rights at the global level is not only premature but is unlikely to be just, until the wide disparities of wealth in our global society have been greatly reduced."[6]

This chapter outlines not only the underdevelopment of the institutional mechanisms of global polity in the field of copyright but also the continued operation and path dependency of institutional structures that resist such development. It pertains to the third element of access to knowledge discussed in Chapter One: access to the processes and institutions governing the regulation of knowledge – in this case, the regulation of intellectual property. In this chapter, I first examine, in historical perspective, the institutional characteristics of the Berne Union as set down in the *Berne Convention* and its historical institutional practices. Second, I examine the institutional characteristics of the general administrative aspects of the secretariat of the Berne Union: BIRPI, which later became WIPO.

The Berne Union

The Berne Union has adopted a number of practices and provisions that are historically rooted in a broader system of colonialism, which the *Berne Convention* serves to extend. First, the *Berne Convention* was negotiated

[3] May and Sell, *Intellectual Property Rights*, 218. [4] Ibid. [5] Ibid. [6] Ibid.

under a system that allowed imperial powers to control, on behalf of the metropole as well as colonial territories, multiple votes. Second, the *Berne Convention* contained, and still contains, a "colonial clause" allowing one country to bring another territory that it controls in to the convention. Third, a number of provisions and practices have stood in the way of Union countries' ability to exit the convention, creating a ratcheting or trap-like effect that has prevented the development of alternative norms and models.[7]

While WIPO now operates under a one-country one-vote system, and while decolonization has reduced (but not ended) the importance of the colonial clause, the provisions that stand in the way of countries' ability to exit the *Berne Convention* have only multiplied. Approximately 85 percent of countries worldwide now participate in the Berne system of international copyright, a significant number of which had no independent control of their own initial adhesion. The second part of this chapter examines some of the institutional factors that keep the norms established in times of colonialism locked in.

Colonial voting

Up to the 1948 revision of the *Berne Convention*, the Berne Union permitted the delegation of an imperial country to send extra delegates to "represent" a second and even a third colony or territory, sometimes thus achieving multiple votes. France, an imperial power, thus gained extra votes at Berne negotiations through its colonies and, in at least one case, the extra votes were determinative; in the 1880s, when Tunisia was represented by Louis Renault, who was also a member of the French delegation, the additional vote of France on behalf of Tunisia was a deciding one on the question of translation rights.[8] Later, in 1896, French delegates represented Bulgaria, France, Tunisia, and Montenegro,[9] giving France several potential votes, though votes were not recorded, so it is not known what effect this had.[10] In 1908, a French delegate represented Tunisia;[11] in 1928, one of the French delegates also stood as delegate for Morocco, Tunisia,[12]

[7] John Braithwaite and Peter Drahos, "Ratcheting Up and Driving Down Global Regulatory Standards," *Development* 42, 4 (1999), 109–114.

[8] In rejecting the 1884 draft of the article on translation rights. Actes 1885, 44. The Haitian delegate also voted with the French. See Chapter 6.

[9] Actes 1896, 86. [10] Actes 1896. [11] Actes 1908, 134 and 144.

[12] Actes 1928, 133, 135, and 137.

Lebanon,[13] and Syria;[14] and even as late as 1948, Morocco and Tunisia were represented by the French delegation, which as a result had three votes.[15]

As well as the multiple votes that France was permitted to have on behalf of itself and its colonies, it was also the practice at some diplomatic conferences to allow, from time to time, one country or territory to vote on another's behalf, even in the absence of a formal imperial relationship. For example, Liberia was represented by William Koentzer, a German Imperial Advisor and Consul General of the Republic of Liberia, at the 1886 meeting to sign the *Berne Convention*,[16] and Liberia acceded to the *Berne Convention* twenty years later in 1908, though formally independent, under signature of the German delegation to the 1908 diplomatic conference to revise the *Berne Convention.*[17]

Alongside the obvious problems and conflicts entailed where one state represents another, there were also additional problems of colonial, settler, and puppet governments, and their relative ability to represent the populations they ruled.[18] The question of representativeness also arises in examining, as discussed in Chapter 8, the composition of delegations and their relative representativeness of various domestic interest groups, as state delegations often included representatives of rights-holder groups, while rarely did they include representatives of user communities or traditional knowledge holders.

13 Ibid., 137.

14 Ibid., 170. Both Syria and Lebanon had acceded to the Berlin Act of the *Berne Convention* in 1924 and the Rome Act in 1933, both under the supervision of France under League of Nations Mandate. Ricketson and Ginsburg, *International Copyright*, 1078 and 1102–1104. Most votes are only recorded as tallies, except for very few cases. In one, France and Tunisia are recorded as each voting on the same side but Morocco, and Syria and Lebanon were not recorded as voting (Actes 1928, 235).

15 Actes 1948, 58–59. While most votes gave only the final tally, in one instance France, Morocco, and Tunisia are recorded as each voting. Even with the extra votes, on this occasion they did not prevail (Actes 1948, 163). On the topic of the accessions of Tunisia and France to the *Berne Convention*, see Ricketson and Ginsburg, *International Copyright*, 1078.

16 U.S. Department of State, "U.S. Relations with Liberia," www.state.gov/r/pa/ei/bgn/6618.htm (accessed March 27, 2015).

17 Ricketson and Ginsburg, *International* Copyright, 82; Levitsky, "The Union of Berne at 100," 367.

18 At least one puppet state has acceded to the convention without objection by the secretariat of the Union: Slovakia in 1944. Ricketson and Ginsburg, *International Copyright*, 1080.

The colonial clause

Prior to the 1950s, much of the *Berne Convention*'s territory was made up of areas under colonial rule to which the *Berne Convention* had been declared to apply. This was made possible by the inclusion of the "colonial clause" or "territorial clause" of the *Berne Convention.*[19] The territorial clause was first proposed and put in place in the *Berne Convention* during its initial negotiation in the 1880s.[20] The British also reserved the power to separately denounce the convention on behalf of one or more of their colonies or possessions.[21] At the founding of the convention, Spain, France, and the UK declared their accessions to apply to their colonies; in 1909 Germany did the same; Denmark, the Netherlands, Portugal, and South Africa were added to the list of colonial powers making use of the territorial clause on their accession to the 1908 Berlin Act of the *Berne Convention*; under the 1928 act Japan, Australia, New Zealand, and Belgium were added to the list of colonial powers making use of the clause to bring in territories under their control.[22]

Those countries brought in to the Union through the territorial clause were considered to be "countries of the Union" without, in most cases, either the obligations or privileges of membership.[23] In most cases, such "countries of the Union" neither paid membership dues nor participated in the negotiation of the *Berne Convention* (although some exceptions, including those just noted, applied). Questions have also been raised as to whether the residents of colonial territories were considered to be "authors" to whom the convention applied, or whether such territories were simply obligated to protect the authors of member states.[24]

Despite the purported opposition of the United Nations to colonization – seen, for instance, in its 1960 *Declaration on the Granting of Independence to Colonial Countries and People* – this clause remains part of the present convention, allowing one state to declare the applicability of the convention to "all or part of those territories . . . for the external relations of which it is responsible."[25] The Appendix to the *Berne Convention*

[19] See also Ricketson and Ginsburg, *International Copyright*, 1107–1117.

[20] Actes 1885, 53. See also Ricketson and Ginsburg, *International Copyright*, 1108–1109.

[21] Bannerman, *Struggle for Canadian Copyright*, 39–41.

[22] Ricketson and Ginsburg, *International Copyright*, 1111–1117.

[23] Peukert "The Colonial Legacy," 11–12. [24] Ibid., 11–13.

[25] *Berne Convention*, 1971, Article 31(1); *Declaration on the Granting of Independence to Colonial Countries and Peoples Adopted by General Assembly resolution 1514 (XV) of 14 December 1960* (New York: United Nations, 1960).

also contains a territorial clause allowing a state to declare the Appendix applicable to such territories in cases where their situation is analogous to those regarded as a developing country under the established practice of the General Assembly of the United Nations.[26] The *Universal Copyright Convention* contains a similar clause.[27]

Controversy arose around such territorial clauses during the mid-twentieth-century wave of independence, and some country representatives objected to them during the 1967 round of negotiations of the *Berne Convention.* At that time, the Stockholm Protocol was under negotiation, and the UK proposed a territorial application clause for the Stockholm Protocol, which would allow the Protocol, as well as the convention, to be applied to territories not responsible for their own foreign relations.[28] The delegations of Tunisia, Czechoslovakia, India, and Israel objected to the inclusion of this clause.[29] When the matter came to a vote, the Tunisian delegate (Mustapha Fersi, a legal advisor from the Ministry of Culture) voted against it, considering that "in the very near future all peoples would be in a position to ratify international conventions themselves."[30] The Indian delegate (Sher Singh) declared that he suspected that the territorial clause was an effort on the part of industrialized countries to secure some benefit for themselves under the protocol that was designed to accord benefits to developing countries.[31] The Israeli delegate, Ze'ev Sher,[32] while objecting to "any form of government which was not the result of self-determination and therefore to the application of any convention which recognized that governments might hold responsibility for the foreign relations of territories," also saw the territorial clause of the Stockholm protocol as a "special case, as such territories "should be assisted in providing appropriate legislation which might be used after independence had been attained," and Israel therefore abstained from voting on the territorial clause of the Protocol, which was adopted fourteen votes to two, with nine abstentions.[33]

[26] *Berne Convention,* 1971, Protocol, Article 2(5).

[27] UCC 1952, Article 13; UCC 1971 Article 13. [28] Records 1967, 998, item 2515.

[29] Ibid., 1198 item 23. [30] Ibid., 998, item 2516. [31] Ibid., 998, item 2521.

[32] Like N'Diaye, Senegal's delegate at the Paris revision conferences in 1971, Sher became an important voice focused on the particular problems and opportunities created by intellectual property laws in developing countries. Sher's work in this capacity included public talks (see "Israeli Expert, Invited by U.S., Gives Views in Washington on Patents," *Jewish Telegraphic Agency* 21, October, 1965), and articles (see "Reflections on Copyright in Developing Countries," *Bulletin of the Copyright Society of the USA* 201 (1968–1969)).

[33] Ibid., 998–999, items 2515–2531.

The territorial clause of the Stockholm Protocol was retained in the 1971 Berne Appendix, as was the main territorial clause of the *Berne Convention*.[34] However, a clause was also added to the 1971 convention: "[t]his Article shall in no way be understood as implying the recognition or tacit acceptance by a country of the Union of the factual situation concerning a territory to which this Convention is made applicable by another country of the Union by virtue of a declaration under paragraph (1)."[35] A similar clause was also added to the *Universal Copyright Convention* the same year.[36] This addition was made at the suggestion of the Director General of WIPO in light of continuing objections in principle to territorial clauses voiced by the Hungarian delegation and supported by the People's Republic of the Congo.[37] No debate is recorded to have occurred concerning the inclusion of the territorial clause of the *Berne Convention* at the 1971 diplomatic conference, the matter having been discussed and resolved by the inclusion of the additional clause at the simultaneous conference to revise the *UCC*.[38] As a result, even after the major waves of postwar decolonization, the "colonial clause" remained in force.

Blocked exit

As former colonies gained independence, it became important to determine whether those territories to which the *Berne Convention* had applied as colonies would continue to be bound by the convention. BIRPI took the position of presuming that the convention continued to apply unless the country declared its exit.[39] This was simply a presumption that allowed those countries that ultimately declared continued adherence to "benefit" from unbroken application of the convention.[40] Prior to an actual declaration of continued adherence or accession on the part of the newly independent country, BIRPI refrained from including said country on lists of member states and the like.[41] However, BIRPI also took positive action to invite newly independent countries to declare their positions, and many either declared continued adherence or acceded to the

[34] Ibid., 998, item 2515; *Berne Convention*, 1971, Article 31(1).

[35] *Berne Convention*, 1971, Article 31(4).

[36] UCC 1971, Article 13(2).

[37] *UCC Records* 1971, 151–152, items 689–697.

[38] *Records* 1971, 139, 144, and 156.

[39] Peukert "Intellectual Property," 11–12; Ricketson and Ginsburg, *International Copyright*, 1128–1129.

[40] Ricketson and Ginsburg, *International Copyright*, 1129.

[41] Ibid., 1132.

convention.[42] BIRPI's policy of allowing continued adherence, and inviting accession, was intended to prevent the shrinkage of the Union as a result of decolonization. It was very successful at achieving this effect; only four states (Indonesia in 1960, Syria in 1962, Upper Volta in 1969, and Mauritius in 1971) denounced the *Berne Convention* on independence, and three declared that they did not consider themselves to be bound by the convention (South Vietnam, South Korea, and Cambodia).[43]

The UCC, when it was established in 1952, contained a "safeguard clause" governing its relationship to the *Berne Convention.* Under this clause, aspects of which were previously discussed in Chapter 6, member states of the UCC who were also members of the Berne Union agreed that countries that withdrew from the Berne Union after 1950 would not be protected under the UCC either.[44] This clause was put in place to discourage countries from exiting the *Berne Convention* in favor of the UCC and thus adopting generally lower levels of protection than those guaranteed under the *Berne Convention.* This clause, combined with the presumption of continued adherence, meant that newly independent countries were forced to accept Berne Union membership without having had any effective voice in the proceedings, and without any regard for the appropriateness of the *Convention* to the country's needs or to its state of readiness.

Indonesia and Syria, despite having been brought into the *Berne Convention* by colonial powers, were treated as denouncing the *Berne Convention* in 1960 and 1962 in a way that would have evoked the safeguard clause. BIRPI, according to Lazar, treated these as denunciations in order to deter other newly independent countries from leaving the Berne Union.[45] Lazar calls this neocolonialism:

> '[n]eo-colonialism' may be an apt euphemism for this phenomenon.... [BIRPI adopted] a 'liberal' construction of the Convention texts to secure Article 26 countries as contracting members, and, once that was achieved, the text was interpreted strictly in defining their obligations to provide high

42 Ibid., 1127.

43 Peukert "Intellectual Property," 11–12; Ricketson and Ginsburg, *International Copyright*, 1121–1122; 1125. See Ricketson and Ginsburg, *International Copyright*, for additional detail and cases of non-application.

44 UCC 1952, Article 17.

45 Lazar, "Developing Countries," 25. Syria rejoined the Berne Union in 2004 and Upper Volta did so as Burkina Faso in 1976. Ricketson and Ginsburg, *International Copyright*, 1094 fn. 208.

> protection and in classifying certain actions as 'withdrawals' sufficient to invoke the Berne Safeguard Clause.[46]

Other countries' uncertain status, upon independence, as members (or not) of the Berne Union had significant implications; were they determined to be members who then either denounced or declared non-adhesion to the Berne Union, they would be subject to the safeguard clause and thus virtually expelled from international copyright relations.[47] This is perhaps seen most clearly in the case of Ghana who, after independence from the UK in 1957, enacted copyright legislation incompatible with the Berne Union, thereby implying non-adherence to the *Convention*, and then acceded to the UCC in 1962. The Union threatened to see these actions as a denunciation that would have triggered the safeguard clause. Ultimately, this did not come to pass, and Ghana remained a member of the UCC but did not join WIPO until 1991. Nonetheless, this example demonstrates the precariousness of developing countries in relation to the regime of BIRPI/WIPO.[48]

The safeguard clause was modified when both the UCC and the *Berne Convention* were revised in 1971, but this modification did not affect the penalties put in place for countries exiting the *Berne Convention*.[49] Portugal, Czechoslovakia, and Brazil had argued for the complete abolition of the safeguard clause, but were unsuccessful.[50]

The *Berne Convention* has become the only model of international copyright, in part, because of the fact that it has been made extremely difficult, for most developing countries, to exit. Many countries were brought into the *Berne Convention* by colonial powers; many were prevented, on threat of expulsion from international copyright relations, from exiting the convention by the safeguard clause; and, as well, some countries were prevented from denouncing the convention when they attempted to do so as colonies. This was the case for Canada, which, as a British dominion, attempted to denounce the *Berne Convention* in 1899 but was prevented from so doing by the British imperial government.[51] As a result, many Berne Union members began as virtual captives of the system, coerced into membership by the rules that they had no part in

[46] Ibid., 18. [47] Ibid., 17. [48] Ibid., 28.
[49] UCC 1971, Appendix Declaration relating to Article 17.
[50] *UCC Records* 1971, 152–153; Ricketson and Ginsburg, *International Copyright*, 1201.
[51] Bannerman, *The Struggle for Canadian Copyright.*

establishing, and unable to exit except in face of the severe penalty of expulsion from international copyright relations.

The secretariat

Funding and control

Until the formation of WIPO in 1970, the secretariat of the Berne Union was housed within the Swiss Government, which appointed the staff of the secretariat and its Director General and supervised the finances of the bureau.[52] Prior to 1970, the representatives of member states of the Berne Union normally met only at diplomatic conferences, usually convened approximately every twenty years, for the revision of the *Berne Convention.*[53] Only after the formation of WIPO, governed by a General Assembly of member states, did the member states of WIPO control the administration and operations of its secretariat; prior to that, the Swiss government appointed staff and supervised the finances of the office.[54] It has been through the vehicle of the General Assembly, and through the committees it establishes, that member states generally have become much more active in the oversight of the organization, for example, in proposing and putting in place the Development Agenda for WIPO.

The greater involvement of member states in the administrative aspects of the organization, which itself has grown enormously, has meant different things for different groups. It has meant that member states, both powerful and less powerful, have taken on roles once played by the Swiss government and the hosts of diplomatic conferences, such as overseeing financial and agenda-setting roles in the organization. In recent years, this has led, on one hand, to efforts by member states and developing countries to exert more oversight and reform efforts. It has also has led to stalemates as the various country groups conflicted over organizational direction.[55]

While the transformation of BIRPI into a member state-controlled institution increased the involvement of member states, including

[52] Bogsch, *The First Twenty-Five Years*, 22–26. [53] Ibid., 26.

[54] Swiss Federal Archives E2001D#1000/1553#7840* (4–51), E2003A#1970/115#109* (4–102).

[55] Catherine Saez, "Inauspicious Start to Gurry's Second term as IP Policymaking Hits Wall at WIPO," *IP-Watch*, October 1, 2014, www.ip-watch.org/2014/10/01/inauspicious-start-to-gurrys-second-term-as-ip-policymaking-hits-wall-at-wipo/ (accessed March 27, 2015).

developing countries, other transformations have, according to some accounts, reduced that control. The first transformation is financial: when BIRPI was founded in 1893, it had a staff of seven and expenses of 38,073 Swiss francs (CHF), or the equivalent of approximately 1 million USD in today's currency, and was funded by member state contributions.[56] Today, WIPO operates with a budget of 673,993,000 CHF, or 672 million USD.[57] Its budget is no longer primarily funded by member states but, in a large part, by fees paid by users of the international intellectual property system; 95 percent of WIPO's budget for the 2014–2015 biennium came from income generated on fees paid on international filing of patent, trademark, and industrial design applications.[58] Member states continue to pay fees, but these make up a relatively minor portion of WIPO's budget.

Since WIPO's budget thus comes, in a large part, from intellectual property owners, it is pertinent to ask whether private interests and intellectual property owners have a significant influence on the operations of the organization. The extent of this influence on the secretariat remains to be extensively examined, but the question of whether WIPO is now beholden to the most active companies in the PCT system (such as Philips Electronics, Siemens, Robert Bosch GmbH, Procter & Gamble, Ericsson, and Matsushita Electric Industrial Co.) has been a source of concern.[59] It may arguably be the case that, despite the formal institutionalization of member state control, the institutional culture, networks of knowledge, and funding of WIPO by major transnational IP rights-holders places powerful limits on reform, exerting epistemic and cultural influence over the organization. It may also be that such restraints are supported by the main intellectual property-exporting member states.

A second factor that has reduced the control over the organization exerted by member states is its growing bureaucracy, which can make it difficult for developing country representatives, NGOs, and other observers to participate. Much of the work at WIPO occurs in permanent and temporary committees that often meet several times a year.

56 Actes 1896, 206.

57 WIPO, *WIPO Program and Budget for the 2014/15 Biennium* (Geneva: WIPO, 2013), 14.

58 CIEL, *A Citizen's Guide to WIPO*, 13; WIPO, *Results, Budget and Performance*. www.wipo.int/about-wipo/en/budget/ "Developed" countries, in recognition of WIPO's role in the implementation of the TRIPs Agreement, increased their budget contributions "to facilitate the capacity building and legislative advice functions of the organization"; May, *The World Intellectual Property Organization*, 53.

59 CIEL, *A Citizen's Guide to WIPO*, 13 and 19; May, "Direct and Indirect Influence," 39–56.

Growing bureaucracy

Prior to the formation of WIPO, the preparatory work for revision of the *Berne Convention* was done by BIRPI in conjunction with the government hosting the conference. However, at the diplomatic conference of 1948 to revise the *Berne Convention*, it was decided to set up a Permanent Committee of the Berne Union to meet at regular intervals between revision conferences.[60] Permanent committees were seen as a way of monitoring changes and events, and of undertaking the work of the maintenance and improvement of the international copyright system, and especially of adopting recommendations and making preparations for the revision of conventions.[61]

The Permanent Committee of the Berne Union was composed of representatives of twelve member states, chosen to ensure regional distribution. It was replaced, in 1971, with an Executive Committee of the Berne Union, which operated on a similar basis.[62] Much of the work of establishing and revising international copyright treaties has now passed to WIPO's *Standing Committee on Copyright and Related Rights* (SCCR), established in 1998, in which all member states of WIPO and the Berne Union are invited to participate.[63]

The establishment of the standing committee system in 1998 (under which the SCCR and three other new standing committees were established) has, on one hand, allowed for broad participation by member states and observers; not only were the full range of member states granted membership, but WIPO also proposed to finance the participation of some member states.[64] On the other hand, full and equal participation in the SCCR and the expanding bureaucracy of WIPO has proved impossible for many member states and observers. Only those NGOs and developing countries that can afford to maintain an office in Geneva or regularly send representatives can fully participate in the meetings.[65] As Gross observes:

[60] UNESCO. Executive Board. *Proposals of the Director-General Concerning Article IX of the Preliminary Draft of the Universal Copyright Convention*. 30/EX/12. (Paris: UNESCO, 1952), 3; Actes 1948, 425–426.

[61] Ibid., 2–3. [62] *Berne Convention*, 1971, Article 23.

[63] WIPO, Standing Committee on Copyright and Related Rights (Geneva: WIPO, n.d.), www.wipo.int/policy/en/sccr/ (accessed March 27, 2015).

[64] WIPO Standing Committee on Copyright and Related Rights, *Organizational and Procedural Matters and Overview of Substantive Issues* SCCR/1/2 (Geneva: WIPO, 1998), 2.

[65] Robin Gross, "The World Intellectual Property Organization (WIPO)," in *Global Information Society Watch*, eds. Karen Banks, Roberto Bissio, Willie Currie, Anriette Esterhuysen,

> the less wealthy countries cannot afford to send large delegations to Geneva, and instead send a single person who might be responsible for covering all the activities of WIPO, WHO, UNESCO, the ILO, and other UN agencies. These representatives are less likely to be specialists in intellectual property rights and less likely to be aware of a diversity of viewpoints on issues. And representatives from the poorest nations remain in their capital city and rely on communications with Geneva to try to keep on top of what is happening at WIPO. However, official final committee reports and meeting notes can take from six to nine months to be published by WIPO and are therefore always out of date with the actual negotiations.[66]

This can also be seen in the role of the Pacific Islands Forum Secretariat (PIFS), whose office in Geneva represents a number of Pacific Island states at different international organizations, including WIPO; many of the states are small LDCs and would otherwise be unable to afford permanent representatives in Geneva.[67] Such an arrangement is valuable to its members but also highlights the limits of their participation, illustrating the constraints that bureaucratic proliferation has imposed upon developing nations.

In addition, while member state representatives participate as members of these committees, the chairs of the committees have a great deal of power, for example, to decide whether or not a consensus has been reached (see below discussion of consensus).[68] Chairs also decide which proposals are incorporated into treaty texts, which are dropped, and how proposals are discussed. Furthermore, they decide whether, and when, observer groups and NGOs may speak at committee meetings.[69]

In addition to the establishment of standing committees in 1998, WIPO has grown in other ways. Not only has the membership of WIPO grown to 188 as of present writing, its bureaucracy has also grown enormously, making it significantly larger than most UN agencies.[70] The WIPO Academy, as mentioned in Chapter 7, was established in 1998 to provide extensive education programs in intellectual property.[71] Further start-up

Chat Garcia Ramilo, and Magela Sigillito (Melville: Association for Progressive Communications and Humanist Institute for Cooperation with Developing Countries, 2007), 67. Ibid., 72.

66 Ibid., 72.

67 Chakriya Bowman, "The Pacific Island Nations: Toward Shared Representation," in *Managing the Challenges of WTO Participation: 45 Case Studies*, eds. Peter Gallagher, Patrick Low, and Andrew L. Stoler (Cambridge, Cambridge University Press, 2005), 450.

68 Gross, "The World Intellectual Property Organization," 70. 69 Ibid., 65.

70 Gross, "The World Intellectual Property Organization," 65.

71 WIPO, *WIPO Academy*, www.wipo.int/academy/en/ (accessed March 27, 2015).

or national academies are in the process of being established.[72] WIPO has also established a number of regional offices.[73] The Development Agenda has led to a new Development Sector within the secretariat, created from what had formerly been called the Technical Assistance and Capacity Building Sector. As well, between 2009 and 2012, a number of WIPO Technology Innovation and Support Centers (TISCs) were established "with the aim to contribute to reducing the knowledge gap between developed and developing countries."[74]

While member states achieved greater control over WIPO as a result of its transformation into a member state-controlled organization, its bureaucratic growth has also made oversight and control difficult. This is especially true for NGOs and developing country states.

Transparency

The growth of WIPO's bureaucracy has facilitated a degree of organizational transparency: WIPO makes meeting documents available online in multiple languages, often before the meetings take place, it webcasts some of its meetings, it publishes transcripts and reports of meetings, and it admits a significant number of observers to its meetings.[75]

At the same time, while its transparency may be greater than that of many other international organizations, WIPO also lacks transparency on a number of levels. Although some meetings are webcast and minuted, many of the real negotiations take place in "informal" sessions, which are not recorded and minuted, and to which observers are not admitted.[76] Some negotiations are also done at regional meetings, which have sometimes been kept secret, and to which not all member states are invited.[77] As well, as noted in Chapter 7, lack of transparency in the technical assistance that WIPO provides to developing countries has been identified as a problem.[78]

In general, the complexity of WIPO's governance structure, the number and range of bodies that make up the organization, the number and

[72] WIPO, *Start-Up Academies*, www.wipo.int/academy/en/about/startup_academies/ (accessed March 31, 2015).

[73] WIPO. *Regional Bureaus*, www.wipo.int/eds/en/.

[74] WIPO, *Independent Evaluation Report of the Technology and Innovation Support Centres (TISCs)* CDIP/9/5 (Geneva: WIPO, 2012), Annex, 5.

[75] McIntosh, "WIPO Transparency Wins Praise."

[76] Ibid.; Gross, "The World Intellectual Property Organization," 72.

[77] Gross, "The World Intellectual Property Organization," 70–72.

[78] Ibid., 72.

range of topics of negotiation and discussion, and the rules and procedures involved in participating in the organization all make the task of participation, especially by less powerful states and NGOs, difficult.[79]

Relationship with the UN

WIPO's relationship with the UN has also transformed the organization in ways that both support and detract from developing countries' influence in the organization. First, WIPO's mandate, as discussed in Chapter 2, has been reenvisioned by some; its mandate to "promote . . . intellectual property throughout the world and to harmonize national legislation in this field" under the *WIPO Convention* sometimes conflicts with WIPO's mandate under its agreement with the United Nations to "promote creative intellectual activity and to facilitate the transfer of technology to developing countries in order to accelerate economic, social and cultural development."[80]

Second, the system of consensus voting at WIPO, inherited from the UN, has been a force of moderation at WIPO, stalling both the IP maximalist positions of countries like the United States, but also standing in the way of the adoption of principles of access. While the founding *WIPO Convention* establishes that the WIPO General Assembly makes decisions by majority, WIPO committees operate on the basis of consensus and much of the preparatory and norm-setting work occurs in these committees.[81]

Consensus voting at WIPO thwarted the creation of the maximalist copyright treaty that American negotiators set out to obtain in the 1990s negotiation of the WIPO Internet Treaties.[82] However, while consensus voting can enable less powerful states to block motions of which they do not approve, it also means that it is impossible to take forward initiatives

[79] CIEL, *A Citizen's Guide to WIPO*, 6. Similar problems occur at the WTO: Carolyn Deere Birkbeck, "Developing Country Coalitions in the WTO: Strategies for Improving the Influence of the WTO's Weakest and Poorest Members Policy Brief for the IDEAS Centre," (Geneva: IDEAS, 2011), 2.

[80] See CIEL, *A Citizen's Guide to WIPO*, 11–12. *WIPO Convention*, Article 3; *Agreement between the United Nations and the World Intellectual Property Organization* (Geneva: WIPO, 1974); Deere, *The Implementation Game* 45.

[81] *Convention Establishing the World Intellectual Property Organization*, Article 6(3); Gross, "The World Intellectual Property Organization." See also Ricketson and Ginsburg, *International Copyright*, 1014–1015.

[82] Haggart, *Copyfight*, 114.

of which great powers do not approve. This was the case with many of the original proposals of the Friends of Development.[83]

At the same time, there are many instances where the principle of consensus is not fully followed at WIPO, or where it is thwarted by those who wish to push matters through. For example, the recommendation adopted at the conclusion of the 2006 session of the WIPO SCCR to convene a diplomatic conference to conclude the drafting of a new broadcasting treaty was adopted despite clear objections of several countries including India, Brazil, Argentina, Chile, Bolivia, Iran, and South Africa.[84] Here, the chair claimed to have "silent approval" of the recommendation.[85] Geoffrey Yu, then Deputy Director General of WIPO, acknowledged in a 2006 presentation that, at WIPO, an unorthodox view of "consensus" that allows the views of the minority to be overridden is broadly accepted:

> traditionally in WIPO, we try to avoid voting because it is divisive and it shows up that an idea is not embraced by everybody. So we prefer to go the route of consensus building. The only difficulty with consensus building is that different people have different understandings of what is consensus: whether it means that one person or five persons can hold up discussion, or whether we can live with a situation where more than five members are unhappy, but the majority would be happy and, therefore, there is consensus. This is a shifting definition and we have so far avoided the pitfall of trying to define it; we have managed to live with it reasonably well. For us at the international level, getting everyone aboard is still the best approach.[86]

Third, WIPO also inherited from the UN the system of regional groups. One of the strategies used by groups to formulate positions and coalitions on the complex range of issues under consideration is the formation of regional negotiating groups. Prior to the fall of communism, three country groups existed at WIPO, and in the UN system more generally: The Group of 77 (the group of developing countries, formed from the merger of what had been the Group A of Afro-Asian countries and the Group C of Latin American countries), Group B of Western countries (the Stockholm Group, a small number of Group B countries particularly active on copyright, was also active prior to 1996 on an information-sharing basis, though they were not a coalition in the sense of formally

[83] Braithwaite and Drahos, *Global Business Regulation*, 569–571.

[84] CIEL, *A Citizen's Guide to Copyright*, 10; Gross, "The World Intellectual Property Organization," 70.

[85] Gross, "The World Intellectual Property Organization," 70.

[86] Yu, "The Structure and Process of Negotiations," 1452.

expressing joint positions at WIPO), and Group D of socialist countries. These three groups have now been replaced by a series of regional groups: Group B of industrialized countries, the African Group, the Group of Latin American and Caribbean countries (GRULAC), the Asian Group, the Group of Central European and Baltic States, the Group of Eastern European and Central Asian Countries, and China, which is considered a group unto itself.[87] Whereas, prior to 1996, Group B did not express joint statements or positions, it now does, as do the other regional groups. As such, the regional group system has become integral to the structure of negotiations at WIPO, with the expression of regional group positions being central.

While regional groupings of member states make sense for some matters, such as the allocation of seats on committees with limited membership, the allocation of chair positions, or the delivery of technical "assistance" on a regional basis, regional grouping also comes with significant drawbacks, especially for developing countries. This is, in a large part, because interests in matters of intellectual property do not generally coincide with particular regions.[88] Regional groups often struggle to find "sufficient commonality of interest to present a compelling position to negotiating partners."[89] This is, in part, because, while there may be various commonalities between industrialized or developing countries, each regional group contains countries from both categories.[90] Abdel Latif notes that the regional group system can allow the will of a majority of developing countries to be overcome by small numbers of countries, or individual countries, within each group that block the majority position.[91] This very problem has prevented the Asian Group and GRULAC from playing a larger role in the substantive deliberations of the TRIPs Council.[92] It is also particularly problematic in the negotiations leading up to diplomatic conferences, which tend to take place on a regional basis.[93]

It may be noted that Group B is not a "regional" group per se, but is a group of industrialized countries from various regions. For that reason, many of the shortcomings that are associated with regional grouping do

[87] Abdel Latif, "Developing Country Coordination in International Standard-Setting," 31–34; Yu, "The Structure and Process of Negotiations," 1445–1453.

[88] Abdel Latif, "Developing Country Coordination in International Standard-Setting," 32; Deere Birkbeck, "Developing Country Coalitions," 11.

[89] Deere Birkbeck, "Developing Country Coalitions," 11.

[90] Abdel Latif, "Developing Country Coordination in International Standard-Setting," 32.

[91] Ibid. [92] Ibid., 33. [93] Ibid., 33–34.

not come into play for Group B, further magnifying their influence. On the other hand, the African Group, a regional group, has also been able to take an active role on substantive issues.[94]

The establishment of the Friends of Development group and the Development Agenda Group is significant because, while not formally recognized as groups within the WIPO system, they represent cross-regional coalitions of developing countries that have been able to take active roles on substantive issues.[95] While optimists see the rise of coalitions of developing countries in general as "attenuating the asymmetries of power," at least in a WTO context, more pessimistic analysts argue that such coalitions "have diminished the appearance but not the reality, of exclusion from the process" and that "optimism about the rise of coalitions at the WTO is giving unwarranted legitimacy to a negotiating process that remains fundamentally flawed in terms of opportunities for effective representation and participation by small and weak countries, particularly given the realities of their own resource, power and organizational constraints."[96]

Because of the problems associated with regional groupings, Abdel Latif recommends that WIPO should reconsider the involvement of regional groups in the work of the organization, and that cross-regional groupings at WIPO be further institutionalized.[97] Deere Birkbeck notes that coalitions can be regional, issue-based, or based around characteristics or like-mindedness; of these, she finds that issue-based coalitions are often perceived to be the most effective.[98] The Development Agenda Group and the Friends of Development, as issue-based coalitions as well as coalitions that are based on a degree of like-mindedness, may be two successful examples of effective coalitions of the sort suggested by Abdel Latif and Deere Birkbeck. At the same time, such coalitions are clearly not a panacea; Chapter 7 above raised questions about the extent to which such coalitions have been successful in furthering principles of access at WIPO.

Conclusions

The *Berne Convention* was founded in the heyday of colonialism, and many of its original colonial features – the norms set during the days that France had multiple votes, the colonies clause, and the safeguard

[94] Ibid., 33. [95] Ibid., 33. [96] Deere Birkbeck, "Developing Country Coalitions," 3.
[97] Abdel Latif, "Developing Country Coordination in International Standard-Setting," 34.
[98] Deere Birkbeck, "Developing Country Coalitions," 4.

clause – are still in place. These features' importance is reduced due to decolonization, but their effects remain since they have constructed, in combination with the *TRIPs Agreement*, a system from which there is virtually no exit and to which alternatives have been eliminated, making alternate norms and principles of access difficult to imagine.

The transformation to a member-state-controlled UN agency has brought with it more formal opportunities for member state oversight, and increased potential for developing country involvement. However, the transformation of WIPO's funding model, the growth of its bureaucracy, its questionable implementation of consensus voting, and its reliance on regional negotiating groups all contribute to the maintenance of the *status quo* at WIPO.

WIPO's institutional norms mitigate against transformation of the status quo. In this light, the successes achieved by the A2K movement to date appear all the more remarkable.

CONCLUSION

> [T]he moment of truth is fast approaching for the international intellectual property system: Can it evolve from a system serving predominantly the interests of inventors and authors and intellectual property-based industries of developed countries to a more inclusive system that addresses the needs of users and consumers everywhere and of developing countries?[1]

This question, posed by Ahmed Abdel Latif, a founder of the A2K movement and former Egyptian delegate to WIPO, is a crucial one for the A2K movement. Despite the increasing involvement of developing countries and access-oriented NGOs in WIPO negotiations, the principles of access to news, scientific information, educational materials, and translations have narrowed, rather than broadened, over the course of the long history of the Berne system of international copyright. The A2K movement's successes have challenged these trends. However, we do not yet know whether the decades ahead will be known as the age of A2K, or the age of the A2K problem.

We can point to three broad reasons for the gradual loss of principles of access in the history of the Berne system of international copyright. First, we can point to ideas. Principles of access are negotiated within the broader context of competing ideas and visions of development, as promoted by interested actors in state, market, and civil society sectors, and as mediated by the institutions in which they are negotiated. A variety of ideas and visions of development, as seen in Chapter 2, have been reflected in the history of international copyright. In the Berne system, a vision of copyright as a "power tool" of national economic development has been grafted onto a system originally designed almost exclusively to develop not whole economies, but copyright owners' rights. "Development" originally meant the development of international society and an international union for the protection of copyright. This "work of civilization," cast what it deemed at the time to be "uncivilized" countries

[1] Abdel Latif, "Change and Continuity," 54.

out of the "realm of legality," recognizing those outside neither as authors of works nor as authors of law.[2]

The A2K movement thus faces a legacy of colonialism and neocolonialism as it attempts to confront an international copyright system with a history and an institutional framework that has eroded, rather than expanded, principles of access to knowledge. As discussed in Chapter 3, the principle of access to scientific works, once passionately articulated by Louis-Joseph Janvier, was abandoned in light of the globalization, privatization, and commercialization of science. The need to disseminate scientific knowledge, obvious in the 1880s just as knowledge about infectious disease, immunology, and preventive medicine began to show the promise of its tremendous impact, gave way to increasing privatization of scientific knowledge and visions of the development of its potential economic value.

The principle of access to educational works, discussed in Chapter 4, was similarly narrowed. Many Western copyright systems have taken the encouragement of education and learning as a central purpose of copyright, thus connecting copyright to national, economic, and cultural development. The need for access to educational materials appeared all the more pressing following the postwar phase of decolonization. However, the rise of a worldview that saw some societies and peoples as "developed," and others as "underdeveloped" meant that the latter came to be exclusively regarded as the beneficiaries of narrow principles of access to educational works that would flow, in the form of Western knowledge containers, from the North to the South.[3] The failure of the measures established under this worldview in 1971 to adequately ensure access to educational works has left an information famine that continues to plague schools and educational institutions, alongside a failure to recognize traditional knowledge and alternative norms of knowledge governance. The principle of access to works in translation, discussed in Chapter 6, also fell prey to this worldview, allowing only narrow provisions for providing access to translation.

The principle of access to news befell the same fate, as noted in Chapter 5. When the *Berne Convention* was founded in the days of imperialism, the dominant vision of development was connected to the expansion of imperialism and the diffusion of imperial ideology, facilitated by widespread access to imperial news services like Reuters. Copyright in news was not

[2] Actes 1886, 153; Anghie, "Finding the Peripheries," 31.
[3] Escobar, *Encountering Development.*

a priority, and indeed went against the norms of the press in core countries at the time. At the same time, copyright in telegraphic news was, in some cases, established – especially where such copyright could be used as a tool against anti-imperial or nationalistic publications. Later, multinational news corporations adopted a more proprietary view of news. Principles of access to news in international copyright thus narrowed alongside the rise of media conglomerates and market-oriented visions of development and media hegemony.

A second reason for the loss and reduction of principles of access is the inclusion and exclusion of particular interest groups from negotiations, affecting the priorities and visions of development that dominated within the Union, as described in Part II of this book. The ability to participate in the construction of such visions, and to be a "nodal point" on the international networks where visions of the future of international copyright are constructed, has recently allowed the A2K movement to have significant impact.[4] However, while developing countries and NGOs promoting user rights gained an increasing presence at international copyright negotiations, they entered a field in which many of the relevant battles had already been lost. In recent decades of copyright norm-setting, NGOs' roles in agenda-setting and participation in negotiations have been reduced. NGOs are less often embedded in state delegations, where they have fuller access to negotiators, and their proposals are seldom taken as part of the conference preparatory material – two advantages that ALAI, as the dominant NGO in the early days of the Berne Union, had had. Further, some NGOs promoting principles of access have had difficulty obtaining, or been rejected for, observer status at WIPO. WIPO thus isolates itself from key "nodal points" promoting alternative models of international copyright.

The increasing number of developing countries that have come to participate in international copyright negotiations, in the face of narrowed ideas of what access principles were appropriate and to whom they should be applied, has done little to shift the balance between principles of access and principles of protection. By the time most developing countries entered international copyright negotiations in the 1950s and 1960s, many principles of access to knowledge, which had been widely used by the core members of the *Berne Convention*, had been significantly narrowed.

At the same time, as Part I of this book shows, developing country state delegations were not historically the sole promoters of principles of access. Developing country delegates have been successful primarily when

[4] Lyotard, *The Postmodern Condition.*

they have been backed by "developed" countries. The UK and Germany played important roles in establishing some access principles. British colonial ties, in the developing countries of Canada, India, and other British colonies, had enrolled a powerful member of the Berne Union into a project of "less is more" international copyright. Thus, one of the problems that the A2K movement often faces today is the abandonment by more powerful states of the project and principles of access to knowledge.

It may be, as noted in Chapter 8, that proponents of principles of access in international copyright seek, in NGOs and middle or emerging countries, a set of heroic underdogs to advocate principles of access. Neither NGOs nor middle powers, however, consistently fit this ideal. Middle powers have played important roles in maintaining existing principles of access, but have failed to coalesce into a group or coalition of their own. Their role, nevertheless, has been important in maintaining and extending principles of access.

A third reason for the loss and reduction of principles of access, as discussed in Part III, is that institutional factors, including Berne and UCC norms that locked countries in to the Berne system of international copyright, have eliminated alternatives to the Berne system of copyright. The growing bureaucracy of WIPO, along with a flawed system of consensus and a regional group system inherited from the United Nations, all mitigate against efforts to create change.

Alan Story, Colin Darch, and Debora Halbert argue that "the focus needs to become not on how to take over WIPO – an unlikely scenario indeed – or how to reform it, but rather on it how to abolish it and start building a new organisation from the ground up."[5] New organizations and alternatives are important not only in and of themselves but also, as we have seen, because they place pressure for change on existing institutions. Historically, change in the Berne Union and WIPO has often been driven by competition from outside regimes and institutions.

As noted in Chapter 10, the mechanisms for the realization of a global polity in the global governance of copyright are "severely underdeveloped."[6] The principles of access to scientific knowledge, education, news, and works in translation are severely underdeveloped at the international level; the participation of developing countries, NGOs, and indigenous peoples has been highly inadequate and unequal; and many of the institutional structures in place either reflect or continue to reinforce

[5] Story, Darch, and Halbert, *The Copy/South Dossier*, 87.
[6] May and Sell, *Intellectual Property Rights*, 218.

colonial and neocolonial structures. As a result of the shortcomings of global governance, based in broader material inequalities, the workings of global copyright governance are, as May and Sell note, "unlikely to be just."[7] Even so, we are reluctant to see WIPO as *simply* a continuation of the inequalities of empire. WIPO's ability to encompass its margins and to include the excluded, contains *in principle*, the potential to mitigate neocolonial tendencies.[8]

A2K x 3

A Canadian delegate in 1971 proclaimed, "We are all developing countries."[9] Recent economic, social, technological, and cultural changes have been dramatic in many countries and not only in those typically referred to as "developing." The potentials for both increased access to, and increased ownership of, science and culture are at heights never before seen.

The A2K movement, in light of such potentials, must focus on three things. Not only is access to knowledge premised, first, on access to *ideas*: access to the sources of knowledge to memory and databanks, to copyright works, to corpora of scientific and technological knowledge; it is also related, second, to the recognition of the *interests* of particular groups and their legitimate right to have a voice: the ability to be recognized as a source of knowledge, to influence the direction and shape of the discourse that defines what knowledge is, what knowledge is valued, and what knowledge is recognized as being knowledge.[10] Third, access to knowledge involves access to the processes and *institutions* such as educational, scientific, political, and regulatory institutions that are central to the production of knowledge. It may involve, also, the construction of new and competing institutions, or the transformation of existing institutions that, as noted throughout these chapters, may be highly resistant to transformation.

Path dependency and critical junctures

Today, the hope of realizing technological and human potential by making knowledge more accessible rests on the ability to innovate and transform

[7] Ibid. [8] Pahuja, "The Postcoloniality of International Law," 460.

[9] *Records of the Conference for Revision of the Universal Copyright Convention*, UNESCO *House, Paris*, July 5–24, 1971, 105.

[10] Lyotard, *The Postmodern Condition*, 67.

both intellectual property systems and non-property methods of knowledge governance. However, the history of international copyright is the history of disappearing alternatives. Principles of access to news, scientific knowledge, educational materials, and works in translation, among other principles of access, were once entirely within reach: the evidence of their possibility was inscribed in national and international law. However, the narrowing of the path of international copyright and the elimination of alternative paths, both normatively and institutionally, have led to growing levels of path dependency. Such path dependency mitigates against innovation in national and international copyright.

The narrowing of ideas, principles, and models is one form of path dependency. The exclusion or marginalization of groups, such as indigenous peoples, or the Pirate Party International, from or within negotiations creates a second form of path dependency that entrenches the interests, knowledge, and voices of some at the core of international norm-setting, tending to reinforce existing approaches. Institutional features that prohibit exit from the international copyright regime, require entry, or grant power to entrenched players, create a third form of path dependency.

While path dependency is pervasive in politics, in the dynamic area of international intellectual property, there is no shortage of critical junctures that can spark meso-level change. Some critical junctures are routine, occurring in the agenda-setting and negotiation phases of international copyright norm revision. Others are sparked by the initiative of specific players who act to set seeds for the growth of new norms, new players, and new institutions. Others still are the result of opportunities seized out of the unintended consequences of prior events.

The future of access to knowledge rides not on some tidal wave of inevitable progress but on the long-term efforts of A2K advocates to work against the current and against time, as the scope of possible alternatives threatens to further narrow. Having achieved an historic step in the establishment of the *Marrakesh Treaty*, the A2K movement's further success depends, in part, on the construction of common interests in access, held between more powerful state, civil society, and market actors, and between developing and "developed" countries. Success also depends on retaining and creating spaces for innovation and alternative models of knowledge governance. A shared future of A2K, or of the A2K problem, rests in the balance.

BIBLIOGRAPHY

Archival sources

Library and Archives Canada

Department of External Affairs fonds, RG25
  G-1, Vol. 1491, file 278, pt. B
  G-1, Vol. 1491, file 278, pt. III
  Vol. 1490, file 1827–278, pts. 1 and 2
  Vol. 5169, file 5582-U-2–40
  Vol. 10902, file 55–19-WIPO 1970, vols. 4, 5–1, and 5–2
  Vol. 10904, file 55–19–4-BERNE, pts. 5–1, 6–1, and 6–2
Department of Industry, Trade, and Commerce fonds, RG 20
  Vol. 91, file 22655, Vol. 1
Department of Justice fonds, RG13
  A-2, Vol. 85, file 892–217
Secretary of State fonds, RG6
  RG6 A3, Vol. 214, file: "Copyright Conference at Berne, 1886."

National Archives of Australia

Attorney-General's Department, Central Office fonds
  Series A2863 Control 1912/20 Part 2 F Copyright Act 1912

National Archives of Ireland

Department of Foreign Affairs fonds
  DFA/408/51
  DFA/408/136
  DFA LN 6/5

National Archives of South Africa

National Archives Repository (Public records of former Transvaal Province and its predecessors as well as of magistrates and local authorities) (TAB)

CS Vol. 154 Ref. 13027/02: newspapers using Reuter's telegraphic news without authority or payment

LD Vol. 411 Ref. AG1881/03 Part 1 Admission into the Transvaal of British Copyright Works

National Archives Repository (public records of central government since 1910) (SAB)

BTS System 01 Reference 38/6 Part 7 International Copyright Convention

Swiss Federal Archives

Department of Foreign Affairs fonds

Int. Büro für gewerbl., lit., u. künstl. Eigentum. Geschäftsberichte, 1943–1945 (Dossier) E2001D#1000/1553#7840* (4–51)

Department of International Organizations (1950–1972) (1945–1980) fonds

Activité, travaux – Généralités Rapports de gestion (1955–1957) E2003A#1970/115#109* (4–102)

United States National Archives and Records Administration

General records of the Department of State fonds, RG59

Records relating to international copyright matters, 1923–1959, Entry 5211 150–68–32–1 Box 1

Secondary sources

Abdel Latif, Ahmed. "Change and Continuity in the International Intellectual Property System: A Turbulent Decade in Perspective," *WIPO Journal* 3 no. 1 (2011): 36–55.

"The Emergence of the A2K Movement: Reminiscences and Reflections of a Developing-Country Delegate," In *Access to Knowledge in the Age of Intellectual Property*, 99–125. Edited by Gaëlle Krikorian and Amy Kapczynski. Cambridge, Mass.: Massachusetts Institute of Technology Press, 2010.

About Three Percent. www.rochester.edu/College/translation/threepercent/index.php?s = about (Accessed on March 27, 2015).

Abelson, Harold et al. *Report to the President: MIT and the Prosecution of Aaron Swartz.* Cambridge, MA: Massachusetts Institute of Technology, 2013.

Akpan, M.B. "Black Imperialism: Americo-Liberian Rule over the African Peoples of Liberia 1841–1964," *Canadian Journal of African Studies* 7 no. 2 (1973): 217–236.

Allen, Gene. "News as Property: The Case of Associated Press, 1942–1945," Paper presented at the *Annual Meeting of the International Communication Association*, May 25, 2014, Seattle.

Anderson, Carol. "International Conscience, the Cold War, and Apartheid: The NAACP's Alliance with the Reverend Michael Scott for South West Africa's Liberation, 1946–1951," *Journal of World History* 19 no. 3 (2008): 297–325.

Anderson, Tim. *6 Reasons Open Access Matters to the Medical Community*. Washington, DC: The Right to Research Coalition, 2011.

Anghie, Antony. "Colonialism and the Birth of International Institutions: Sovereignty, Economy, and the Mandate System of the League of Nations," *New York Journal of International Law* 34 no. 3 (2002): 513–633.

"Finding the Peripheries: Sovereignty and Colonialism in Nineteenth-Century International Law," *Harvard International Law Journal* 40 no. 1 (Winter 1999): 1–71.

Argentina and Brazil. *Proposal by Argentina and Brazil for the Establishment of a Development Agenda for WIPO.* WO/GA/31/11. Geneva: WIPO, 2004.

Arsenault, Amelia and Manuel Castells, "Switching Power: Rupert Murdoch and the Global Business of Media Politics," *International Sociology* 23 no. 4 (2008): 488–513.

Armstrong, Chris, Jeremy de Beer, Dick Kawooya, Achal Prabhala, and Tobias Schonwetter, eds. *Access to Knowledge in Africa: The Role of Copyright*. Cape Town: University of Cape Town Press, 2010.

Ashcroft, Bill, Gareth Griffiths, and Helen Tiffin, eds. *The Post-Colonial Studies Reader*. London: Routledge, 1985.

Baig, Assed. "Malala Yousafzai and the White Saviour Complex." *Huffington Post*, 15 July 2013.

Bannerman, Sara. "The Development Agenda at WIPO: Where Is Canada?" In *Innovation, Science and Environment: Canadian Policies and Performance 2008–2009*, 190–208. Edited by Glen Toner. Montreal and Kingston: McGill-Queen's University Press, 2008.

The Struggle for Canadian Copyright: From Imperialism to Internationalism. Vancouver: University of British Columbia Press, 2013.

"The World Intellectual Property Organization and the Anti-Counterfeiting Trade Agreement Threat (WIPO and the ACTA Threat)," *International Journal of Technology Policy and Law* 1, no. 1 (2012): 3–14.

Bannerman, Sara and Blayne Haggart. "Historical Institutionalism in Communication Studies," *Communication Theory* 25, no. 1 (2015): 1–22.

Baker, Gavin. "Open Access and the New WIPO Director." www.gavinbaker.com/blog/2008/09/23/open-access-and-the-new-wipo-director/ (Accessed March 27, 2015).

Barton, John H. and Keith E. Maskus. "Economic Perspectives on a Multilateral Agreement on Open Access to Basic Science and Technology," *SCRIPT-Ed* 1, no. 3 (September 2004): 369–387.

Basalamah, Salah. "Compulsory Licensing for Translation: An Instrument of Development," *IDEA* 40 (2000): 503.

Le droit de traduire: une politique culturelle pour la mondialisation. Ottawa: Les Presses de l'Université d'Ottawa, 2008.

Battiste, Marie. "Post-colonial Remedies for Protecting Indigenous Knowledge and Heritage," Chapter 15 in *Teaching as Activism: Equity Meets Environmentalism*, 224–232. Montreal and Kingston: McGill-Queens University Press, 2005.

Bellido, Jose. "Latin American and Spanish Copyright Relations (1880–1904)," *The Journal of World Intellectual Property* 12 no. 1 (2009): 1–39.

Benkler, Yochai. *The Wealth of Networks: How Social Production Transforms Markets and Freedom.* New Haven: Yale University Press, 2007.

Bently, Lionel. "Copyright and the Victorian Internet: Telegraphic Property Laws in Colonial Australia." *Loyola of Los Angeles Law Review* 38 (2004–2005). 71–176.

"Copyright, Translations, and Relations between Britain and India in the Nineteenth and Early Twentieth Centuries," *Chicago-Kent Law Review* 82 no. 3 (2007): 1181–1240.

Bently, Lionel and Brad Sherman. "Great Britain and the Signing of the Berne Convention in 1886," *Journal of the Copyright Society of the USA* 48 no. 3 (2001): 311–40.

Bettig, Ronald V. *Copyrighting Culture: The Political Economy of Intellectual Property.* Westview Press, 1996.

Birnhack, Michael D. *Colonial Copyright: Intellectual Property in Mandate Palestine.* Oxford: Oxford University Press, 2012.

"The Idea of Progress in Copyright Law," *Buffalo Intellectual Property Law Journal* 1 (2001): 1–66.

Boateng, Boatema. *The Copyright Thing Doesn't Work Here: Adinkra and Kente Cloth and Intellectual Property in Ghana.* Minneapolis: University of Minnesota Press, 2011.

Bogsch, Arpad. *The First Twenty-Five Years of the World Intellectual Property Organization from 1967 to 1992.* Geneva: International Bureau of Intellectual Property, 1992.

Bowker, Richard Rogers. *Copyright: Its History and Its Law.* Boston and New York: Houghton Mifflin, 1912.

Bowman, Chakriya. "The Pacific Island Nations: Toward Shared Representation," In *Managing the Challenges of WTO Participation: 45 Case Studies*, 450–458. Edited by Peter Gallagher, Patrick Low, and Andrew L. Stoler. Cambridge: Cambridge University Press, 2005.

Bowrey, Kathy, and Jane Anderson. "The Politics of Global Information Sharing: Whose Cultural Agendas Are Being Advanced?" *Social & Legal Studies* 18 (December 2009): 479–504.

Braithwaite, John, and Peter Drahos. *Global Business Regulation.* Cambridge: Cambridge University Press, 2000.

"Ratcheting Up and Driving Down Global Regulatory Standards," *Development* 42 no. 4 (1999) 109–114.

Brazil, Ecuador and Paraguay. *Proposal by Brazil, Ecuador and Paraguay, Relating to Limitations and Exceptions: Treaty Proposed by the World Blind Union (WBU).* SCCR/18/5. Geneva: WIPO, 2009.

"Budapest Open Access Initiative." www.budapestopenaccessinitiative.org/read (Accessed March 27, 2015).

Burke, Peter. *A Social History of Knowledge: from Gutenberg to Diderot.* Cambridge: Polity Press, 2000.

Burns, John. "Media Player," *SundayTimes.co.uk*, November 16, 2013.

Canada. House of Commons of Canada. *Debates of the House of Commons, Fifth Session – Thirteenth Parliament 11–12 George V., 1921*, Vol. CXLVI. Ottawa: F.A. Acland, 1921.

Canagarajah, A. Suresh. *A Geopolitics of Academic Writing.* Pittsburgh: University of Pittsburgh Press, 2002.

Carlsson, Ulla. "The Rise and Fall of NWICO – and Then? From a Vision of International Regulation to a Reality of Multilevel Governance," from *EURICOM Colloquium in Venice – Information Society: Visions and Governance*, May 5–7, 2003.

Carroll, Michael. "The Struggle for Music Copyright," in *Villanova University School of Law: School of Law Working Papers*, Paper 31 (Villanova, PA: Villanova School of Law, 2005), 956, http://law.bepress.com/villanovalwps/papers/art31.

Cassedy, Claire. "KEI Comments regarding USTR Public Interest Trade Advisory Committee." *Knowledge Ecology International*, March 25, 2014, http://keionline.org/node/1983 (accessed March 27, 2015).

Center for International Environmental Law. *A Citizen's Guide to WIPO.* Washington, DC, and Geneva: Center for International Environmental Law, 2007.

Chakrabarty, Dipesh. *Provincializing Europe: Postcolonial Thought and Historical Difference.* Princeton, NJ: Princeton University Press, 2009.

Chang, Ha-Joon. *Kicking Away the Ladder: Development Strategy in Historical Perspective.* London: Anthem Press, 2002.

Chapman, Audrey R. "A Human Rights Perspective on Intellectual Property, Scientific Progress, and Access to the Benefits of Science," Paper presented at *WIPO Panel Discussion on Intellectual Property and Human Rights*, November 8, 1998. Geneva: WIPO, 1998.

Chile. *Proposal by Chile on the Analysis of Exceptions and Limitations.* SCCR/13/5. Geneva: WIPO, 2005.

Proposal by Chile on the Subject "Exceptions and Limitations to Copyright and Related Rights." SCCR/12/3. Geneva: WIPO, 2004.

Chon, Margaret. "Intellectual Property 'From Below': Copyright and Capability for Education," *UC Davis Law Review* 40 no. 3 (2007): 805–854.

"Postmodern Progress: Reconsidering the Copyright and Patent Power," *DePaul Law Review* 43 no. 1 (1993): 97–146.

Clark, Ian. *The Hierarchy of States.* Cambridge: Cambridge University Press, 1989.

Commission on Intellectual Property Rights. *Integrating Intellectual Property Rights and Development Policy: Report of the Commission on Intellectual Property Rights.* London: WIPO/WTO/TRIPS, 2002.

Consumers International. *Copyright and Access to Knowledge: Policy Recommendations on Flexibilities in Copyright Laws.* Kuala Lumpur: Consumers International Asia Pacific Office, 2006.

Coombe, Rosemary. "The Recognition of Indigenous Peoples' and Community Traditional Knowledge in International Law," *St. Thomas Law Review* 14 (2001): 275–285.

CPTech. *Treaty on Access to Knowledge, Draft of 9 May 2005.* www.cptech.org/a2k/a2k_treaty_may9.pdf (Accessed March 31, 2015).

CP Tech. *Access to Knowledge.* www.cptech.org/a2k/a2k-debate.html (Accessed March 27, 2015).

Dayan, Joan. *Haiti, History and the Gods.* Berkeley and Los Angeles, Calif.: University of California Press, 1995.

Deere, Caroline. *The Implementation Game: The TRIPS Agreement and the Global Politics of Intellectual Property Reform in Developing Countries.* Oxford: Oxford University Press, 2008.

Deere Birkbeck, Carolyn. "Developing Country Coalitions in the WTO: Strategies for Improving the Influence of the WTO's Weakest and Poorest Members Policy Brief for the IDEAS Centre." Geneva: IDEAS, 2011.

Deere Birkbeck, Carolyn and Santiago Roca. *An External Review of WIPO Technical Assistance in the Area of Cooperation for Development.* CDIP/8/INF/1/ANNEX1. Geneva: WIPO, 2011.

Deschamps, Christine, Kay Raseroka, Barbara Kirsop, Jean-Jacques Pierrat, Georges Malamoud, Barbara Aronson, and Manfred Spiesberger. "Round Table: Open Access Issues for Developing Countries," *Information Services and Uses* 23 no. 2–3 (2003): 149–159.

Doyle, Cathal and Jérémie Gilbert. "Indigenous Peoples and Globalization: From 'Development Aggression' to 'Self-Determined Development,'" *European Yearbook of Minority Issues* 7 (2008/2009): 219–262.

Downes, David. "Using Intellectual Property as a Tool to Protect Traditional Knowledge: Recommendations for Next Steps," *Center for International Environmental Law (CIEL)* Discussion Paper. Madrid: CIEL, 1997.

Drahos, Peter. *A Philosophy of Intellectual Property.* London: Ashgate, 1996.

"'IP World' – Made by TNC Inc.," In *Access to Knowledge in the Age of Intellectual Property*, 197–216. Edited by Gaëlle Krikorian and Amy Kapczynski. New York: Zone Books, 2010.

"When the Weak Bargain with the Strong: Negotiations in the World Trade Organization," *International Negotiation* 8 (2003): 79–109.

Drahos, Peter, and John Braithwaite. *Information Feudalism: Who Owns the Knowledge Economy?* London: Earthscan Publications, 2002.

Drahos, Peter and Susy Frankel. "Indigenous Peoples' Innovation and Intellectual Property: The Issues," Chapter 1 in *Indigenous Peoples' Innovation: Intellectual Property Pathways to Development*, 1–29. Edited by Peter Drahos and Susy Frankel. Canberra: Australian National University E Press, 2012.

Escobar, Arturo. *Encountering Development: The Making and Unmaking of the Third World.* Princeton, New Jersey: Princeton University Press, 1995.

Eyers, James. "Facing up to the IP Tsunami," *Australian Financial Review*, August 11, 2009.

Ficsor, Mihály J. "Commentary to the Marrakesh Treaty on Accessible Format Copies for the Visually Impaired," *Copyright See-Saw.net* (2013). www.copyrightseesaw.net/archive/?sw_10_item=50 (Accessed March 27, 2015).

Finnemore, Martha and Michael N. Barnett. "The Politics, Power and Pathologies of International Organizations," *International Organizations* 53 no. 4 (1999): 699–732.

Flynn, Sean. "Special 301 and Global Administrative Law," In *Balancing Wealth and Health: The Battle over Intellectual Property and Access to Medicines in Latin America*, 225–246. Edited by Rochelle Dreyfuss and César Rodríguez-Garavito. Oxford: Oxford University Press, 2014.

Foundation for Aboriginal and Islander Research Action. *Submission to the WIPO Secretariat on Indigenous Peoples' Effective Participation in WIPO on GRTKF.* Geneva: WIPO, 2011.

Fraser, Nancy. "Behind Marx's Hidden Abode: For an Expanded Conception of Capitalism," *New Left Review* 86 (March 2014): 55–72.

Friends of Development. *Proposal to Establish a Development Agenda for the World Intellectual Property Organization (WIPO): An Elaboration of Issues Raised in Document. WO/GA/31/11.* IIM/1/4 Annex. Geneva: WIPO, 2005.

Fuhrmans, Vanessa. "New German Bill is Key Win for Google," *Wall Street Journal Europe*, 4 (March 2013).

Gandhi, Leela. *Postcolonial Theory: A Critical Introduction.* New York: Columbia University Press, 1998.

Geneva Declaration on the Future of WIPO. www.futureofwipo.org/ (Accessed March 27, 2015).

Ghosh, S. B. and Anup Kumar Das. "Open Access and Institutional Repositories – A Developing Country Perspective: A Case Study of India," In *72nd IFLA Council and General Conference*, Seoul, August 20–24, 2006.

"Googling the News; European Publishers Want to Fleece Their Online Middleman," *The Wall Street Journal Online*, November 7, 2012.

Green, Leslie. "Legal Positivism," In *Stanford Encyclopedia of Philosophy*, Fall 2009 edition. Edited by Edward N. Zalta. http://plato.stanford.edu/archives/fall2009/entries/legal-positivism/ (Accessed March 27, 2015).

Greenleaf, Graham and Catherine Bond. "'Public Rights' in Copyright: What Makes Up Australia's Public Domain?" *Australian Intellectual Property Journal* 23 (2013): 111–138.

Gross, Robin. "The World Intellectual Property Organization (WIPO)," In *Global Information Society Watch*, 65–73. Edited by Karen Banks, Roberto Bissio, Willie Currie, Anriette Esterhuysen, Chat Garcia Ramilo, and Magela Sigillito. Melville: Association for Progressive Communications and Humanist Institute for Cooperation with Developing Countries, 2007.

Gurry, Francis. "Opening Speech by Francis Gurry, Director General, World Intellectual Property Organization, to the Marrakesh Diplomatic Conference," June 17–28, 2013. www.wipo.int/about-wipo/en/dgo/speeches/dg_dc2013.html (Accessed March 27, 2015).

Haggart, Blayne. *Copyfight: The Global Politics of Digital Copyright Reform*. Toronto: University of Toronto Press, 2014.

Halbert, Debora J. *Resisting Intellectual Property*. London and New York: Routledge, 2005.

The State of Copyright: The Complex Relationships of Cultural Creation in a Globalized World. London and New York: Routledge, 2014.

Handa, Sunny. "A Review of Canada's International Copyright Obligations," *McGill Law Journal* 42 no. 4 (1997): 961–990.

Hannum, Hurst. "New Developments in Indigenous Rights," *Vanderbilt Journal of International Law* 28 (1988), 649–678.

Hargreaves, Ian. *Digital Opportunity: Review of Intellectual Property and Growth*. London: Department for Business, Innovation, and Skills, 2011.

Heclo, Hugh. "Ideas, Interests, and Institutions," In *The Dynamics of American Politics: Approaches & Interpretations*, 366–392. Edited by Lawrence C. Dodd and Calvin Jillson. Boulder: Westview Press, 1994.

Idris, Kamil. *Intellectual Property: A Power Tool for Economic Growth*. Geneva: WIPO, 2003.

Incomindios. "Statement Presented by Ambassador Ronald Barnes to the 50th General Assembly of WIPO on Behalf of Incomindios," *IP-Watch*, October 4, 2012. www.ip-watch.org/weblog/wp-content/uploads/2012/10/WIPO-GA-50-Incomindios-statement.pdf (Accessed March 27, 2015).

"Israeli Expert, Invited by U.S., Gives Views in Washington on Patents," *Jewish Telegraphic Agency*, October 21, 1965.

Janke, Terri. "Managing Indigenous Knowledge and Indigenous Cultural and Intellectual Property," In *Australian Indigenous Knowledge and Libraries*, 83–93. Edited by Martin Nakata and Marcia Langton. Sydney: Sydney University Press, 2005.

Johnson, C.F. "The Origins of the Stockholm Protocol," *Bulletin of the Copyright Society of the USA* 18 (1970): 91–108.

Jordaan, Eduard. "The Concept of a Middle Power in International Relations: Distinguishing between Emerging and Traditional Middle Powers," *Politikon* 30 no. 2 (2003): 165–181.

Jordans, Frank. "German Publishers Opt to Stay on Google News for Now, as New Copyright Law Comes into Effect," Associated Press Newswires, August 1, 2013.

"Jose Maria Torres Caicedo," *Famous Americans.* http://famousamericans.net/josemariatorrescaicedo/ (Accessed March 27, 2015).

Kampelman, Max M. "The United States and International Copyright," *American Journal of International Law* 41 no. 2 (1947): 406–429.

Kapczynski, Amy. "The Access to Knowledge Mobilization and the New Politics of Intellectual Property," *Yale Law Journal* 117 no. 804 (2008): 804–885.

Ketzan, Erik. "Rebuilding Babel: Copyright and the Future of Machine Translation Online," *Tulane Journal of Technology & Intellectual Property* 9 (Spring 2007): 205–234.

Kim, Chin. "Librarians and Copyright Legislation: The Historical Background," *American Libraries* 2 no. 6 (June 1971): 615–622.

King, David A. "The Scientific Impact of Nations," *Nature* 430 no. 6997 (July 15, 2004): 314.

Kirsop, Barbara and Subbiah Arunachalam. *Open Access Archiving: The Fast Track to Building Research Capacity in Developing Countries.* London: Science and Development Network, 2005,

Knutsson, Benjamin. "The Intellectual History of Development: Towards a Widening Potential Repertoire," *Perspectives* 13 (April 2009): 2–46.

Koskenniemi, Martti. *The Gentle Civilizer of Nations: The Rise and Fall of International Law, 1870–1960.* Cambridge: Cambridge University Press, 2002.

Ladd, David. "Address: Copyright and the Re-Emergence of the Middle Kingdom," *American Bar Association, Section of Patent Trademark and Copyright Law Proceedings* 94 (1984): 94–97.

Lazar, Alan H. "Developing Countries and Authors' Rights," *Copyright Law Symposium* 19 (1971): 1–42.

Leonard, Karen Isaksen. *Immigrant Faiths: Transforming Religious Life in America.* Walnut Creek: AltaMira Press, 2005.

Levitsky, Serge L. "The Union of Berne at 100: What Keeps the Superpowers at Bay? Thoughts and Apprehensions," In *Law and the Gorbachev Era: Essays in Honour of Dietrich André Loeber*, 271–373. Dordecht: Martinus Nijhoff, 1988.

Livingstone, Victoria. "Google, Duolingo, and the Problems of Internet Translation," *Fairobserver.com*, March 28, 2014. www.fairobserver.com/region/north_america/google-duolingo-problems-internet-translation-67312/ (Accessed March 27, 2015).

Löhr, Isabella. "Selling Books: The League of Nations and the Globalization of Intellectual Property Rights in the 1930s," Paper presented at the *11th Annual Conference of the European Business History Association*, September 13–15, 2007.

"Louis Joseph Janvier," Lehman College, Île en île. www.lehman.cuny.edu/ile.en.ile/paroles/janvier.html (Accessed March 27, 2015).

Lyotard, Jean-François. *The Postmodern Condition: A Report on Knowledge.* Minnesota: University of Minnesota Press, 1984.

MacBride, Sean. *Many Voices, One World: Communication and Society, Today and Tomorrow: The MacBride Report.* Paris: UNESCO, 1980.

Mann, David. "WIPO – Advancing Access to Information for Print Disabled People," Paper presented at the *67th Council and General Conference of the International Federation of Library Associations and Institutions (IFLA)*, August 16–25, 2001.

May, Christopher. "Direct and Indirect Influence at the World Intellectual Property Organization," In *Business and Global Governance*, 39–56. Edited by Mortgen Ougaard and Anna Leander. London and New York: Routledge, 2010.

"The World Intellectual Property Organization," *New Political Economy* 11 no. 3 (2006): 435–445.

The World Intellectual Property Organization: Resurgence and the Development Agenda. London: Routledge, 2007.

May, Christopher and Susan K. Sell. *Intellectual Property Rights: A Critical History.* Boulder and London: Lynne Rienner, 2006.

McChesney, Robert. "Will the Last Reporter Please Turn out the Lights?" In *News 2.0. Can Journalism Survive the Internet?* Edited by Martin Hirst. Crows Nest, N.S.W.: Allen & Unwin, 2011.

McIntosh, Toby. "WIPO Transparency Wins Praise, Gaps Remain," *Freedominfo . org*, January 7, 2014. www.freedominfo.org/2014/01/wipo-transparency-wins-praise-gaps-remain/ (Accessed March 27, 2015).

Médecins Sans Frontières, *Trans-Pacific Partnership*, www.msf.ca/en/trans-pacific-partnership (accessed March 12, 2015).

Mick, Jason. "Quick Note: Google Translate Helps Irish Paramedics Deliver a Baby," *DailyTech.com*, 12 February 12, 2015, www.dailytech.com/Quick+Note+Google+Translate+Helps+Irish+Paramedics+Deliver+a+Baby/article37155.htm (accessed March 27, 2015).

Milan, Stefania. *Social Movements and Their Technologies: Wiring Social Change.* New York: Palgrave Macmillan, 2013.

Morin, Jean-Frédéric. *Mapping Prevailing Ideas on Intellectual Property: Preliminary Findings from a Survey.* Geneva: ICTSD, 2013.

"Paradigm Shift in the Global IP Regime: The Agency of Academics," *Review of International Political Economy* 21 no. 2 (2014): 275–309.

Morin, Jean-Frédéric and Edward Richard Gold. "An Integrated Model of Legal Transplantation: The Diffusion of Intellectual Property Law in Developing Countries," *International Studies Quarterly* 58 (2014): 781–792.

Morin, Jean-Frédéric and Sara Bannerman. "Tigers and Dragons at the World Intellectual Property Organization (WIPO)," In *Rising Powers in Multilateral Institutions.* Edited by Dries Lesage and Thijs Van de Graaf. Basingstoke: Palgrave Macmillan, 2015.

N'Diaye, N'Déné. "The Influence of Copyright on Cultural Development in the Developing Countries," *RIDA* 86 (1975).

"The Berne Convention and Developing Countries," *The Columbia-VLA Journal of Law & the Arts* 47 (1986–1987).

Nielson, Lynge. *Classifications of Countries Based on Their Level of Development: How It Is Done and How It Could Be Done.* Washington, DC: IMF, 2011.

Neufeld, Mark. "Hegemony and Foreign Policy Analysis: The Case of Canada as Middle Power," In *Readings in Canadian Foreign Policy: Classic Debates and New Ideas*, 94–107. Edited by Duane Bratt and Christopher J. Kukucha. New York: Oxford University Press, 2006.

New, William. "WIPO Approves 15 New Observers, Including DNDi, COHRED; Pirate Parties Rejected," *IP-Watch*, September 25, 2013. www.ip-watch.org/2013/09/25/wipo-approves-15-new-observers-including-dndi-cohred-pirate-party-rejected/ (Accessed March 27, 2015).

"Experts Debate Access to Knowledge," *IP-Watch*, February 15, 2005. www.ip-watch.org/2005/02/15/experts-debate-access-to-knowledge/ (Accessed March 27, 2015).

Norris, Pippa. *Democratic Phoenix: Reinventing Political Activism.* Cambridge: Cambridge University Press, 2002.

Ntahokaja, Jean-Baptiste. "Rapport présenté par M. l'Abbé Ntahokaja (Burundi) Rapporteur général," *Droit d'Auteur* 76 no. 10 (October 1963): 250–259.

Ntahokaja, Jean-Baptiste. *African Study Meeting on Copyright: Report. RADA/10.* Paris: UNESCO, 1963.

Pahuja, Sundhya. "The Postcoloniality of International Law," *Harvard Journal of International Law* 46 no. 2 (2005): 459–469.

Paranaguá, Pedro. "Strategies to Implement WIPO's Development Agenda: A Brazilian Perspective and Beyond," Chapter 11 in *Implementing the World Intellectual Property Organization's Development Agenda*, 140–157. Edited by Jeremy de Beer. Waterloo, ON: Wilfrid Laurier University Press, CIGI, IDRC, 2009.

"Pays scandinaves," *Le Droit D'Auteur* 5, no. 9 (September 1892): 115–118.

Perkins, Kenneth. *The History of Modern Tunisia.* Cambridge: Cambridge University Press, 2004.

Peukert, Alexander. "Intellectual Property: The Global Spread of a Legal Concept," *Goethe Universität Faculty of Law Research Paper No. 2/2013* (Forthcoming in *Legal Cultures, Legal Transfer, and Legal Pluralism*), http://ssrn.com/abstract=2218292 (Accessed July 17, 2015).

"The Colonial Legacy of the International Copyright System," In *Staging the Immaterial: Rights, Style and Performance in Sub-Saharan Africa.* Edited by Mamadou Diawara and Ute Röschenthaler. Oxford: Sean Kingston, http://ssrn.com/abstract=2057796 (Accessed July 17, 2015).

Pierson, Paul. *Politics in Time: History, Institutions, and Social Analysis.* Princeton and Oxford: Princeton University Press, 2004.

Pimienta, Daniel, Daniel Prado, and Álvaro Blanco. *Twelve Years of Measuring Linguistic Diversity on the Internet: Balance and Perspectives.* Paris: UNESCO, 2009.

Pinedo, Emma. "Spain to Force Search Engines to Pay to Display Some Content," *Reuters News*, February 14, 2014.

Pirate Parties International. *About the PPI.* Brussels: PPI, 2015. www.pp-international.net/about (Accessed March 31, 2015).

Elected Pirates. Brussels: PPI, 2015. http://wiki.pp-international.net/Elected_Pirates (Accessed March 31, 2015).

Plischke, Elmer. *U.S. Department of State: A Reference History.* Westport, Conn.: Greenwood, 1999.

Poppeliers, Natalia Taylor. "Cultural Rights and Library Development and Discourse in Sub-Saharan Africa: Is the Colonial Legacy Still Alive?" In *Beyond Article 19: Libraries and Social and Cultural Rights*, 41–84. Edited by J. B. Edwards and S. P. Edwards. Duluth, MN: Library Juice Press, 2010.

Putnis, Peter. "The Struggle over Copyright in News Telegrams in Australia, 1869–1912," In *When Journalism Meets History 2003*, 58–68. Edited by Sybil Nolan. Melbourne: RMIT Publishing, 2004.

Rahmatian, Andreas."Neo-Colonial Aspects of Global Intellectual Property Protection," *The Journal of World Intellectual Property*, 12, 1 (2009), 40–74.

Read, Donald. "Reuters: News Agency of the British Empire," *Contemporary Record* 8 no. 2 (2008): 195–212.

Ress, Manon. *Timeline: Addressing Copyright Related Barriers to Overcoming Reading Disabilities.* Washington, DC: Knowledge Ecology International, 2009.

Ricketson, Sam. "The Birth of the Berne Union," *Columbia-VLA Journal of Law and the Arts* 11 no. 9 (1986): 9–32.

Ricketson, Sam. *WIPO Study on Limitations and Exceptions of Copyright and Related Rights in the Digital Environment.* SCCR/9/7. Geneva: WIPO, 2003.

Ricketson, Sam, and Jane Ginsburg. *International Copyright and Neighbouring Rights: The Berne Convention and Beyond*, 2nd edition. London: Oxford University Press, 2006.

Rife, Martine Courant. "The Fair Use Doctrine: History, Application, and Implications for (New Media) Writing Teachers," *Computers and Composition* 24 (2007): 154–178.

Roit, Natasha. "Comment: Soviet and Chinese Copyright: Ideology Gives Way to Economic Necessity," *Loyola Entertainment Law Journal* 6 (1986): 53–71.

Saez, Catherine. "Crisis at WIPO over Development Agenda; Overall Objectives in Question," IP-Watch, May 25, 2014.

"Inauspicious Start to Gurry's Second Term as IP Policymaking Hits Wall at WIPO," IP-Watch, October 1, 2014.

Samuelson, Pamela. "The U.S. Digital Agenda at WIPO," *Vanderbilt Journal of International Law* 37 (1996): 369–439.

Shaheed, Farida. *Report of the Special Rapporteur in the Field of Cultural Rights: Copyright Policy and the Right to Science and Culture.* A/HRC/28/57. New York: United Nations, 2014.

Report of the Special Rapporteur in the Field of Cultural Rights: The Right to Enjoy the Benefits of Scientific Progress and Its Applications. A/HRC/20/26. New York: United Nations, 2012.

Shashikant, Sangeeta. "The Doha Declaration on TRIPS and Public Health: An Impetus for Access to Medicines," In *Access to Knowledge in the Age of Intellectual Property*, 141–159. Edited by Gaëlle Krikorian and Amy Kapczynski. New York: Zone Books, 2010.

Schechner, Sam. "Google Settles with Belgian Newspapers amid European Copyright Fights," *Dow Jones Institutional News*, December 13, 2012.

Schiller, Herbert. "Genesis of the Free Flow of Information Principles," In *Communication and Class Struggle*, Volume I: Capitalism, Imperialism, 345–353. Edited by Armand Mattelart and Seth Siegelaub. New York: International General, 1979.

Schwartz, Maxime. "The Life and Works of Louis Pasteur," *Journal of Applied Microbiology* 91 no. 4 (2001): 597–601.

Sell, Susan K. "*Cat and Mouse: Forum-Shifting in the Battle over Intellectual Property Enforcement*," Paper presented at the *American Political Association Meeting*, Toronto, September 3–6, 2009.

Power & Ideas: The North–South Politics of Intellectual Property and Anti-Trust. New York: State University of New York Press, 1998.

Private Power, Public Law: The Globalization of Intellectual Property Rights. Cambridge: Cambridge University Press, 2003.

Shepard, Marietta Daniels. "International Dimension of US Librarianship," *ALA Bulletin* 62 no. 6 (June 1968): 699–710.

Sher, Ze'ev. "Reflections on Copyright in Developing Countries," *Bulletin of the Copyright Society of the USA* (1968–1969): 201.

Sherman, Brad. "From the Non-Original to the Ab-Original: A History," In *Of Authors and Origins: Essays on Copyright Law*, 111–130. Edited by Brad Sherman and Alain Strowel. Oxford: Clarendon Press, 1994.

Shiva, Vandana. "TRIPs, Human Rights, and the Public Domain," *The Journal of World Intellectual Property* 7 no. 5 (2004): 665–673.

Steele, James H. and Peter J. Fernandez, "History of Rabies and Global Aspects," In *The Natural History of Rabies*, 2nd edition, 1–26. Edited by George M.Baer. Boca Raton, FL: CRC Press, 1991.

Story, Alan. "Burn Berne: Why the Leading International Copyright Convention Must Be Repealed," *Houston Law Review* 40 no. 3 (2003): 763–803.

Story, Alan, Colin Darch, and Debora Halbert. *The Copy/South Dossier: Issues in the Economics, Politics, and Ideology of Copyright in the Global South*. Canterbury, UK: Copy/South Research Group, 2006.

Štrba, Susan Isiko. *International Copyright Law and Access to Education in Developing Countries: Exploring Multilateral Legal and Quasi-Legal Solutions*. Leiden: Martinus Nijhoff, 2012.

Stamatopoulou, Elsa. "Indigenous Peoples and the United Nations: Human Rights as a Developing Dynamic," *Human Rights Quarterly* 16 no. 1 (1994): 58–81.

Suljak, Nedjelko D. "Right to Translate and International Copyright Conventions," *Law Library Journal* 62 (1969): 47–57.

Sunder, Madhavi. "The Invention of Traditional Knowledge," *Law and Contemporary Problems* 70 (Spring 2007): 97–124.

Swartz, Aaron. *Guerilla Open Access Manifesto*, July 2008, https://ia600808.us.archive.org/17/items/GuerillaOpenAccessManifesto/Goamjuly2008.pdf.

Taubman, Antony. "Preface: Indigenous Innovation: New Dialogues, New Pathways," Preface to *Indigenous Peoples' Innovation: Intellectual Property Pathways to Development*, xv–xxiv. Edited by Peter Drahos and Susy Frankel. Canberra: Australian National University E Press, 2012.

Tawfik, Myra. "History in the Balance: Copyright and Access to Knowledge," In *In the Public Interest: The Future of Canadian Copyright Law*, 69–89. Edited by Michael Geist. Toronto: Irwin Law, 2005.

Truman, Harry S. Inaugural Address, January 20, 1949.

Tworek, Heidi. "Protecting News before the Internet," In *Making News: Historical Perspectives on the Political Economy of the Press in Great Britain and the United States since 1688*. Edited by Richard R. John and Jonathan Silberstein Loeb. Oxford: Oxford University Press, 2015.

Tworek, Heidi and Christopher Buschow, "History Lessons: Why Germany's 'Google Tax' Won't Work," *Nieman Reports*, October 3, 2014. http://niemanreports.org/articles/history-lessons-why-germanys-google-tax-wont-work/ (Accessed March 27, 2015).

Thelen, Kathleen and Sven Steinmo. "Historical Institutionalism in Comparative Politics," In *Structuring Politics: Historical Institutionalism in Comparative Analysis*, 1–32. Edited by Sven Steinmo, Kathleen Thelen, and Frank Longstreth. Cambridge: Cambridge University Press, 1992.

"Urges Revision of Copyright Laws: Official of British Society says Canada Backward in Protection Legislation: Development Retarded," *Montreal Gazette*, December 6, 1920.

United Kingdom. *Imperial Conference, 1926: Summary of Proceedings*. Cmd. 2768. London: His Majesty's Stationery Office, 1926. http://parlipapers.chadwyck.com.

Minutes of Proceeding of the Imperial Copyright Conference, 1910. Microfilm reels B-2392 to B-2393. Library and Archives Canada.

UNESCO, *Candidates for Election to Executive Board: Curriculum Vitae, Professor Nathaniel V. Massaquoi 8C/NOM/9*. Paris, 1954.

Information Received from Entities of the United Nations System and Other Intergovernmental Organizations: World Intellectual Property Organization E/C.19/2012/5 23 February 2012. United Nations Economic and Social Council, 2012.

The Administrative Obstacles to the Universal Free Flow of Culture, Deriving from the Existence of Copyright. Free Flow Com./14 Paris: UNESCO, October 13, 1947.

UNESCO, Executive Board. *Proposals of the Director-General Concerning Article IX of the Preliminary Draft of the Universal Copyright Convention*. 30/EX/12. Paris: UNESCO, 1952.

42nd Session. *Report of the Director-General on the Activities of the Organization* (March–November 1955). 42 EX/43. Paris: UNESCO, 1955.

United Nations, *United Nations Declaration on the Rights of Indigenous Peoples*. United Nations, 2007.

UNESCO Constitution, art. 1(1).

The Millennium Development Goals, www.undp.org/mdg/? (Accessed March 1, 2015).

United Nations Permanent Forum on Indigenous Issues. "Indigenous Forum Holds Dialogue with World Intellectual Property Organization; Speakers call for Reform, Greater Inclusion of Indigenous in Decision-Making." United Nations Economic and Social Council, May 10, 2012.

Recommendations of the North American Indigenous Peoples' Caucus to the Eleventh Session of the United Nations Permanent Forum on Indigenous Issues. United Nations Permanent Forum on Indigenous Issues, 2012.

Report on the Eleventh Session 7–18 May 2012 E/C.19/2012/13. New York: United Nations Economic and Social Council, 2012.

Declaration on the Rights of Indigenous Peoples. http://undesadspd.org/IndigenousPeoples/DeclarationontheRightsofIndigenousPeoples.aspx (Accessed March 27, 2015).

U.S. Department of State. "U.S. Relations with Liberia," May 5, 2015. www.state.gov/r/pa/ei/bgn/6618.htm (Accessed July 17, 2015).

United States. *Papers Relating to the Foreign Relations of the United States, Transmitted to Congress with the Annual Message of the President*, December 9, 1891. Washington, DC: Government Printing Office, 1892.

United States, National Institutes of Health. *Policy on Enhancing Public Access to Archived Publications Resulting from NIH-Funded Research*. http://grants.nih.gov/grants/guide/notice-files/NOT-OD-05-022.html (Accessed March 1, 2015).

Venuti, Lawrence. *The Scandals of Translation: Towards an Ethics of Difference*. New York: Routledge, 1998.

von Lewinski, Silke. "Copyright in Central and Eastern Europe: An Intellectual Property Metamorphosis," *Fordham Intellectual Property Media & Entertainment Law Journal* 8 no. 1 (1997): 39–61.

von Lewinski, Silke, ed. *Indigenous Heritage and Intellectual Property: Genetic Resources, Traditional Knowledge and Folklore*, 2nd edition. Alphen aan den Rijn: Kluwer Law International, 2008.

Wiesmann, Gerrit. "Axel Springer Expects Google Fee for Web Content," *Financial Times*, Asian edition, March 7, 2013.

Willinsky, John. *The Access Principle: The Case for Open Access to Research and Scholarship*. Cambridge: Massachusetts Institute of Technology Press, 2006.

WIPO, About WIPO Lex. www.wipo.int/wipolex/en/about.html (Accessed March 27, 2015).

Accredited Observers. Geneva: WIPO, n.d. www.wipo.int/members/en/organizations.jsp?type=NGO_INT (Accessed March 27, 2015).

Berne Notification No. 92 Accession by the Russian Federation. Geneva: WIPO, December 9, 1994. www.wipo.int/treaties/en/notifications/berne/treaty_berne_162.html (Accessed March 27, 2015).

Chair's Conclusions, Twenty-Eighth Session of the Standing Committee on Copyright and Related Rights. SCCR/28/REF/CONCLUSIONS. Geneva: WIPO, 2014.

Committee on Development and Intellectual Property, Thirteenth Session, Draft Report. CDIP/13/13 Prov. Geneva: WIPO, 2014.

Coordination Committee, Fourteenth Session (11th Ordinary), WO/CC/XIV/5 (Geneva: WIPO, 1980).

Coordination Mechanisms and Monitoring, Assessing and Reporting Modalities, 2010. www.wipo.int/ip-development/en/agenda/coordination˙mechanisms.html (Accessed March 27, 2015).

Evaluation Report. CDIP/9/7 Annex. Geneva: WIPO, 2012.

Project Evaluation: Intellectual Property Technical Assistance Database. CDIP/9/4. Geneva: WIPO, 2012.

Evaluation Report of the Project on Intellectual Property and the Brain Drain. CDIP/13/6. Geneva: WIPO, 2014.

General Report of the Assemblies of the Member States of WIPO. A/51/20. Geneva: WIPO, 2013.

Independent Evaluation Report of the Technology and Innovation Support Centres (TISCs). CDIP/9/5. Geneva: WIPO, 2012.

Information Note for the Panel of Indigenous and Local Communities. WIPO/GRTKF/IC/23/INF/6. Geneva: WIPO, 2012.

Intellectual Property and Genetic Resources, Traditional Knowledge and Traditional Cultural Expressions: An Overview. Geneva: WIPO, 2012.

Matters Concerning Intellectual Property and Genetic Resources, Traditional Knowledge and Folklore – An Overview. IGC/01/03. Geneva: WIPO, 2001.

Observers. www.wipo.int/members/en/admission/observers.html (Accessed March 27, 2015).

Organizational and Procedural Matters and Overview of Substantive Issues. SCCR/1/2. Geneva: WIPO, 1998.

Progress Reports. CDIP/8/2. Geneva: WIPO, 2011.

Project Evaluation – Development Agenda Recommendation 2: Conference on "Mobilizing Resources for Development." CDIP/9/3. Geneva: WIPO, 2012.

Projects of Implementation of Development Agenda Recommendations. www.wipo.int/ip-development/en/agenda/projects.html (Accessed March 27, 2015).

Provisional Committee on Proposals Related to a WIPO Development Agenda (PCDA). PCDA/3/3 Prov. Geneva: WIPO, 2007.

Regional Bureaus. www.wipo.int/eds/en/ (Accessed March 27, 2015).

Report from the Thirty-First (15th Extraordinary) Session of the WIPO General Assembly. WO/GA/31/15. Geneva: WIPO, 2004.

Report of the Twentieth Session of the Intergovernmental Committee on Intellectual Property and Genetic Resources, Traditional Knowledge and Folklore. WIPO/GRTKF/IC/20. Geneva: WIPO, 2012.

Report of the Twenty-Second Session of the Intergovernmental Committee on Intellectual Property and Genetic Resources, Traditional Knowledge and Folklore July 9–13 2012. WIPO/GRTKF/IC/22. Geneva: WIPO, 2012.

Standing Committee on Copyright and Related Rights. Geneva: WIPO, n.d. www.wipo.int/policy/en/sccr/ (Accessed March 27, 2015).

Standing Committee on Copyright and Related Rights. *Provisional Working Document Towards an Appropriate International Legal Instrument (in Whatever Form) on Limitations and Exceptions for Educational, Teaching and Research Institutions and Persons with Other Disabilities Containing Comments and Textual Suggestions.* SCCR/26/4 Prov. Geneva: WIPO, 2013.

Standing Committee on Copyright and Related Rights, Twenty-Eighth Session, Chair's Conclusions. SCCR/28/REF. Geneva: WIPO, 2014.

Standing Committee on Copyright and Related Rights, Twenty-Seventh Session, Provisional Report. SCCR/27/9PROV. Geneva: WIPO, 2014.

Standing Committee on Copyright and Related Rights, Updated Report on the Questionnaire on Limitations and Exceptions. SCCR/21/7. Geneva: WIPO, 2010.

Start-Up Academies. Geneva: WIPO, n.d. www.wipo.int/academy/en/about/startup_academies/ (Accessed March 31, 2015).

Study on Copyright Limitations and Exceptions for Libraries and Archives. SCCR/29/3. Geneva: WIPO, 2014.

Technical Assistance. Geneva: WIPO, n.d. www.wipo.int/global_ip/en/activities/technicalassistance/ (Accessed March 27, 2015).

The Case for a Treaty on Exceptions and Limitations for Libraries and Archives: Background Paper by IFLA, ICA, EIFL and Innovarte. SCCR/23/3. Geneva: WIPO, 2011.

The 45 Adopted Recommendations under the WIPO Development Agenda. www.wipo.int/ip-development/en/agenda/recommendations.html (Accessed March 27, 2015).

www.wipo.int/tk/en/resources/faqs.html (Accessed March 27, 2015).

Tunis Model Law on Copyright for Developing Countries. Paris and Geneva: UNESCO and WIPO, 1976.

Traditional Knowledge and Intellectual Property – Background Brief www.wipo.int/pressroom/en/briefs/tk_ip.html (Accessed March 30, 2015).

WIPO Academy. Geneva: WIPO, n.d. www.wipo.int/academy/en/ (Accessed March 27, 2015).

WIPO Academy Education and Training Portfolio. Geneva: WIPO, 2015.

WIPO Indigenous Fellow: One Year Fellowship (2013), Renewable for One Further Year (2014): Call for Expressions of Interest. Geneva: WIPO, 2012.

WIPO Program and Budget for the 2014/15 Biennium. Geneva: WIPO, 2013.

WIPO Report on Fact-Finding Missions on Intellectual Property and Traditional Knowledge (1998–1999). Geneva: WIPO, 2001.

Treaties and Contracting Parties: Berne Convention: Japan. www.wipo.int/treaties/en/remarks.jsp?cnty_id=975C (accessed March 27, 2015).

Wolfers, Michael. *Politics in the Organization of African Unity.* London: Methuen, 1976.

World Bank. *Nongovernmental Organizations in World Bank-Supported Projects.* Washington, DC: World Bank, 1999.

World Blind Union. "Policy Position agreed by the World Blind Union (WBU), the Daisy Consortium and IFLA Libraries for the Blind Section (LBS)." www.worldblindunion.org/English/our-work/Position&20Statements/wbu&20ifla&20lbs&20and&20daisy&20Joint&20Policy&20Position.doc (Accessed March 27, 2015).

Yu, Geoffrey. "The Structure and Process of Negotiations at the World Intellectual Property Organization," *Chicago-Kent Law Review* 82 no. 3 (2007): 1445–1453.

Yu, Peter K. "Intellectual Property and Asian Values," *Marquette Intellectual Property Law Review* 16 no. 2 (2012): 329–399.

"The Rise and Decline of the Intellectual Property Powers," *Campbell Law Review* 34 no. 3 (2012): 525–577.

Yousafzai, Malala. "Address on Education to the United Nations General Assembly," July 12, 2013. www.theguardian.com/commentisfree/2013/jul/12/malala-yousafzai-united-nations-education-speech-text.

INDEX

CAMBRIDGE INTELLECTUAL PROPERTY AND INFORMATION LAW

Titles in the series (formerly known as *Cambridge Studies in Intellectual Property Rights)*

Brad Sherman and Lionel Bently
The Making of Modern Intellectual Property Law

Irini A. Stamatoudi
Copyright and Multimedia Products: A Comparative Analysis

Pascal Kamina
Film Copyright in the European Union

Huw Beverly-Smith
The Commercial Appropriation of Personality

Mark J. Davison
The Legal Protection of Databases

Robert Burrell and Allison Coleman
Copyright Exceptions: The Digital Impact

Huw Beverly-Smith, Ansgar Ohly and Agnès Lucas-Schloetter
Privacy, Property and Personality: Civil Law Perspectives on Commercial Appropriation

Catherine Seville
The Internationalisation of Copyright Law: Books, Buccaneers and the Black Flag in the Nineteenth Century

Philip Leith
Software and Patents in Europe

Geertrui Van Overwalle
Gene Patents and Clearing Models

Lionel Bently, Jennifer Davis and Jane C. Ginsburg
Trade Marks and Brands: An Interdisciplinary Critique

Jonathan Curci
The Protection of Biodiversity and Traditional Knowledge in International Law of Intellectual Property

Lionel Bently, Jennifer Davis and Jane C. Ginsburg
Copyright and Piracy: An Interdisciplinary Critique

Megan Richardson and Julian Thomas
Framing Intellectual Property: Legal Constructions of Creativity and Appropriation 1840–1940

Dev Gangjee
Relocating the Law of Geographical Indications

Andrew Kenyon, Megan Richardson and Ng-Loy Wee-Loon
The Law of Reputation and Brands in the Asia Pacific Region

Annabelle Lever
New Frontiers in the Philosophy of Intellectual Property

Sigrid Sterckx and Julian Cockbain
Exclusions from Patentability: How the European Patent Office is Eroding Boundaries

Sebastian Haunss
Conflicts in the Knowledge Society: The Contentious Politics of Intellectual Property

Helena R. Howe and Jonathan Griffiths
Concepts of Property in Intellectual Property Law

Rochelle Cooper Dreyfuss and Jane C. Ginsburg
Intellectual Property at the Edge: The Contested Contours of IP

Normann Witzleb, David Lindsay, Moira Paterson and Sharon Rodrick
Emerging Challenges in Privacy Law: Comparative Perspectives

Paul Bernal
Internet Privacy Rights: Rights to Protect Autonomy

Peter Drahos
Intellectual Property, Indigenous People and their Knowledge

Susy Frankel and Daniel Gervais
The Evolution and Equilibrium of Copyright in the Digital Age

Edited by **Kathy Bowrey and Michael Handler**
Law and Creativity in the Age of the Entertainment Franchise

Sean Bottomley
The British Patent System and the Industrial Revolution 1700–1852: From Privileges to Property

Susy Frankel
Test Tubes for Global Intellectual Property Issues: Small Market Economies

Jan Oster
Media Freedom as a Fundamental Right

Sara Bannerman
International Copyright and Access to Knowledge

Lightning Source UK Ltd.
Milton Keynes UK
UKOW06n1845220216

268901UK00002B/42/P

9 781107 023062